NURSES AND NURSING

The Person and the Profession

Edited by Pádraig Ó Lúanaigh

Routledge
Taylor & Francis Group

LONDON AND NEW YORK

First published 2017
by Routledge
2 Park Square, Milton Park, Abingdon, Oxon OX14 4RN

and by Routledge
711 Third Avenue, New York, NY 10017

Routledge is an imprint of the Taylor & Francis Group, an informa business

British Library Cataloguing-in-Publication Data
A catalogue record for this book is available from the British Library

Library of Congress Cataloging in Publication Data
Names: Ó Lúanaigh, Pádraig, MSc(Psych), editor.
Title: Nurses and nursing : the person and the profession / edited by Pádraig Ó Lúanaigh.
Other titles: Nurses and Nursing (Ó Lúanaigh)
Description: Abingdon, Oxon ; New York, NY : Routledge, 2017. | Includes bibliographical references and index.
Identifiers: LCCN 2016055031| ISBN 9781138189195 (hbk) | ISBN 9781138189201 (pbk.) | ISBN 9781315641744 (ebook)
Subjects: | MESH: Nursing | Nurses
Classification: LCC RT51 | NLM WY 100.1 | DDC 610.73--dc23
LC record available at https://lccn.loc.gov/2016055031

ISBN: 978-1-138-18919-5 (hbk)
ISBN: 978-1-138-18920-1 (pbk)
ISBN: 978-1-315-64174-4 (ebk)

Typeset in Bembo by Saxon Graphics Ltd, Derby

MIX
Paper from
responsible sources
FSC   FSC® C013056
www.fsc.org

Printed and bound in Great Britain by
TJ International Ltd, Padstow, Cornwall

CONTENTS

ABOUT THE CONTRIBUTORS

Professor Lisa Bayliss-Pratt PhD, RN Nursing Director, Health Education England, London, UK

Lisa was appointed as Director of Nursing at Health Education England (HEE) in 2012. In this role she has responsibility for leading national policy, workforce planning, and the commissioning of multi-professional education and training for the non-medical healthcare workforce. Her achievements include the establishment of the Shape of Caring Review, development and piloting of pre-degree care experience for aspirant nurses and leading the 'return to practice' initiative. Lisa's work also includes the creation of a three-tiered dementia education and training framework through which over 100,000 members of NHS personnel received dementia awareness training – achieving a key Government Mandate requirement. Lisa also led the development of the 'Fundamentals of Care' certificate for support/care workers across health and social care in England. Before joining HEE, Lisa led on strategic and operational work throughout a number of senior nursing roles at both regional and national levels. Lisa is also a trustee of the Foundation of Nursing Studies.

Professor Mike Cook EdD, MSc (Quality Mgmt), MSc (Education Mgmt), Cert Ed DipN (Lond), FHEA Professor of Healthcare Leadership and Management, University of Bedfordshire, UK

Mike has over 35 years' experience of the NHS, as a clinician, an academic and service commissioner. He is passionate about improving healthcare through the provision of high-quality education, research and consultancy that provide positive results. His research and publications are focused on healthcare and leadership. He currently provides Executive Coaching to a wide range of clients and supports the NIHR CLAHRC (East of England) Fellowship programme.

Ms Jennifer Cunningham MSc, BSc (Hons), RPN Lecturer in Mental Health Nursing, Waterford Institute of Technology, Ireland

Jennifer is a Lecturer in Mental Health Nursing in the Department of Nursing and Health Care at Waterford Institute of Technology. She has lecturing experience at undergraduate and postgraduate level in the areas of nursing and health care. She is the Course Leader for the Postgraduate Diploma in Nursing programme at WIT. She holds a professional qualification in mental health and has clinical experience in a range of areas in the mental health setting including acute, community, rehabilitation and care of the older adult. She has gained extensive research experience through her work on EU-funded research and participation in HSE national project work. She is currently completing a PhD in the area of workforce planning in mental health services in Ireland. Her research interests include mental health, workforce planning, skill mix, policy and work-related stress.

Ms Liz Fenton MSc, BSc (Hons), RN Professional Nurse Advisor, Health Education England, London, UK

Liz joined Health Education England (HEE) in July 2015 as the Professional Nurse Advisor in the Directorate of Education and Quality. Having completed nurse training at King's College Hospital, London, Liz qualified as a Registered Nurse in 1981 and subsequently held a number of clinical and leadership roles in both acute and community settings including at board level. Passionate about quality improvement, Liz works with the Care Quality Commission as a Specialist Advisor and is an elected member of the Community Hospitals Association leadership team. Liz undertakes national and international peer accreditation, benchmarking services against best practice, most recently in Portugal and Dublin.

Dr Jacquie Kidd PhD, RN Senior Lecturer, University of Auckland, New Zealand

He mihinui mahana ki a koe. Ko Ngāpuhi raua ko Ireland and France oku iwi. Ko Ngati Hineira raua ko Te Uri Taniwha oku hapu. Kia ora!

Jacquie is a Senior Lecturer at the University of Auckland. She is of Maori, Irish and French descent, and brings a strong oral tradition of storytelling to teaching postgraduate mental health nurses and an eclectic mix of research projects. In general, Jacquie works with research that pushes the boundaries of how knowledge is created, using kaupapa Māori approaches, autoethnography, and arts-based, creative research practices. Her programme of research focuses broadly on the health literacy practices of people in the mental health and/or Māori health arenas, and on the health of the nursing workforce. A key part of her research practice includes supporting vulnerable or marginalised groups to develop and sustain their own research knowledge.

Tena koe, tena koe, tena ra tatou.

Mr Roy Lilley NHS writer, broadcaster, commentator and conference speaker, London, UK

Roy built up his first enterprise from scratch, turning it into a multi-million pound turnover business. Roy's position as a former chair of an NHS Trust and a commentator and analyst of healthcare policy has contributed to his unparalleled reach over social media in the NHS. You can follow Roy on Twitter @RoyLilley.

He has been voted the top UK speaker on NHS topics twice and is listed in the Debrett's most influential people in healthcare. Roy is the Founder of the Academy of Fabulous NHS Stuff (www.fabnhsstuff.net), a repository which has become a social movement and is seen as the change platform for the NHS and Social Care. He is also a publisher of the e-newsletter for NHS managers (www.nhsmanagers. net).

Roy is a frequent broadcaster and writer on health, current affairs and social issues and speaks at conferences and seminars throughout the UK and overseas. He has written for the *Guardian, Sunday Times, Telegraph* and many national newspapers, journals and management periodicals. Roy is the author of over twenty books on health and health service management.

Ms Maureen Morgan OBE, RN, RHV Senior Fellow in Clinical Leadership, Keele University and UK Nursing and Midwifery Council member

Maureen is Senior Fellow in Clinical Leadership. Prior to this post she was Professional Officer for Policy and Practice in the Chief Nursing Officer team at the Department of Health, London. A nurse and health visitor, Maureen has held a number of management and executive positions in the NHS, and was awarded an OBE in 2012.

Ms Helen Myers MSc, BSc, RN, MACN Senior Research Assistant, School of Nursing & Midwifery, Edith Cowan University, Perth, Australia

Helen is a registered nurse with a clinical background in mental health nursing. For the last 18 years she has worked in acute care nursing, both in the clinical and university setting, implementing research projects focused on improving the quality and safety of patient care. Helen has extensive experience in quantitative research methods, statistical analysis, survey design and administration, and clinical research. She has conducted research in the areas of fall prevention, patient satisfaction, patient outcomes, nurse staffing and skill mix, nursing practice environment, cancer care, and economic evaluation.

Dr Kay Norman EdD, MSc, PGDHE, BSc (Hons), RGN Principal Lecturer – Adult Nursing, Institute of Health and Society, University of Worcester, UK

Kay's nursing background is within the Community Nursing field (adult) with a particular focus on General Practice Nursing. Kay has continued to work within clinical practice since commencing her educator role in 2000, predominantly as a practice nurse/contraception and sexual health nurse.

Her research interests relate to the image and perceptions of nursing, with recent work focusing on young people's perceptions of nursing as a career and the image of nursing in general. This also relates to her current interest in the 'recruitment and retention' aspect of nursing and young people's decision-making voice. Kay's previous research has related to the development of leadership and management roles within nursing and the impact of this on decision-making processes relating to healthcare services. Kay's teaching interests include mentorship, leadership and management in healthcare, community and primary care nursing, health promotion, and qualitative research methods.

Dr Pádraig Ó Lúanaigh EdD, MSc(Psych), BSc(Hons), DipHE(Mid), AdvDipEd, PGDE, RN, RM, RHV, FHEA Deputy Director of Nursing, Norfolk and Norwich University Hospitals Foundation NHS Trust, Norwich, UK

With over 28 years' experience of working within health and higher education, Pádraig has a broad and integrated range of experiences gained from working in organisations across the UK, Australia and New Zealand. With professional registrations as a nurse, midwife and health visitor and experience of working in primary and secondary care, he has a credible knowledge of leading provider and operational aspects of healthcare services. Pádraig has held teaching and leadership roles in education, complemented by strategic leadership and health policy experience in central government and strategic health organisations. Pádraig continues to publish and research a range of topics reflecting his professional background.

Mr Robert Parry MSc, BSc, RN, RMN UK Nursing and Midwifery Registrant Council member

Robert, a registered adult and mental health nurse, was Associate Director of Nursing and Midwifery at NHS Education for Scotland 2008–2015 leading latterly on workforce development and education in supporting the integration of health and social care. Prior to this he held a number of senior academic posts, including Dean of the Faculty for Health and Social Care at the University of Hull.

Professor Elizabeth Rosser DPhil, MN, Dip N Ed, Dip RM, RN, RNT, PFHEA Deputy Dean Education and Professional Practice, Bournemouth University, UK

As Professor of Nursing and academic lead for education in Bournemouth, Elizabeth has a particular research interest in the health and social care workforce. As Principal Fellow of the Higher Education Academy, she is an experienced educationalist passionate about the integration of education and professional practice and she has published widely on issues related to nurse education.

Elizabeth has a particular interest in culturally relevant care, having worked for six years as nurse/midwife in Colombia, South America. More recently she has been involved in a number of workforce research projects both within the UK and in Brazil. Elizabeth has a keen interest in supporting the developing professional both at the prequalifying level through the lifelong learning process to consultant nurse and beyond, towards achieving excellence in patient care.

Dr Allison Squires PhD, RN, FAAN Assistant Professor, Deputy Director, International Education & Visiting Scholars, Rory Meyers College of Nursing, New York, USA

Allison studies health workforce capacity building, primarily in low- and middle-income countries. Recent studies and collaborations have focused on primary care workforce development and obesity management strategies, inter-professional education in geriatrics, health workforce migration policy in Latin America, and projects promoting evidence-based practice among frontline healthcare providers. To date, her research has occurred in 30 countries. She is a health labour markets consultant for the World Bank and a Fellow with the Migration Policy Institute.

Mr Harry Jacobs Summers Senior Advisor, The Truth About Nursing, USA

Harry has served as senior advisor to The Truth About Nursing since its founding. He is co-author of *Saving Lives: Why the Media's Portrayal of Nursing Puts Us All at Risk* and many articles on nursing and the media. Harry has a BA from Columbia University and a JD from Georgetown University. Since 1998, he has been a litigation attorney with the Federal Election Commission in Washington, DC. Harry spent several years in USAID-funded legal positions in Cambodia, serving as an American Bar Association Legal Advisor to the Cambodian Ministry of Commerce and a Program Officer at The Asia Foundation. He also spent a year in New Zealand on a Fulbright scholarship at the University of Auckland. www.truthaboutnursing.org/.

Ms Sandy Summers RN, MSN, MPH Founder and Executive Director, The Truth About Nursing, USA

Since 2001, Sandy has led the effort to change how the world views nursing by challenging poor media depictions of nurses. Sandy is the co-author of *Saving Lives: Why the Media's Portrayal of Nursing Puts Us All at Risk*, which has won awards from the Sigma Theta Tau International Honor Society and the *American Journal of Nursing*. She has also written many articles and op-eds on nursing. Sandy speaks frequently on nursing's image and empowering nurses to change how they are perceived. She has Master's degrees in Nursing and Public Health from Johns Hopkins University (2002) and a Bachelor of Science in Nursing from Southern Connecticut State University (1984). Sandy has convinced many major corporations to remove or improve advertisements that presented damaging images of nursing. In 2013 she worked with others to convince MTV to ameliorate the damage done by its television show *Scrubbing In*, which focused on the personal lives of a group of travel nurses. That same year she convinced American Family Care, a chain of quick clinics, to stop advertising in a way that suggested that NPs are inferior to physicians. www.truthaboutnursing.org/.

Professor Di Twigg PhD, MBA, B Health Sc (Nsg) Hons, RN, RM, FACN
Dean, School of Nursing & Midwifery, Edith Cowan University, Perth, Australia

Di combines her extensive experience in Health Service leadership with more recent research and policy development to make a research contribution to issues related to nursing workforce, hospital staffing and cost-effective care. She is recognised for her work in relation to nursing workforce and patient outcome research which specifically relates to safe staffing levels and the relationships between staffing, patient, organisational and economic outcomes. Since joining academe in 2010, this work has attracted over AU$1,680,000 research funding, resulted in over 30 peer-reviewed papers, a number of keynote presentations and has been used by industry and industrial organisations to argue for safe staffing levels. Professor Twigg was appointed to the National Nursing and Midwifery Education Advisory Network, an advisory body responsible for the provision of advice to Australian Health Ministers on issues relating to the planning and coordination of education, employment and immigration for nurses and midwives.

Professor John S.G. Wells PhD, MSc, BA (Hons), PGDipEd, RNT, RPN
Head of the School of Health Sciences, Waterford Institute of Technology, Ireland

John trained as a mental health nurse at St George's Hospital School of Nursing at Springfield Hospital in London. He then held a number of clinical and management positions in mental health services including Staff Nurse in Child and Adolescent Psychiatry, Community Mental Health Nurse, and Ward Manager, Acute Psychiatric Admissions at the Maudsley and Bethlem Hospital and Springfield Hospital in London. He took up his first academic appointment in 1991 as a Lecturer in Mental Health Nursing at the Maudsley Hospital School of Nursing. This was followed in 1993 with an appointment as a Lecturer in Nursing at King's College, University of London, where he remained until 1998 when he moved to Ireland and took up a lectureship in Psychiatric Nursing based in the Waterford Institute of Technology.

FIGURES

FIGURES

TABLES

FOREWORD

The relationship between the nurse and the patient, relative, resident, user or carer defines the health service. Nurses work at the frontline, in the shop window, at the beginning, the middle and the end. The work of nurses is not just in 'our hospital' or practice; their work is international. Nurses see us at our lowest and highest. Frightened and euphoric. Nurses are, also, much more than a soothing hand or a friend in need. They are, increasingly, technocrats, specialists and experts in their work.

This book is long overdue; it examines the relationships, the personal attributes and influences on the profession that are redefining the profession. Not least the interface between the nurse, other professionals and patients. Written in a refreshing style the book creates a dialogue between the reader and the contributors and asks some tough questions. We all know without nursing our health and care services have no future but what, in the context of health technology and workforce pressures, is the future for nursing?

What do nurses think about their future? More of the same or more of something quite different?

Nursing is international. We have seen that at home; the pressures of poor workforce planning and demand for more nurses means the NHS has looked overseas to find new personnel. It might be fair to say the authorities have been surprised at the skills and training of nurses from parts of Europe, their language skills and their willingness to be mobile.

It is the pressures for more nurses that may have more of a defining hand than we thought. Is it sustainable to expect all nurses to be degree trained? For years voices, the voices saying close the door to those able to bring vocation, care and compassion to their work but not academia, are voices we ignore at our peril.

Pressures of social media and technology put nurses in the frontline of delivering a very different health system. Improvements in health technology have opened the way to nurse consultants and practitioners.

For most of us it is the interface between nursing and patients that defines the quality experience. Spectacular quality failures in the English NHS system have been laid at the door of nursing. It is probably true that nurses should have been more vocal but fear and the memory of the fate of previous whistle-blowers proved a discouragement. This begs the question: what was the role of the regulator in the care and safety of the public? The conclusion is the regulators failed. Is there a role for regulation in nursing? Beyond a register of accreditation and competency can regulators hope to make complex healthcare safer? The evidence would appear to say no.

What works and what doesn't, where can we look for best practice and avoid reinventing the wheel? This fascinating book draws on international best practice, research, commentary and common-sense.

Essential reading.

Roy Lilley
London, England.
October 2016

PREFACE

The idea for this textbook was born on a lazy Sunday afternoon as I was thinking about and questioning where nursing was going and what nursing would be in the future. An unusual thought possibly, but it resulted from a conversation I had with nursing colleagues as we contemplated what the next 20 years of our careers held for us. I was frustrated and concerned that I was struggling to think or picture what the future of nursing would be. The result of my inability to imagine the future of nursing is this book.

I have been fortunate to have met and worked with many true professionals during my career and these are the people I have turned to for help in capturing what nursing is and what the future may hold for nurses. The authors who have contributed to this book have found time in their busy lives to share their experience and knowledge and this collection of nursing experience provides the reader with a rich mix of nursing perspectives and ideas.

As I planned this book to explore nursing, it became obvious to me very quickly that the future of nursing will be determined by individual nurses themselves – nurses *are* nursing and just as we, as people bring to nursing our personal qualities we also *become* nurses as our professional lives shape us as individuals.

Often when I sit down to read a book I am still excited by the expectation of 'getting knowledge' and finding out what I need to know. However, the reality is that in terms of professional nursing practice, we must each individually create our own practice knowledge and understanding. Each chapter in this book has identified reflection sections; places where you are encouraged to stop, reflect and think about what you think. Having invested your money purchasing and time reading this book, I would encourage you to honestly and actively make use of the reflect moments since this is where the real learning and understanding is in this book. I see nursing practised every day and when I see nursing done well it is truly beautiful and each chapter in this book is intended to help you think about and define your own practice to become the nurse you want to be.

This book is split into three parts and while designed to be read in a structured way from chapter 1 to 11, each chapter may also be read on its own.

Part I has four chapters that will provide you with a foundational understanding of nursing and provides you with an opportunity to think about the kind of nurse you are or want to be.

Part II consists of three chapters that are designed to help you think about yourself and provides you with knowledge and skills to develop you own nursing practice.

Finally, Part III concludes the book and the focus for the four chapters broadens out from individual nursing practice and looks at the wider contexts that have both direct and indirect impact and influence on your practice.

At times the content of this book may appear negative, and frequently the contributors have made reference to 'scandals' in health where nursing was severely criticised. It is precisely for this reason that this book is so important now. As individual nurses and as the profession of nursing, we must have the clarity of expression, vision and confidence to demonstrate and describe the difference that quality nursing practice makes to the health of individuals, communities and global populations. This book is designed to challenge you, provide some of the evidence and support you to develop your own convincing argument for what nursing is.

Nursing is complex and the environments we work in are ever-changing and present on a daily basis challenges and competing demands which cause us stress, frustration and at times despair.

Equally, I am reminded when reading this book that when nurses work together, question and think about what they do, the result is something of value that supports safe, positive and quality patient and client experiences – the beauty of nursing. I hope this book supports you to understand and enhance your own beautiful nursing care.

Pádraig Ó Lúanaigh
Norwich, England
October 2016

ACKNOWLEDGEMENTS

The quality and relevance of this textbook was enhanced and developed thanks to the peer reviews provided by nursing student and registered nurse colleagues who gave their time freely to read draft work and provided valuable feedback.

We wish to thank the following individuals: Carolina Antunes, Julie Boyd, Sharon Martin and Tania Silcock, and all those colleagues whose own nursing practice has influenced each of us to become the nurses we are today.

PART I

Understanding nursing and nurses

1

NURSING'S PUBLIC IMAGE

Toward a professional future

Sandy Summers and Harry Jacobs Summers

Why this chapter is important

The media in all its forms is a powerful influencer of public opinion and understanding. This chapter explores how nurses and nursing have been portrayed in the news, on television, in films and online. Through the use of real-life examples from the media this chapter helps the reader to understand how they themselves and the public may understand nurses and their work. From the angelic angel to the battle-axe matron or sex-crazed naughty nurse, the inaccurate portrayal of nursing through the media has had an impact on nurses' ability to be taken seriously, respected for their expertise and professionalism or influential in policy decision making. The chapter provides useful suggestions on ways individual nurses and collectively the profession can work to ensure that an accurate representation of nurses and the work they do is conveyed to the public.

Chapter trigger question: Does the media portrayal of nurses and nursing have any actual influence over nursing practice and the strength of the profession?

Key words: image of nursing, media, public understanding of nursing, influencing policy

---

Introduction

This chapter examines nursing's public image, especially as reflected in recent media, explaining why the image matters and proposing ways to improve public understanding. Readers should consider the gap between the skilled, autonomous nursing profession they know and the feminine stereotypes that remain common.

Of course, both image and reality have evolved since the time of Florence Nightingale, when the idea of nurses' unassailable virtue helped to establish the modern profession in a world in which physicians held sway. Yet as we'll see, nursing's image is still plagued by stereotypes that reflect the limits of these roots, including the unskilled handmaiden, the naughty nurse, the battle-axe, and the angel itself. Nursing's future depends on closing the gap between these images and the life-saving reality of the profession.

Consider the kind of nurse you want to be. Don't you wish your idea of that excellent nurse clinician, educator, research or advocate was featured on TV, or at least that society better understood the real nursing role?

Reflect 1.1

- Spend a few moments thinking about how nurses are portrayed in the media and reported in the news.
- What kind of words and descriptions are used to describe nurses in the press?

A 7 September 2016 story in the *New York Times*, 'Doctors in Aleppo Tend to Scores of Victims in Gas Attack', reported that as talks between the warring factions in Syria continued, 'doctors in the city of Aleppo were still treating people in intensive care' after an apparent chlorine gas attack sickened more than 100. According to the piece, 'doctors said they believed' that the house of one victim had been struck directly and 'doctors were still working to confirm the final death toll'. There was no mention of any specific health workers *but physicians*. Other elite media have taken a similar approach to Aleppo stories. In a BBC item on the 29th of that same month, 'Aleppo doctors facing Armageddon', the noted British volunteer surgeon David Nott conveyed his concern for the 'doctors and surgeons' with whom he had worked. Whether the idea is that only physicians are providing significant care, that only their experiences and views matter, or that 'doctors' is a convenient shorthand for all health workers, the result is to remove nurses from the scene.

Even when nurses appear in such media reports, it may reinforce stereotypes. Consider a 13 August 2016 CNN website report headlined 'Aleppo's angel: A nurse's devotion to Syria's children'. The 'angel' was Malaika, a young head nurse in the neonatal unit at the Aleppo Children's Hospital. In addition to context on the war, the piece described Malaika and a physician trying to perform CPR on a dying infant who had lost his oxygen supply after a government airstrike on the hospital. And the nurse got a few powerful quotes, including her description of the strike as 'a war crime'. Yet readers are most likely to remember that she is an 'angel' characterised by 'devotion': the classic imagery under which nursing skill, knowledge and strength is buried. As the report made sure to note, 'malaika' means 'angel' in Arabic. And even in a piece partly about a nurse and her sacrifices – Malaika has kept working despite her own shrapnel wounds and the departure of her family – a key point was that 'only 35 doctors' are left in Aleppo. How many nurses are left? Does that matter?

Reflect 1.2

- Was the image of the nursing 'angel' one you thought about in the previous Reflect?
- What are your views on the portrayal of nurses in the way detailed – does this help the public to understand the work nurses do?

Stereotypical images affect not only nurses' sense of professional identity but the respect and resources they receive for their work. Public health research shows that the popular media, even fictional television, has a real effect on society's health-related views and actions. And because real nurses play such a critical role people across the globe suffer adverse health outcomes when nurses lack the resources they need (Truth About Nursing, 2008). We have only 16 million nurses across the globe, instead of the 75 million we would need to achieve adequate nurse-to-population ratios. Current nursing staffing ratios are dangerous – leading to errors, deaths, nurse burnout, and other ill-effects of the undervaluation of nursing, which is inherently challenging and stressful.

Nurses should explore ways to address this problem. These include projecting the image of a policy-oriented professional, educating health care colleagues, and shaping global and local media content, through a wide range of advocacy and creative efforts.

A brief history of nursing's image

The most enduring stereotypes of nursing are one-dimensional notions of femininity – the angel, the handmaiden, the harlot, and the battle-axe. All these stereotypes can be traced to the roots of the modern profession in the mid-nineteenth century, when reformers like Nightingale organised groups of females to provide intimate care to strangers. To be accepted, those early nurses had to be virtuous and non-threatening to physicians; if nurses failed to conform, it was a problem.

The most common vision of nursing well into the twentieth century was the angel of mercy, an image that often carried a maternal tinge. Many examples can be seen in *Pictures of Nursing*, a collection of historic postcards assembled by nurse Michael Zwerdling and curated in a 2014 exhibit at the US National Institutes of Health by media scholar Julia Hallam (Hallam & Zwerdling, 2015).

As the twentieth century progressed, nurses were increasingly portrayed as the faithful and even heroic assistants of physicians. In Frank Borzage's 1932 film *A Farewell to Arms*, based on Ernest Hemingway's 1929 novel, nurses were virtuous love interests of military men in World War I; strict head nurses enforced morality and deference to physicians.

After World War II, nurses tended to be presented as deferential assistants of expert physicians. In the 1950s and 1960s, according to communications scholar Joseph Turow, the American Medical Association actually vetted scripts, ensuring that Hollywood products presented physicians in a good light. (Turow, *Playing Doctor: Television, Storytelling, and Medical Power*, 2010). The ABC television show *Marcus Welby* (1969–76) featured a lead character who handled even psychosocial aspects of care nurses traditionally regarded as their own. Health scholars Beatrice and Philip Kalisch dubbed this 'Marcus Welby syndrome' (Kalisch & Kalisch, 1986). The post-War era did produce a popular series of youth novels about Cherry Ames, a bright, adventurous young nurse who travelled from job to job solving mysteries (Wells & Tatham, 1943–1968).

Social changes following this era included sexual liberation and more career opportunities for women, who began to enter medicine. Popular views of nursing seemed to retreat toward feminine extremes, including the naughty nurse and the battle-axe, that reflected male fantasies and fears. Sexualised nurse characters became a staple in pornography and eventually in advertising. And the idea that nurses were mainly looking for romance with physicians took root. In Robert Altman's 1970 film *M*A*S*H*, based on Richard Hooker's 1968 novel, military nurse Margaret 'Hot Lips' Houlihan was a rule-bound martinet who suffered sexual mockery from the film's cynical surgeon heroes. Milos Forman's 1975 film *One Flew Over the Cuckoo's Nest*, based on Ken Kesey's 1962 novel, featured the notorious Mildred Ratched, a sociopathic nurse who tortured patients in the psychiatric unit she controlled (Truth About Nursing, 2014).

In the final decades of the twentieth century, some media did present nurses as serious, competent professionals. However, even the best of it tended to reinforce the idea that nurses were skilled, reliable assistants to the physicians whose work mattered most, many of them now female. This was true in everything from the elite news media to influential television dramas, like NBC's *St. Elsewhere* (1982–88), the BBC's *Casualty* (1986–present), and NBC's *ER* (1994–2009), all of which offered relatively realistic views of gritty urban hospital care.

Early twenty-first century media products have given some cause for hope. Some news media sources have run powerful, accurate reports on nurses. In an October 2014 *Guardian* piece, three nurses gave long first-person accounts of their work caring for Ebola patients in West Africa. And several television shows focused on nurses have appeared, most notably Showtime's *Nurse Jackie* (2009–15), about a troubled but expert present-day New York emergency nurse, and the BBC's *Call the Midwife* (2012–present), about nurse midwives providing autonomous care for the poor in post-World War II London. Other shows set in the distant past have offered fair portrayals, such as PBS's US Civil War drama *Mercy Street* (2016–present). Even some non-health care shows have included strong nurse characters, including the time-travelling Claire Randall on Starz's *Outlander*, assassin Mary Morstan on the BBC's *Sherlock*, and nurse-to-the-superheroes Claire Temple, who appears on recent Netflix Marvel shows such as *Luke Cage* (Truth About Nursing, 2016a).

But a few helpful products and characters are not enough. Most influential current entertainment media that includes substantial portrayals of modern health care still reflects the idea that nurses are at best skilled assistants to heroic, expert physicians. That is true in shows that focus on health care and those that do not, which can still include deceptively influential portrayals. Extreme recent examples of Marcus Welby syndrome include ABC's surgical soap *Grey's Anatomy* (2005–present) and Fox's diagnosis-focused *House* (2004–12), which lack nurse characters. But even shows that do have fairly strong nurse characters, like NBC's *Chicago Med* (2015–present), generally revolve around the physicians who dominate in clinical matters. And sitcoms often mock nursing, notably the egregious Fox/Hulu OB/GYN show *The Mindy Project* (2012–present), whose regular nurse characters are mostly stooges (Truth About Nursing, 2016b).

The nursing image should be much better …

Reflect 1.3

- Think about the range of film and television examples mentioned. If you have previously watched any of these, had you considered how nurses were portrayed?
- Do you think that the media portrayal of nurses has a real impact on actual nurses and nursing?

Why the nursing image matters

The media strongly affects our health-related views and actions, including those related to nursing. There is abundant evidence of the media's general influence on society. One study found that after cable television was introduced in certain areas of rural India, women reported having more autonomy and less bias against female children (Jensen & Oster, 2009). And a study found that death rates from female-named hurricanes were far higher, evidently because people respected and feared those with female names less and failed to get out of their paths (Jung, Shavitt, Viswanathan, & Hilbe, 2014). Of course, a hurricane name, like a television drama, is basically a fictional description of something real.

Those in the field of health communication study and manage health-related messaging in the media. In a 2002 report for the Kaiser Family Foundation, scholars Joseph Turow and Rachel Gans explained that media products from news coverage to fictional television affect what people believe about the health care system. Indeed, they argued persuasively that fictional media may be even more influential, since it generally reaches a larger audience with more compelling dramatic themes (Turow & Gans, *As Seen on TV: Health Policy Issues in TV's Medical Dramas.* Available at http://bit.ly/2eRpPil, 2002). Thus, health advocates often work with the entertainment media to improve what the media tells the public about health issues. In October 2013, American Public Media's *Marketplace* radio show reported that the University of Southern California's Hollywood, Health & Society had received a grant from The California Endowment to persuade television shows to do plotlines about the Affordable Care Act (Obamacare) (Posel, 2013).

Some research has measured the effects of the media on views of nursing, particularly nursing careers. In 2000, JWT Communications did a focus group study of 1,800 primary and secondary school students. The study found that the respondents got their strongest impression of nursing from the popular television drama *ER*. Consistent with that show's overall depictions of nurses as skilled but peripheral physician subordinates, the youngsters believed that nursing was a job for girls, that it was technical work 'like shop' and that it was not appropriate for private school students, who were expected to aim higher (JWT Communications, 2000).

A 2008 study by researchers at the University of Dundee (Scotland) examined the views of academically advanced primary school students. Again, respondents got their main image of nursing from television. The Dundee study found that the media discouraged these students from pursuing nursing and suggested that a nursing career would not be 'using their examination grade to maximum benefit'. One student noted: 'In *Casualty* some nurses are portrayed as brainless, sex-mad bimbos out to try to romance doctors and get a doctor for a husband' (Neilson & Lauder, 2008).

In 2012, a study at University College Dublin (Ireland) examined the ten most popular nurse-related videos on YouTube. Researchers found that four of the videos showed nursing as skilled and caring; all of these were posted by nurses. The remaining six videos presented nurses as stupid, incompetent, and/or sex objects. All of these six were drawn from television or ads (Kelly, Fealy, & Watson, 2012).

And a 2013 study at the University of Western Sydney (Australia) surveyed 484 nursing students about the health-related television shows they watched. Most students reported that the shows depicted nurses as handmaidens doing tasks of little consequence while physicians did the important things in clinical settings. And the students' most-watched show? – *Grey's Anatomy* (Weaver, Salamonson, Koch, & Jackson, 2013).

Other research has focused on specific television programmes. A 2014 study found that the MTV reality show *16 and Pregnant*, along with its *Teen Mom* sequels, had not only increased the level of online activity on the relevant topics, but also reportedly 'led to a 5.7 percent reduction in teen births in the 18 months following its introduction' accounting for 'around one-third of the overall decline in teen births in the United States during that period' (Kearney & Levine, 2014).

Accordingly, the most popular hospital shows have led to significant research. In 2009, University of Alberta researchers found that many physician residents and medical students had picked up incorrect intubation techniques from *ER* and other shows (Brindley & Needham, 2009). And a 2008 Kaiser Family Foundation study showed that an embedded 'edutainment' plotline on *Grey's Anatomy* had substantially increased viewers' understanding of maternal HIV transmission (Kaiser Family Foundation, 2008). *Grey's* itself helped spread the word about the study's findings, with the show's 'director of medical research' telling *TV Guide* that the show took its influence on its large audience 'very seriously' (Colihan, 2008).

So why do powerful media creators still fail to present a more realistic image of nursing? Of course nurses themselves bear some responsibility. They must do more to educate others about the value of their work. Critical factors also include that nursing remains overwhelmingly female but has not gained much support from feminists or 'progressive' media creators, who see the job as a backwater and may feel they are already doing enough to advance social equality; that nursing also has insufficient support from most physicians, who often benefit from nursing's media marginalisation; and that entrenched professional stereotypes persist even among the media elite. One nursing scholar told us that several years ago, producers from a hospital show that was popular around the world had consulted the scholar for key plot information. But the producers were shocked to learn that this globally recognised expert was a *nurse*. And despite the expert's friendly but spirited advocacy for nursing on their call, the producers refused to strengthen their portrayal of nursing, insisting that their audience cared only about physicians.

These views affect nursing practice. A 14 September 2015 piece in the *Calgary Herald*, 'Nurses say lack of resources affecting their ability to properly care for patients', reported an alarming rise in moral distress among nurses in Alberta due to insufficient time and other resources. Those conditions do not arise randomly. They are the result of policy and economic decisions made by humans, based on their views on the value of nursing. And those views are what must change.

Stereotypes affecting nursing's public image

Are nurses low-skilled workers?

Perhaps the most common stereotype of nursing is that nurses lack significant skills. Imagery reinforcing that notion ranges from explicit disrespect – we have seen more than one comparison of nurses to monkeys – to more subtle forms. Those include crediting physicians for nursing work, suggesting that nursing can be performed by anyone, and simply ignoring nursing, even when it plays a key role in a particular care setting.

Some media items do present nurses as serious professionals. That is more common in the news media, especially the print press, where nurses have appeared as expert life-savers, clinical leaders, and health innovators. A short 20 February 2016 piece in the *Dorset Echo*, 'Nurse leading the battle with sepsis' reported that Dorset County Hospital's 'sepsis project nurse' Ann Bishop has spent years raising awareness of the deadly condition. Portrayals of nursing skill have appeared consistently on several recent television shows, notably *Nurse Jackie* and *Call the Midwife*, in which characters have saved lives using their nursing knowledge, holistic focus, and creative patient advocacy. In the 22 March 2010 episode, nurse Jackie Peyton used her extraordinary interpersonal skills to persuade a reluctant insurance company to cover an expensive surgery to re-attach several fingers – which the patient had a particular need for, since she was deaf. Even Hollywood films may offer something helpful. Disney's 2014 blockbuster *Big Hero 6* featured Baymax, a robotic 'nurse' who repeatedly saved the main character's geek squad with advanced health knowledge and problem-solving ability. Baymax was a far cry from the real-life robotic care assistants who are sometimes mislabelled 'nurses' (Truth About Nursing, 2016c).

Unfortunately, a lot of the most prominent media regularly suggest that nurses are low-skilled. That trend is notable in some globally influential television products, particularly those that focus on the professional status of female and minority physician characters. Since 2005, that has been the case with *Grey's Anatomy*, which gives the impression that advanced hospital care is provided almost exclusively by surgeons. Those physicians even perform exciting tasks in which nurses play a key role in real life, such as defibrillation, triage, psychosocial care, patient advocacy and education. Meanwhile, the nurse characters rarely speak. One March 2016 episode had a flashback to the show's premiere, in which a patient had insulted one surgeon by saying that the patient's previous caregiver had not been so clueless, 'and that was, like, a *nurse*' (Truth About Nursing, 2013a).

The Mindy Project has given its regular nurse characters a lot more attention, but sadly it has revealed them to be human punchlines. All the sitcom's characters are silly, but the physicians get some respect based on their professional status, whereas the nurses tend to be bizarre, ignorant peasants who provide incidental splashes of comic colour. The main nurse character is Morgan Tookers, a well-meaning but unnerving ex-convict who had to be told by one of the physicians in an April 2014 episode that he couldn't be 'promote[d] to doctor' (Truth About Nursing, 2013c).

Non-fictional television also includes such messaging. A September 2015 episode of the daytime talk show *The View* featured an attack on a Miss America contestant who had chosen to highlight her nursing at the contest. Co-host Joy Behar wondered what the nurse was doing with 'a doctor's stethoscope' (Truth About Nursing, 2015a). An October 2012 segment of *The Daily Show with Jon Stewart* stressed that returning US military veterans were being denied civilian jobs based on needless technical requirements. Stewart insisted that military medics were overqualified to be school nurses. He mocked school nursing as being all about 'kickball' and 'tummy aches', although in reality, the work involves managing a range of serious conditions like diabetes, asthma, and allergies (Meyer, 2012).

And even the elite news media regularly undervalues nursing skill. A 14 June 2016 *New York Times* report about the tragic shooting at an Orlando, Florida nightclub, 'Orlando injuries were severe, but trauma care was nearby' included quotes from seven named physicians and not a single nurse. Nurses were mentioned in lists of providers – like one that specified how many persons in several different physician specialties were involved but simply said there were 'countless nurses'. The piece also had statements like 'doctors had to act more aggressively than they normally would', with no comparable statements about nurses.

Similarly, an April 2016 US National Public Radio piece about efforts to manage the Zika virus in Brazil featured a barrage of statements suggesting that physicians were the only type of health professional dealing with the mosquito-borne virus. The report focused on the work of two local neuro-paediatricians and included many statements about what 'doctors believe' how 'lots of doctors are helping out' and what 'doctors have been telling' NPR (Garcia-Navarro, 2016).

Yet a few news reports show that nurses are doing this type of work. Indeed, the *Guardian* ran a piece by a Brazilian nurse telling how she and her Red Cross colleagues go door to door to raise awareness of Zika. The *Guardian* piece resisted pronouncements about what 'nurses say' so while it offered a good quick portrait of one public health nurse saving lives, it was not a blast of exclusionary professional deification, as many of the physician-focused pieces are (Ribeiro, 2016).

Still, judging from much of the media, nursing is not a skilled profession. The broad use of 'nursing' to encompass breastfeeding and unskilled tending reinforces this sense, as does the use of terms like 'baby nurse' and 'maternity nurse' to refer to infant caregivers who may have little or no health training. Observers might well ask whether almost *anyone* could be nurse.

Reflect 1.4

- Review your local newspapers or media for health-related stories or feature articles.
- Are nurses presented as 'the experts' in any of the examples you can identify?
- Can you identify any reasons why nurses are not frequently used or quoted as 'experts' in news stories?

Are nurses physician handmaidens?

Nursing is an autonomous profession with its own scientific basis and scope of practice, but the view that nurses exist mainly to serve physicians – that they are 'handmaidens' – is widely held. This image fits easily with the unskilled one, but it is a distinct problem. And it remains even though many physicians are now female and more nurses are male (Truth About Nursing, 2015b).

It can be hard to find fictional media about health care that is free of the idea that nurses report to physicians. Even items that portray nursing skill, like *Nurse Jackie*, often include suggestions that the physicians control nursing care. Depictions seem most likely to convey autonomy when nurses are practising away from a hospital, like the nurse midwives on *Call the Midwife*. That show's season five, episode three featured Patsy Mount diagnosing a typhoid outbreak in a large close-knit family, and then, after the matriarch was found to be the carrier, arranging a modern flat for her nearby. Some reporting also presents nurses in this way. In July 2016 *The New Yorker* ran a long, detailed portrait of a hospice nurse that gave a good sense of her autonomy (MacFarquhar, 2016).

However, the handmaiden remains dominant in popular television programming. *Grey's Anatomy* presents a vision of hospital care in which nurses are silent, nameless bit players who exist to take orders ('Yes, doctor, right away!'); fetch physicians; hand things to physicians; or fiddle with equipment to assist physicians. Often, the nurse characters seem to look at the surgeons with something like awe, or even fear. In fact, some of the actors playing nurses are actually on-set technical advisers, real-life nurses showing the actors playing physicians how to do the work nurses do in real life. In a 7 May 2015 episode, a surgical resident told a group of interns that her number one rule was to 'listen' to the nurses and 'do whatever the nurses say', an example of what we might call 'TV producer irony' – if *Grey's* physicians actually did only what nurse characters on the show said to do, the physicians wouldn't do anything at all.

Nurse characters in most recent Hollywood shows fall somewhere between the timid servitude of *Grey's* and the more robust skilled-assistant mode exemplified by *ER*. For example, on NBC's *Chicago Med* and CBS's *Code Black*, nurse characters actually think, talk, and act as trusted aides-de-camp. But they still exist to serve commanding physicians rather than patients.

The handmaiden appears in a range of other media. In April 2015, the *Sesame Street* character Elmo and US Surgeon General Vivek Murthy appeared in a public service announcement video to promote vaccinations. The spot made a gentle joke of Murthy's many credentials, and he provided authoritative information about vaccines. There was also a short appearance by 'Nurse Jane' who gave Elmo a vaccination but said little. When Elmo asked if the shot would hurt, it was *Murthy* who answered and deftly distracted Elmo from the pain by encouraging him to sing. The Jane character seemed to be there to perform simple tasks for the physician, so he could handle the important patient education and public health policy (Weiss, Silverman, & Rubin, 2015).

Reflect 1.5

- A number of 'handmaiden' examples have been provided in this section of the book.
- How different is the reality of the nurse–doctor relationship in your experience compared to the media portrayal?

The assistant image is especially pernicious because nurses cannot fulfil their obligation as patient advocates if they are seen as physician subordinates and have an accordingly low status. One result is potentially deadly errors – a leading cause of death. The handmaiden stereotype also contributes to poor relations with physicians, who may feel they need not treat nurses with respect, leading to nursing burnout. And the image affects who chooses to become a nurse. Do college-educated career-seekers want a job that involves silently serving a different profession that gets all the glory?

Are nurses sexually available in the workplace?

Imagery that links nursing with female sexuality – the 'naughty nurse' – remains common worldwide in advertising, sexually oriented material, and television. In 2006 Agence France Presse reported that a poll had found that 54 per cent of British men had sexual fantasies about nurses – more than about any other group (Agence France Presse, 2006). A related notion is that nurses are unusually focused on romance in the workplace, with many looking to marry or at least hook up with physicians. Female nurses have long been considered potential romantic objects for male physicians, but the idea that nurses are obsessed with sex really emerged with the 1960s. It is another stereotype rooted in feminine extremes, in this case the whore rather than the angel. Perhaps nurses, managing intimate health issues of male patients, must be one or the other.

What's wrong with being a 'hot nurse'? Linking a predominantly female profession to workplace sexuality undermines respect for nursing roles, skills and education. This leads to fewer resources for nursing practice; encourages sexual abuse, which studies show nurses experience at unusually high levels; and undermines efforts to improve gender diversity. Although these images are often defended as humour, jokes are a common way that stereotypes about disempowered groups are reinforced (Truth About Nursing, 2015c). Indeed, in some settings, nurses are actually considered comparable to prostitutes, as an August 2004 piece in the *Times* of London reported was the case in parts of Asia (*The Times*, 2004). *Der Spiegel* covered a German programme to turn prostitutes into nurses (Kleinhubbert, 2006). An August 2010 report by the news service *Al Bawaba* about protests of a naughty nurse character on Egyptian television quoted a nursing professor as saying that the Egyptian media reinforced the common idea that nurses are 'girls with bad reputations who try to seduce doctors and rich patients' (Al Bawaba, 2010).

The advertising industry remains unhelpful. The naughty nurse has been used to sell everything from alcohol to shoes to milk, and the culprits range from huge multinationals to local businesses. A March 2010 piece in the *Daily Mail* reported that a bus company in the West Midlands in the UK had been using naughty nurse ads to tell riders about its route to a local hospital (*Daily Mail*, 2010). In 2014, Unilever began marketing Klondike Kandy Bars with a television ad featuring a sexy candy bar 'nurse' whose seduction of a Klondike ice cream bar 'patient' ostensibly led to the birth of the new product. 'Nurse Candy' reassured her patient: 'I know how to make you feel better!'

The naughty nurse is less common on television than the unskilled handmaiden, but she is there, lurking, especially in sitcoms. In a 7 January 2014 episode of *The Mindy Project*, a physician character played 'nooky hooky' from work with two attractive women in lingerie; he told a colleague that 'my nurses have a few more tests to run'. On 14 June 2010, Dame Helen Mirren appeared on *The Late Show with David Letterman* to promote a film about a Reno brothel. Mirren explained that 'a lot of girls who work in that [prostitution] industry actually come from the nursing industry, which kind of makes sense, because they're used to naked bodies, it's not intimidating to them, you know, the body and the bodily functions, if you like'.

The sexy nurse also persists in other media, ranging from Mariah Carey's 2010 video for 'Up Out My Face' to a vast array of pornography (e.g. the 2012 film classic *Transsexual Nurses 10*), to perennial Hallowe'en costumes. The *Daily Mail* reported that Kate Middleton and Prince William had resolved their relationship difficulties when Kate wore a 'naughty nurse' outfit to a 2007 costume party at William's military barracks. And the rest is history (Moody, 2013).

Are nurses sad females from a bygone era?

Now that women have entered medicine in significant numbers, much of society appears to have concluded that nursing is not good enough for smart, ambitious modern females. Many feminists appear to believe that because nursing was one of the few jobs to which women were traditionally confined, it must be just as limited and insignificant as the men responsible for that confinement believed. But it is critical to properly value the work women have traditionally done, even if it has overtones of 'caring' that male power structures have not valued highly.

Consider a September 2016 appearance by soccer star Abby Wambach on National Public Radio's *Fresh Air*. Wambach asserted that the real impetus for Title IX, the historic US civil rights statute, was that 'a ton of women ... wanted to become doctors, they didn't want to just be a nurse'. Wambach was characterising social attitudes from 1972, but neither she nor *Fresh Air* host Terry Gross suggested that they disagreed – in stark contrast to Wambach's blunt comments rejecting gender inequality in sports (Gross, 2016).

Influential Hollywood shows still reflect those views. The female physician lead characters on *Grey's Anatomy* have sought to distinguish themselves from nurses, who represent the female underclass those able women have gladly left behind. Both *Grey's* (27 March 2005) and *Mindy* (1 October 2013) have shown successful female physicians to be indignant at the erroneous suggestion that they *are* nurses. Of course, that would not happen on the spate of recent shows set many decades in the past – *Call the Midwife* (1950s–1960s), *Breathless* (1960s), *The Crimson Field* (1910s), *The Knick* (1900s), *Mercy Street* (1860s) – before strong, independent women could become physicians.

The media has been more open to men entering nursing than might be expected. There has been fair reporting on the progress of men in the profession, such as an October 2013 *Los Angeles Times* profile of a local man who became a skilled intensive care nurse after a very tough childhood (Bloomekatz, 2013). Strong male nurse characters have appeared in a number of television shows in recent decades, from *Casualty*'s lynchpin Charlie Fairhead to *Nurse Jackie*'s Mohammed 'Mo-Mo' De La Cruz. Even Greg Focker of the *Meet the Parents* films was, despite all the comic misadventures, a skilled professional with some authority.

But there is still plenty of stereotyping of men in nursing as failing to embody traditional notions of masculinity. Some male nurse characters have been pointedly weak, even on shows that feature strong female nurses, like *Nurse Jackie*. Other shows have enjoyed the role reversal of female physicians wielding authority over attractive male nurses, as with the midwife character Dell on the *Grey's* spin-off *Private Practice* (2007–2013). And some male nurse characters are wannabe physicians. In the 13 May 2010 episode of *Private Practice*, Dell was shown to be elated about his acceptance to medical school, just before the show killed him off.

Some portrayals of men in nursing are basically gender insults. The 8 October 2014 episode of the sitcom *Black-ish* featured an African-American physician trying to interest her bright young daughter in a physician career by showing her around the hospital. After mom assigned a male nurse to babysit, the precocious girl told the hapless fellow that he was a 'man who has a woman's job'. The plotline neatly encapsulated the media's problems with gender in nursing.

Are nurses angels of mercy?

The angel image has been with nursing since the nineteenth century, when the profession was often regarded as a religious vocation. Today's most popular entertainment media is generally too jaded to embrace this feminine stereotype, but the image persists in a variety of forms, from passing media references to nurses as 'angels' to the emotional, virtue-oriented imagery that often plagues efforts to honour nurses.

Many nurses embrace angel imagery. So what's wrong with being an angel – shouldn't nurses be caring and compassionate? Yes, of course. But when the public sees nurses as being mainly about 'touching' and 'feeling' rather than advanced skills, it undermines the sense that nurses are modern science professionals who need education, resources, and rest. Maybe they can endure anything, caring for 10 patients for 16 hours with no break. The traditional imperative that nurses serve in modest silence also discourages them from advocating for their patients and themselves. And the image dissuades men from becoming nurses.

Angel imagery still plays a role in the news media. In an August 2011 *Telegraph* piece, Cristina Odone argued that a new UK programme under which nurses wore 'do not disturb' tabards to reduce distractions during drug rounds signalled that nurses now saw patients as a 'nuisance'. Odone claimed that university education had 'professionalised' what had been a vocation, leading the 'angel[s] of the ward' to think they were too good to provide tender loving care (Odone, 2011). In mid-2006, some anonymous physicians published op-eds like 'Why nurses are no angels' which ran in the *Independent*, to dissuade the government from letting nurses play expanded clinical roles. Evidently, these new roles had produced nurses who were lazy, stupid, and uncaring, yet uppity. The obvious answer was to refocus the nurses on basic custodial tasks (Outhwaite, 2006).

But perhaps the most striking examples of the angel appear in salutes to nursing. Since 2002, the global drug company Johnson & Johnson has sponsored the Campaign for Nursing's Future. Some Campaign media has conveyed good information, but it has also relied heavily on sentimental television ads and other media stressing the importance of a 'nurse's touch' (Truth About Nursing, 2011a).

For International Nurses Day, some tributes do convey something of nurses' expertise and advocacy. For 2017, the International Council of Nurses' theme of 'Nursing – A Voice to Lead – Achieving the Sustainable Development Goals' – no angel there. But most imagery still focuses on nurses' compassion and selflessness. In 2015, the University of Texas Medical Branch, a major academic health centre, issued its 'Silent Angel Awards'. Their breakdown:

A: Always thinking of others
N: Numerous acts of kindness
G: Going above and beyond
E: Endless devotion
L: Loved

Nurses Day is held on Florence Nightingale's birthday. During the Crimean War, Nightingale tried to save British soldiers from dying of preventable disease, in part by pressing the government for more resources. The fierce advocate wrote: 'I stand at the altar of murdered men, and, while I live, I shall fight their cause'. What would she make of our 'silent angels'?

Reflect 1.6

- How do you feel about the imagery of nurses as 'angels'?
- Does the use of such imagery and language undermine your professional status or is it just harmless sentiment?

Are nurses with authority battle-axes?

A senior female nurse who uses her authority to inflict harm on patients, colleagues, or the public reinforces the battle-axe stereotype. The most prominent example was the Nurse Ratched character from *One Flew Over the Cuckoo's Nest*, a maternal sociopath who tortured men on an inpatient psychiatric unit. In addition, *M*A*S*H*'s 'Hot Lips' Houlihan was a military officer who did help patients but also tormented colleagues with her obsession for procedure and barely repressed sexual frustration.

The battle-axe continues to appear. The 2012 film *Cloud Atlas*, directed by Andy and Lana Wachowski, and Tom Tykwer based on David Mitchell's 2004 novel, included Nurse Noakes, a malevolent, gender-ambiguous supervisor of a nursing home that imprisoned unwanted relatives. Hospital shows sometimes present a senior nurse as a heartless enforcer of trivial rules that seem to cause more harm than good. Even *Nurse Jackie* did this in its early portrayal of nurse manager Gloria Akalitus (Truth About Nursing, 2015d). Some scary films, like *Nurse 3D* (2014), have included a hybrid character we call the 'naughty-axe', a malevolent sexualised nurse.

One striking recent example of the battle-axe stereotype was a comment by British politician Boris Johnson about Hillary Clinton. In November 2007 Johnson, then a Member of Parliament, published a column in the *Telegraph* in which he remarked that Clinton had a 'steely blue stare, like a sadistic nurse in a mental hospital'. The media raised this statement with Johnson after he was appointed Foreign Secretary in July 2016. No apology ensued (Johnston, 2016).

Are advanced practice nurses just low-cost 'physician extenders'?

In the 1960s, some nurses began to provide certain types of care that physicians traditionally had done. These 'advanced practice registered nurses' (APRNs) include nurse practitioners (NPs), nurse midwives, nurse anaesthetists, and clinical nurse specialists. Today, there are more than 200,000 APRNs in the United States, most with at least a master's degree and increasingly with doctoral preparation. Research shows that APRN care is at least as good as that of physicians (Truth About Nursing, 2016d). APRNs follow a holistic, preventive care model, and they excel at detecting subtle problems and handling chronic conditions. APRNs care for underserved urban and rural populations, but they practice in all settings, offering a cost-effective practitioner care model.

The media's treatment of APRNs has been mixed. Some news reports have given a fair account of APRN practice. The headline of an 18 March 2016 post on *The Washington Post*'s Wonkblog said it all: 'In a fight between nurses and doctors, the nurses are slowly winning'. The piece described how US APRNs were gaining the right, state by state and function by function, to practice without physician 'supervision'. Recently, some US city magazines have begun including nurses in their familiar 'top doctors' pieces. Oregon's *Portland Monthly* has published an annual list of that area's 'Top Doctors and Nurses' with the next slated for January 2017. The feature provides a database of practitioners, and although it is overwhelmingly physicians; it also has many APRNs (*Portland Monthly*, 2016).

There have been a few strong television portrayals, such as those of the NPs on Channel 4's documentary show *24 Hours in A&E* (2011–present), who have been able to display some good technical and psychosocial care. But most depictions have relied heavily on imagery suggesting that APRNs are low-skilled physician wannabes. In the 5 August 2013 episode of Disney XD's tween series *Lab Rats*, one major character exclaimed that his brother had turned into 'Dr. Evil … or should I say Nurse Practitioner Evil, since you flunked out of med school!'

Mattel produced a children's product with a comparable message in 2005. This was a collectible duck doll called the Nurse Quacktitioner, which suggested that NPs are 'quacks', unqualified practitioners who pretend to be physicians. After UK physicians heard about the row, many sent letters urging Mattel to *keep* selling the doll because it *would* promote contempt for NPs, arguing that NPs are inadequate physician substitutes used to cut costs (Truth About Nursing, 2006).

Prominent advertising for healthcare products and services often suggests that practitioner care is provided only by physicians. Doubt it? 'Ask your doctor!'

The news media's treatment of APRNs has also been flawed. News entities rarely consult APRNs as general health experts, and sometimes not even for stories about APRNs. There are often suggestions that APRNs can treat only minor ailments. In a 6 January 2015 op-ed in the *New York Post*, Betsy McCaughey protested a New York State move to expand NP practice, arguing that NPs should not 'play doctor without going to medical school'. McCaughey cited one physician who baselessly said that he had once diagnosed an unexpected condition and speculated that an NP 'would've' missed it.

And on 1 June 2016, Fox News ran a report on a new rule proposed by the US Department of Veterans Affairs (VA) to permit its APRNs to provide the full range of care without physician 'supervision'. The piece stated that the rule would 'allow highly trained nurses to act as doctors, and even administer anaesthesia without a doctor's supervision'. The headline: 'Vets may have to settle for a visit with the nurse at the VA'. The report relied almost entirely on the views of physicians (Rohrbeck & McKelway, 2016). American Association of Nurse Anaesthetists president Juan Quintana, RN, DNP, himself a military veteran, noted that because the physicians 'don't have any evidence of their own to support their arguments, their actions are really quite reckless and selfishly put our nation's veterans in a most precarious position'. Evidently, while Quintana lives he will fight their cause (American Association of Nurse Anesthetists, 2016).

Improving the image of nursing through leadership in advocacy and media

Nurses must take the lead in changing their place in their world. Nurses should recognise their own power and role in health care; project a professional image, from everyday interactions to public advocacy; educate physicians and others in the clinical setting; shape existing media about nursing; and create their own media to explain nursing. Some of these key themes appear later in this text, for example the importance of nurses taking the lead in policy matters, discussed below and in Chapter 11 of this book.

A first step for many nurses will be recognising their own importance. Every day, nurses hold lives in their hands. Nursing is a big deal, and therefore, so are you. But with great power comes great responsibility. And a central responsibility of nursing is to advocate: for patients, yes, but also for nurses themselves, since nurses cannot save others if they are not strong.

We realise the stakes are high for an advocate. In June 2016 Ontario's *London Free Press* reported that a local hospital had fired Vanessa Burkoski, its eminent chief nursing officer, apparently because she also served as president of the Registered Nurses Association of Ontario (RNAO), which had issued a report critical of de-nursification at the province's hospitals (Sher, 2016). But by September, this CNO had a new post at a major Toronto hospital. And after a US Navy nurse was threatened with discharge for declining on ethical grounds to participate in force-feeding of prisoners at Guantanamo Bay Navy Base in Cuba, the American Nurses Association (ANA) sent a forceful letter urging the military to impose no punishment (Cipriano, On Military View of Force-Feeding, 2015b). The Navy nurse prevailed (Cipriano, On Navy Nurse Force-Feeding Decision, 2015c).

Every nurse can project a professional image. Consider your uniform – is it self-respecting? Or does it feature cartoon characters? Be nurse-identified. Introduce yourself as a nurse. Include your surname. Consider 'nursing out loud' – describe your assessments and clinical thought process, so patients, families, and colleagues understand what nursing is. Accept credit for your work. Modesty is a virtue, but not if it undermines nursing by perpetuating the stereotypes described above. Even our language merits attention. Use 'prescriptions' instead of 'orders' to better establish nursing autonomy and refute the idea that physicians direct nursing.

Public advocacy on health issues is also important. Don't wait for permission to speak and ask for improvements, or to advocate. If you feel you need permission – we give it to you! Many nurses have trouble finding their voices. You can start small by contacting local authorities about things like pothole repair. No one disputes they need to be fixed. And when you find you can move the government to protect people even though in this small way, you are on the road to recognising your ability to affect effect change. But this is just the beginning. Consider taking on larger policy issues, as nursing professor Mona Shattell did in a powerful March 2016 *New York Times* op-ed she co-wrote about the health challenges long-haul truckers face (Balay & Shattell, 2016). And how about a run for public office? No group is more qualified to make policy decisions than nurses.

Consider efforts to educate those you work with in the clinical setting: physicians and other colleagues, patients, and family members. In hospitals and schools, work to get nursing the same institutional power and recognition as medicine commands, from governing boards to ethics committees to websites. Work with your webmaster to increase nursing's presence. To improve the understanding physicians have of nursing, consider co-educational programmes, like the one at Dartmouth in which medical students shadow nurses (Dartmouth Medicine, 2005). You can even create short educational videos to educate medical students and physicians about nursing roles, autonomy, and duty to advocate.

It is essential to educate the media about nursing, to encourage more accurate portrayals as well as reduce damaging misinformation. Consider how to attract media coverage. You can collect and pitch stories about nursing, perhaps with roundtables or press releases about nursing, including research about the nursing image, like the studies discussed earlier. Publicise nurses' clinical innovations. In December 2013, Scotland's *Southern Reporter* highlighted the work of a critical care nurse at Borders General Hospital who had developed an effective programme for early identification of at-risk patients (Peebles, 2013). Try to persuade any media contacts, like local health reporters, to put you or your colleagues on their list of health expert sources.

In reacting to media products that have already appeared, first try to catch the media being good. Praise helpful portrayals. Consider giving awards to local media. Persuading the media to reconsider harmful portrayals is more challenging. You can use phone calls; public campaigns, perhaps through Change.org; press releases; and social media, which nurses used to convince MTV to limit the damage done by its 2013 reality show *Scrubbing In* (Truth About Nursing, 2013b). Above all, *be persistent*. In 2007, we learned of Dentyne Ice television commercials in Canada featuring female nurses hopping into bed with male patients. After a week of discussions with Cadbury Schweppes Canada, a letter writing campaign in which we were joined by RNAO, and voicemail messages to the top seven Cadbury executives in the world, we finally received a call from the CEO in London. He apologised, discussed our concerns, and said he was pulling the ad (Truth About Nursing, 2007).

Summary

Nurses should create their own media to explain nursing to the world. Tell your most compelling stories. Write about nursing in blogs, articles, books, and op-eds. In June 2010, we published an op-ed on the BBC News website, 'Is the media image of nursing damaging the profession?' (Yes, it is, we argued.) After the nurse who declined to participate in force-feedings at Guantanamo prevailed, ANA president Pamela Cipriano had a strong May 2015 op-ed in the *Washington Post* urging the military to create a framework for managing such ethical conflicts (Cipriano, Let nurses do the ethical thing: Patients' interests should trump all other obligations, 2015a).

Broadcast media can be more challenging. But a great long-running nurse-hosted radio show is *HealthCetera*, formerly *HealthStyles*, which has been hosted for many years by Diana Mason and Barbara Glickstein on New York City's WBAI. And nurse Maureen McGrath hosts the *Sunday Night Sex Show*, which airs on Vancouver's CKNW. These shows include informed discussions of cutting-edge health issues in which nurses are full-fledged participants.

And with the Internet, there are few limits on our disruptive innovations. In October 2011, we used Xtranormal software to create and post a short video to subvert stereotypes called *Nursing: Isn't That Sweet?!* (Truth About Nursing, 2011b) From online video to social media to life simulation gaming, the future of the nursing image, like the profession itself, is unwritten. It is our job to write it.

References

Agence France Presse, 2006. *Nurses and firemen top fantasy poll*. Available at: http://bit. ly/2fuJjwT. Also see www.truthaboutnursing.org/news/2006/aug/24_fantasy.html.

Al Bawaba, 2010. *Nurses Union demands Ghada Abd Al Riziq's drama be stopped*. Available at: http://bit.ly/2fuRKrX. Also see www.truthaboutnursing.org/news/2010/aug/16_ egypt.html.

American Association of Nurse Anesthetists, 2016. *Study Shows Practice Restrictions and Physician Supervision Have No Impact on Anesthesia Patient Safety*. Available at: http://bit. ly/1XBStHL.

Balay, A. & Shattell, M., 2016. Long-haul sweatshops. *New York Times*, 9 March.

Bloomekatz, A., 2013. A nurse who is healing patients and himself. *Los Angeles Times*, 9 October.

Brindley, P.G. & Needham, C., 2009. Positioning prior to endotracheal intubation on a television medical drama: Perhaps life mimics art. *Resuscitation*, May, 80(5), p. 604.

Cipriano, P., 2015a. Let nurses do the ethical thing: Patients' interests should trump all other obligations. *Washington Post*, 22 May.

Cipriano, P., 2015b. *On Military View of Force-Feeding*. Available at: http://bit.ly/2eSHsyc.

Cipriano, P., 2015c. *On Navy Nurse Force-Feeding Decision.* Available at: http://bit. ly/2fv4Sxe.

Colihan, K., 2008. *Grey's Anatomy Raises Health Awareness.* Available at: http://cbsn. ws/2eWWPZA.

Daily Mail, 2010. *Ooooh Matron! Upset nurses demand bus company removes 'demeaning' advert promoting bus route to hospital.* Available at: http://dailym.ai/2eptEuH. Also see www. truthaboutnursing.org/news/2010/mar/16_oooh.html.

Dartmouth Medicine, 2005. *'Me and my shadow' is mantra for a new medical student elective.* Available at: http://dartmed.dartmouth.edu/summer05/html/vs_mantra.php. Also see Ellen Ceppetelli explain in detail at http://bit.ly/2epMvFK.

Garcia-Navarro, L., 2016. *How To Fight Zika When Your Country Is In Trouble: Improvise.* Available at: http://n.pr/1TKiphv.

Gross, T., 2016. *Why Abby Wambach Doesn't Want To Be Known 'Just As A Soccer Player'.* Available at: http://n.pr/2eM4Ujf. Also see: http://blog.truthaboutnursing.org/2016/ 11/abby_wambach/.

Hallam, J. & Zwerdling, M., 2015. *The Zwerdling Postcard Collection: Pictures of Nursing.* Available at: www.nlm.nih.gov/exhibition/picturesofnursing/.

Jensen, R. & Oster, E., 2009. The power of TV: Cable television and women's status in India. *The Quarterly Journal of Economics*, 124(3), pp. 1057–1094.

Johnston, C., 2016. Britain's new foreign secretary Boris Johnson: a career of insults and gaffes. *The Guardian*, 13 July.

Jung, K., Shavitt, S., Viswanathan, M. & Hilbe, J.M., 2014. Female hurricanes are deadlier than male hurricanes. *Proceedings of the National Academy of Sciences of the USA*, 17 June, 111(24), pp. 8782–8787.

JWT Communications, 2000. *Memo to Nurses for a Healthier Tomorrow.* Available at: http:// bit.ly/2eWJjVK.

Kaiser Family Foundation, 2008. *Television as Health Educator: A Case Study of Grey's Anatomy,* s.l.: Kaiser Family Foundation. Available at: http://bit.ly/2f61cxR.

Kalisch, P. & Kalisch, B., 1986. A comparative analysis of nurse and physician characters in the entertainment media. *Journal of Advanced Nursing*, 11(2), pp. 179–195.

Kearney, M.S. & Levine, P.B., 2014. Media Influences on social outcomes: The Impact of MTV's 16 and Pregnant on teen childbearing. *American Economic Review*, 105(12), pp. 3597–3632.

Kelly, J., Fealy, G.M. & Watson, R., 2012. The image of you: constructing nursing identities in YouTube. *Journal of Advanced Nursing*, 68(6), pp. 1804–1813.

Kleinhubbert, G., 2006. *Prostitute Retraining Program: From Johns to Geriatrics.* Available at: http://bit.ly/2dTQle5.

MacFarquhar, L., 2016. *A Tender Hand in the Presence of Death.* Available at: http://bit. ly/2dVtrTA.

Meyer, D., 2012. *Economic Reintegration for Veterans.* Available at: http://on.cc.com/2e2ohjX.

Moody, M., 2013. *Secrets of the Royal romantic reunion that changed the course of history.* Available at: http://dailym.ai/2er9yQO.

Neilson, G.R. & Lauder, W., 2008. What do high academic achieving school pupils really think about a career in nursing: Analysis of the narrative from paradigmatic case interviews. Available at: http://bit.ly/2f12oEb. *Nurse Education Today*, 28(6), pp. 680–90.

Odone, C., 2011. Nursing is no longer the caring profession. As they rise through the ranks to a desk job, many see patients as a nuisance to be ignored, says Cristina Odone. *The Telegraph*, 28 August.

Outhwaite, A., 2006. Why nurses are no angels: The public loves them. The Government wants to give them more power. If only you knew what nurses are really like, says Dr Lucy Chapman. *Independent*, 19 June.

Peebles, H., 2013. Borders General takes starring role on Danish TV. *Southern Reporter*, 31 December.

Portland Monthly, 2016. *Top Doctors and Nurses 2017*. Available at: www.pdxmonthly.com/pages/top-docs-nurses.

Posel, S., 2013. *Hollywood Deployed to Convince Americans to Sign Up for Obamacare*. Available at: http://bit.ly/2eRoatp.

Ribeiro, R., 2016. *Tackling Zika in Brazil: 'There is fear among the people I meet'*. Available at: http://bit.ly/2f4uG0x.

Rohrbeck, D. & McKelway, D., 2016. *Vets may have to settle for a visit with the nurse at the VA*. Available at: http://video.foxnews.com/v/4923512702001/?#sp=show-clips.

Sher, J., 2016. An Ontario nursing group contends Vanessa Burkoski was fired to silence her about changes affecting patient safety. *London Free Press*, 17 June.

The Times, 2004. *Racists Hit Drive for Nurses*. 24 August Available at: http://tinyurl.com/l335jpg.

Truth About Nursing, 2006. *Some U.K. physicians to Mattel: Keep that anti-nurse hatred coming!*. Available at: www.truthaboutnursing.org/news/2006/jan/09_mattel.html.

Truth About Nursing, 2007. *Getting fresher*. Available at: www.truthaboutnursing.org/news/2007/oct/06_dentyne.html.

Truth About Nursing, 2008. *Q: I get that the public health community and even Hollywood itself believes that the entertainment media has a big effect on real world health. But is there any actual research showing it affects what people think and do about health issues like nursing?* Available at: www.truthaboutnursing.org/faq/hollywood_research.html.

Truth About Nursing, 2011a. *Johnson & Johnson Nurse Television Commercials*. Available at: http://tinyurl. com/pc42jyt.

Truth About Nursing, 2011b. *Nursing: Isn't That Sweet?* Available at: http://bit.ly/1SRJo9n.

Truth About Nursing, 2012. *You will be required to deal with bruising: Jon Stewart ridicules school nursing*. Available at: www.truthaboutnursing.org/news/2012/oct/24_jon_stewart.html.

Truth About Nursing, 2013a. *Grey's Anatomy analyses and action*. Available at: www.truthaboutnursing.org/media/tv/greys.html.

Truth About Nursing, 2013b. *Scrubbing Less: MTV's Scrubbing In agrees to make some positive changes*. Available at: www.truthaboutnursing.org/news/2013/nov/12_scrubbing_in.html.

Truth About Nursing, 2013c. *The Mindy Project reviews*. Available at: www.truthaboutnursing.org/media/tv/mindy_project.html.

Truth About Nursing, 2014. *Reviews and ratings of films featuring nurses*. Available at: www.truthaboutnursing.org/media/films/index.html.

Truth About Nursing, 2015a. *Miss America, Kelley Johnson and The View*. Available at: www.truthaboutnursing.org/news/2015/sep/kelley_johnson_the_view.html.

Truth About Nursing, 2015b. *Q: Are you sure nurses are autonomous? Based on what I've seen, it sure looks like physicians are calling the shots.* Available at: www.truthaboutnursing.org/faq/autonomy.html.

Truth About Nursing, 2015c. *Q: Get a sense of humor! How could jokes possibly affect the way people think about nursing?* Available at: www.truthaboutnursing.org/faq/jokes.html.

Truth About Nursing, 2015d. *Nurse Jackie episode reviews*. Available at: www.truthaboutnursing.org/media/tv/nurse_jackie.html.

Truth About Nursing, 2016a. *Healers and Heroes: Fall 2016 Overview of Nursing on Television.* Available at: http://blog.truthaboutnursing.org/2016/10/healers-and-heroes/.

Truth About Nursing, 2016b. *Media reviews and analysis.* Available at: www.truthaboutnursing.org/media/.

Truth About Nursing, 2016c. *Not your everyday robot.* Available at http://blog.truthaboutnursing.org/2014/11/not-your-everyday-robot/

Truth About Nursing, 2016d. *Do physicians deliver better care than Advanced Practice Registered Nurses?* Available at: www.truthaboutnursing.org/faq/aprn_md.html.

Turow, J., 2010. *Playing Doctor: Television, Storytelling, and Medical Power.* s.l.: University of Michigan Press.

Turow, J. & Gans, R., 2002. *As Seen on TV: Health Policy Issues in TV's Medical Dramas.* s.l.: Kaiser Family Foundation. Available at http://bit.ly/2eRpPil.

Weaver, R., Salamonson, Y., Koch, J. & Jackson, D., 2013. Nursing on television: Student perceptions of television's role in public image, recruitment and education. *Journal of Advanced Nursing,* April, 69(12), pp. 2635–2643.

Weiss, E., Silverman, M. & Rubin, J., 2015. *Shots: Elmo, so good on vaccines and third person self-description, not so good on nursing.* Available at: www.truthaboutnursing.org/news/2015/apr/elmo_vaccines.html.

Wells, H. & Tatham, J.C., 1943–1968. *Cherry Ames Nurse Stories.* New York(NY): Grosset & Denlap.

2

NURSING, A TRUSTED BRAND

Do we dare to care?

Pádraig Ó Lúanaigh

Why this chapter is important

For nurses to be able to demonstrate their contribution and value in providing safe, quality and effective health services they need to be able to articulate and describe their practice. Equally, individual nurses need to be able to identify the core values and attributes that define and inform their own practice. This chapter unpicks and questions the value and appropriateness of the term 'care' in relation to nursing work and challenges the reader to consider how they define and explain their own nursing practice and the impact they have individually on health service provision.

Chapter trigger question: Do you really need to be caring to be a good nurse?

Key words: care, nursing effectiveness, patient experience, compassion

Introduction

In keeping with the overall aim of this book, this chapter is intended to get you to think about your (the person) nursing practice and the kind of nurse you are by exploring and questioning what many argue is the cornerstone of nursing (the profession), the concept of care and caring.

The word 'care' is one of those taken for granted words that we all know and use and this over familiarity does raise issues for nurses and nursing in particular. This chapter will examine the problems associated with defining care and demonstrating a caring attitude and approach to nursing work. In keeping with the other chapters and design of this textbook, you will have an opportunity to explore your own views on how care and caring defines your practice while also considering the limitations and challenges in actually defining and measuring what good nursing care is.

A range of perspectives and theoretical ideas will be used to support the arguments presented and justify the need to rethink how we as nurses define and describe nursing work in the context of organisational cultures and the patient experience.

Care, the contested concept

It is difficult to talk about or even think about the word 'nursing' without adding the term care with it. In the introduction to this chapter I intentionally refer to 'nursing work' and not 'nursing care'. Even writing the term *nursing work* felt clumsy and awkward; as if nursing was more than 'work' and to define it in this way was to reduce nursing activity to something less than it is. The very fact that we use the term 'care' interchangeably when we mean nursing and how 'nursing care' seems so natural a phrase; it may seem odd to even question the value or need to examine the application of care as part of the debate on nurses and nursing.

Care and caring are terms that have been associated with and used to define nursing in popular culture and Chapter 1 in this text presented some of these associations within the media.

Due to the term 'care' being at the heart of how we describe and think about nursing and possibly ourselves, I would like you to take a few minutes to complete a reflect activity at this early stage of the chapter. Complete each activity in order without reading the next instruction.

Reflect 2.1

* First, without spending too much time thinking, write down why you became or want to become a nurse.
* Next write down a list of what nurses do, and finally try to capture in one sentence what nursing is.
* Now, as you reread what you have written, highlight the number of times you used the words, care, caring, compassion, help, kindness or support.
* Mindful of the focus of this chapter you may have purposefully tried to avoid using the words care or caring – if this was the case, I suspect you found this an irritating and more difficult experience to undertake.
* It would be interesting to speak with another colleague who has undertaken the same reflect exercise to see if there are similarities in your use of words and terms.

Of course, it is a reasonable question to ask why it matters how nursing is described or understood and the words used to do this. The reason I believe it matters is that there has been an emerging and intense global questioning about the quality of health care provided with a specific focus on nurses and a dissatisfaction with how nursing care is provided (Watson, 2009). I became aware many years ago that the only people interested in talking about nursing are nurses. However, the public and media have a very keen interest in talking about poor standards and quality of care and in particular nursing care. And there is that word *care* again!

While the term care has been a powerful and useful (if ill-defined) concept for the nursing profession because it engendered trust, safety and benevolence; this pillar of trust and belief has been questioned and damaged by a number of 'health care scandals' where nurses were exposed as failing to provide appropriate or quality care. Such crises in care are not limited to particular countries or health systems and examples are found in Europe, America and Oceania (Reader and Gillespie, 2013).

The debate surrounding the influence and existence of humanitarian values in nursing is long, ongoing and inconclusive. Chapter 1 in this book provides a fascinating insight into the portrayal of nurses and nursing and more importantly how these popular and media representations and images have changed over time. It is of course no coincidence that historically, caring has been associated with women's work and as such was presented as requiring little or no skill, ability or knowledge and as a consequence not valued economically (Stockdale and Warelow, 2000). Equally I believe that taken for granted words such as caring, compassion and empathy in relation to nursing practice have and continue to have changing relevance and importance in defining nursing work. In Chapter 4 you will explore how nursing roles have evolved and changed and yet frequently how we describe the fundamental aspects of nursing work has remained unchanged.

While care is frequently accepted and promoted unquestionably as the 'essence' of nursing (Stockdale and Warelow, 2000) there are those who counter against the value of such a term in modern professional practice. The portrayal of nurses in the media as highlighted in Chapter 1 frequently reverts to the 'battle-axe matron' who appears devoid of any emotion and would surely see any form of care for patients as a weakness and a sign of becoming over-involved and stepping outside a professional boundary. There could be an argument that in the paid relationship that is nursing, to claim to be caring 'suggests hypocrisy and offers only an illusion of caring' (Stockdale and Warelow, 2000, p. 1202). While I find this position slightly harsh there is a need to acknowledge that the nurse–patient/client relationship is a professional one and one where the nurse is in receipt of remuneration for the role and work undertaken.

Equally there is the perspective that the term *care* implies dependency and need and creates an unequally balanced relationship between the individual providing and the person receiving that care. I can see the potential for unhealthy caring relationships and how strong 'doing for' approaches to nursing practice could undermine core elements of the nursing scope of practice such as health promotion, rehabilitation and empowerment of individuals to take responsibility for their own health.

From a nursing perspective care is a difficult concept because it is used in many different contexts. For example, an individual may be '*in care*', you may *care* about global warming, *care* for your pet, *care* for a family member or friend and *care* about the welfare of refugees. So there may be a difference (or not) in caring about or caring for someone or something. Maybe it is simply a case than when you care it is a genuine and enduring thought that may or may not translate into any actual action but is likely to influence how you behave and feel. If we accept this view of caring in nursing then it is possibly reasonable to see caring as being made up of how we think, behave and the attitudes or beliefs and values we hold.

This idea about caring does pose the question; if the personal qualities you have as an individual are the same you have as a nurse or if they are different or indeed if your practice as a nurse is influenced by your personal identity? Obviously your nursing practice is also informed and influenced significantly by professional considerations such as codes of professional conduct. Chapter 5 will help you to examine and understand the impact and role of professional regulation and how factors such as codes of professional conduct further shape and inform your nursing practice.

Should nurses care about care?

The challenge in relation to using care as a shorthand term to describe and represent nursing interventions is the risk associated with differing expectations and understanding of the term. The risk is not solely carried by the nursing profession as the potential misunderstanding can play a direct role in how nurses and those they care for perceive that interaction.

There is considerable evidence in support of the assertion that there is no congruence of perceptions between patients and nurses in regard to which behaviours are considered caring, and very interestingly intended caring is not always perceived as such by the patient or person receiving care (Papastavrou et al., 2011). This understanding of how care is received is in many ways much more important than our concern about how concepts of *care* define nursing. If you do see care as a core element of your nursing practice, how confident are you that you can describe how you demonstrate caring and how those you care for experience this action?

In their systematic review exploring perceptions of caring behaviours, the researchers identified that differing categories of caring interventions were valued by patients and nurses (Papastavrou et al., 2011). Expressive activities such as establishing trusting relationships and offering support were valued and seen as important aspects of 'caring' by nurses, whereas instrumental activities such as physical action-oriented helping behaviours and technical skills were seen as caring more by patients than by nurses. The review by Papastavrou et al. (2011) demonstrates that nurses do not always accurately assess patients' perceptions of the importance applied to the various dimensions of caring, which means that they may plan and implement caring for the patient based on their own nursing assumptions.

It would appear that high-quality nursing requires the development of knowledge, skills, sound judgement and effective nurse–patient communication in meeting the patient's expectations of the behaviours that express and demonstrate caring. It is clearly important to take into account the patient's perspective to link nursing interventions with positive patient outcomes.

How does the term 'care' influence your nursing practice?

When considering your nursing practice, it is important to question how the concept of care influences how you nurse and the kind of nurse you are. In her research examining the results of 49 qualitative reports and 6 concept analyses of caring, Finfgeld-Connett (2006) identified that caring is 'a context-specific interpersonal process that is characterized by expert nursing practice, interpersonal sensitivity and intimate relationships' (p. 196).

Finfgeld-Connett (2006) provides some interesting alternative elements on which to determine nursing work; expert nursing and interpersonal sensitivity delivered within a context of intimate relationships. This work is important because it starts to pull out the actual components of what nurse caring is comprised of. The term 'interpersonal sensitivity' would seem a key component to think about but of course it is equally difficult to describe and observe and may only ever be assessed by the person on the receiving end. And yet, this aspect of interaction between a nurse and the person they are with does seem to get at the essence of nursing for me. For caring to happen, there needs to be someone who is in need and willing to be cared for in an environment that allows care to be provided by expert nurses who are sensitive to the individual they are caring for.

Unlike the debate earlier in this chapter that caring was an unrealistic expectation of a paid professional, I wonder if nurses truly demonstrate care '... by being physically and mindfully present, centring completely on the patient and being emotionally open and available' (Finfgeld–Connett, 2007, p. 199). I suspect that the vast majority of patients want to be in control of their health, rehabilitation and recovery and are not expecting nurses to perform as subservient or surrogate family members. I do, however, think that when patients or clients interact with nurses that are 'physically and mindfully present' their patient experience is of excellent nursing care. Finfgeld–Connett (2007) reminds us that the challenge in being an effective and caring nurse is to be able to '... become deeply involved without succumbing to over emotional, destructive, controlling and self-centred forms of helping' (p. 200)

Reflect 2.2

- Take a few minutes to review the list you made when you started reading this chapter in Reflect 2.1.
- Based on what you have read so far, are there elements of your 'what nurses do' sentence that you wish to change or revise?
- Try to find time to discuss with a colleague the concept of *interpersonal sensitivity* and note if it helps you to define your nursing practice.
- Finally, can you recall times when you were truly 'physically and mindfully present' when engaging with a patient? If so, what was different or allowed

this to happen? Equally are there times when you were not and were simply 'processing' the person or completing tasks?

As you start to consider the complexity of nursing care and what that means, the next section of this chapter explores if it is possible to learn to care and how research studies have helped us understand the experience of learning to care.

Learning to care: Are good nurses born or made?

While terms such as care and compassion have proven difficult to define, they also contribute to the additional debate on whether such values or qualities can be learnt, acquired and indeed measured (Richardson *et al.*, 2015). A research study that interviewed final-year nursing students in the UK looked at how registered nurses influenced student learning in the clinical environment and one of the key findings was the ability of the student participants to distinguish between 'good' and 'bad' nursing (Ó Lúanaigh, 2015). The students in this study described how they were influenced by registered nurse role models who exhibited 'good' nursing. Importantly, the students described how they used their experiences of observing what they considered to be 'bad' nursing as a means of enabling them to know that they did not wish to practise in that way. Indeed 'bad' nurses were described as the nurses the students didn't wish to become. When asked to describe what nursing was, the student participants consistently used the word 'caring' and the researcher concluded that '... it would seem that nursing and the unique contribution of nurses was only recognised when witnessed or experienced by the participants in this study' (Ó Lúanaigh, 2015, p. 455). The student participants appeared to be unable to describe nursing, and the term 'care' was used as a shorthand description for nursing practice that they perceived as good.

This study highlights that while the complexity of nursing and providing care is recognised by nursing students they resort to using terms such as good or bad nursing to try and explain those nurses they admired and respected against those whose practice they did not consider to be caring. In terms of learning how to nurse, the nurses that the students admired were the ones '... perceived as being able to communicate and demonstrate the *tricks of the trade*' and more importantly their nursing practice through the 'little things that matter' (Ó Lúanaigh, 2015, p. 455).

When we think about and discuss the 'little things that matter', I wonder if we are witnessing and describing the *interpersonal sensitivity* that was highlighted in the previous section of this chapter since it has been argued that the 'smallest of nursing actions can convey compassion' (Bramley and Matiti, 2014, p. 2790).

Reflect 2.3

Reflect on those nursing students that spoke about nursing in terms of good or bad nursing and how good nurses were described as those that did the 'little things that matter':

- Think about a nursing colleague you have observed and whose nursing practice you admire and respect.
- What is it that impresses you about their practice? Write down a description of how they work.
- What kind of words did you use to explain your colleague's practice?

For most people, describing what nursing and *caring* nursing is can be a challenging and difficult activity. In their work with first-year nursing students, UK researchers discovered that the participants found it difficult at the start of their studies to describe what care was. Based on the student interviews the following themes were identified to capture how the student participants 'understood' caring in the context of professional nursing:

- caring by *doing tasks* or demonstrating skills with patients;
- caring as a *personal quality*;
- caring by *communicating an understanding of a person's needs*;
- caring as seen *through the media* or through *personal experiences*;
- examples of *uncaring behaviours*, traits or situations.

(Phillips *et al.*, 2015, p. 405)

The first-year students in this study by Phillips *et al.* (2015) had strong views and opinions on why they chose nursing, potentially similar to the reasons you listed in Reflect 2.1. Fundamentally, the students in this study wanted to make a difference in their intended nursing careers. However, as with the work by Ó Lúanaigh (2015) the students in this study struggled '… to articulate their personal values and their understanding of the nature of caring using professional language' (p. 407).

It does not seem unreasonable that those starting out on a career in nursing would struggle to describe care in relation to nursing practice, but this study further identifies the importance of nursing students having the support to develop the ability to articulate what nursing practice is. What was clear from the student group in this study was their motivation to make a difference and provide good nursing care. There is, however, worrying evidence that nursing students demonstrate a decline in caring attributes and attitudes from the second year of their studies (Watson *et al.*, 1999; Murphy *et al.*, 2009) and there are obviously many potential reasons for this; one may well be the poorly articulated understanding of how to maintain and manage caring relationships.

Lyneham and Levett-Jones (2016) drew out four nursing values from their interviews with 14 Australian nursing students at the conclusion of their nursing degree programme. The researchers identified that the student participants had developed professional values and behaviours which appeared to have been strongly influenced once again by good nurse role models. The four professional values or behaviours used to describe good nursing care were:

- being person-centred;

- kindness and caring;
- being in control;
- commitment to learning.

Reflect 2.4

- List the four nursing values identified by Lyneham and Levett-Jones (2016) and try to write down how you demonstrate these in your everyday nursing practice.
- How would someone know you incorporated these four values into your practice if they were simply observing you?
- Do these four values provide a more useful way of describing your nursing practice than the word 'care'?

The person perspective on care: Nursing care defined through the patient experience

The previous section of this chapter posed some of the issues in relation to the use of the term care and caring when applied to nursing practice. We also examined how it appears that nursing students enter their studies with strong ideals and values and how this commitment may wane during the progress of their study. This section is designed to support you to take the views presented earlier and start to think about your own practice by considering care in the context of the patient experience. Through the use of real-life examples of health care, in this section you will get the opportunity to consider other concepts and words that may be as equal if not more important to defining your practice than through the concept of care. Considering care and nursing interventions from the patient or client perspective may in many ways be a more useful way of trying to understand and describe care. In many ways the reality of the impact nursing work has can only be understood through patient experiences as captured through their stories and experiences. A US research study with 199 adults receiving hospital care explored the concept of quality care from a patient's perspective (Larrabee and Bolden, 2001). The study resulted in five themes of good nursing care. On the face of it, each of the themes would seem obvious and in many ways 'common sense'.

Five themes of good nursing care from a patient perspective (ibid.):

- providing for my needs;
- treating me pleasantly and with respect;
- caring about me;
- being competent (accurate, knowledge and skill);
- providing prompt care.

Importantly, the five themes of good nursing while including 'caring about me' are not exclusively dependent on 'care'. Clearly the nurse–patient relationship is much more complex than being a 'caring nurse'. The UK Patients Association reported the need for all patients to be treated in a '… humane and caring way with compassion and dignity, openness and honesty' (The Patients Association, 2015, p. 6). The report goes on to echo the findings from Larrabee and Bolden (2001) when it stresses that 'People want to *feel* equal and cared for and listened to' (The Patients Association, 2015, p.14). The focus on honest and open relationships between patients and nurses is supported by established evidence which demonstrated that the less patients and nurses disagreed on the desirability of clinical outcomes, the more satisfied patients were with their care (Kovner, 1989).

In 2015, The Patients Association in the UK produced a report based on the key themes that emerged from calls to their patient and carer helpline. The following excerpt is taken from that report, called *Why our NHS should listen and be human: This is what the public are telling us.* The account was provided by the granddaughter of Mr Frederick George Tolhurst who died in hospital in 2014:

In the middle of the night my grandad Fred was moved onto a winter pressures ward with half agency nursing and half employed staff. By the time we finally located where my grandfather had gone to, telephoned the ward numerous times with no answer and reached the hospital for visiting time at 3pm my mother did not recognise her own father. His mouth was so dry his tongue was stuck to the roof of his mouth; he struggled to communicate with us, was disorientated and utterly confused. Another contributory factor we found out a few days later was that nurses were mistakenly over-prescribing his epileptic medication, which added to his drowsiness and confusion. When we asked staff about his deterioration in less than a twenty-four hour period spent within the hospital, our concerns were dismissed.

One such case of rude and unpleasant nursing occurred within the first week my grandfather spent on this ward. I buzzed his call bell for him and a health care assistant attended. She said to me, not to my grandfather the patient, in a raised and aggressive tone 'yes what do you want?' When I highlighted to her that my grandfather wished to use the commode, she said 'He will have to wait. I do not have anyone to help me'. When I offered to assist she turned her back to me and walked away.

My Grandad Fred was left acutely dehydrated through the poor care of this hospital. Whenever our family went in to visit he would be gasping for a drink but often fluids and his personal items such as glasses, or food our family had taken to the hospital, were left out of reach. I never saw any blood pressure (BP) checks carried out within visiting hours, which were 3pm to 8pm. Furthermore, vital medication would be placed in front of elderly patients but nurses did not actually check to see if patients were taking these drugs. On a number of occasions, I would administer the drugs that had been left on my grandfather's table as he was unable to see them due to cataracts. Since receiving my grandfather's medical notes after his death, I now know that he had not been properly hydrated for seven days prior to his death, and food charts had been falsified/lost due to staff not having enough time to monitor patients correctly.

This ward at Whipps Cross failed on basic hygiene; the toilets upon entry to the ward often smelt of human waste. Patients including my grandfather would be left unwashed, lying on their backs to prompt sleep and bedside buzzers left in their cradles on the wall so patients would not bother nursing staff. When my Grandad Frederick George Tolhurst (I like writing his full name because it makes me remember the person he was), was mentioned by any nurses, he was 'bed 17', utterly dehumanised, no longer a person with a past and people that loved him. Simply a number, a statistic, void of feelings or emotions.

The night before he died, due to a breakdown in communication with Social Services, our family was told to expect that my grandad should be discharged the next day as he was free of infection and had recovered fully from his fall. The only thing delaying him going home was that he had become constipated. A young registrar prescribed a laxative called Picolax and when my mother highlighted that my grandad was used to more natural methods of constipation relief, eg prunes or dates, this doctor replied with 'Pfft we have something stronger than that'. Grandad Fred was dead less than sixteen hours later.

On Friday 14 March 2014 at 1.50pm in the afternoon I received a call to say my grandfather had been found unresponsive, he died less than ten minutes later of a cardiac arrest, alone and with no family by his bedside. We later found out that he had been calling my mother's name, Anne, all morning due to the distress of having unbearable sickness and diarrhoea, but no-one had contacted us. He died frightened and alone, in unfamiliar surroundings with people he did not trust.

In writing about her grandfather Mr Tolhurst, his granddaughter describes his and her experience as follows; my grandfather was '… utterly dehumanised, no longer a person with a past and people that loved him' (p. 23); '… he died frightened and alone, in unfamiliar surroundings with people he did not trust' (p. 24). This account (and recall, by a relative) is powerful and sobering and in my opinion highlights the importance of ensuring that our practice as nurses never fails any individual. I am unsure and at a loss to describe or find words as to what was missing or absent in this example. We have a choice of words: care, empathy, compassion or humanity. The reality of course is that the words we use are in many ways redundant, since the outcome was so devastating in this example. Mr Tolhurst's experience as described by his granddaughter is one none of us is likely to want for ourselves or our family. So why do these things happen?

Reflect 2.5

- Reflect on how you reacted to reading about Mr Tolhurst's experience of nursing.
- Describe how the account made you feel.
- How do we learn from reading about such poor patient experiences?
- How does the description of Mr Tolhurst's patient experience challenge your personal values and professional nursing identity – *what* is nursing?

Throughout this chapter I have focused predominately on teasing out our understanding of the word 'care'. However, at times I have included the term 'compassion' and this is a word that would appear to have more significance as this chapter has progressed and started to explore the lived experience of patients and those in receipt of poor care. It will be obvious that to explore 'compassion' would require another chapter and many of the debates we have had around the use of the word care would come into play. It is important, however, to be aware and mindful of how compassion differs and may equally enable you to better understand and explain your own nursing practice. As we reflect on why nurses chose to neglect and abuse patients or adopt bad nursing care there seems to be a fundamental issue with their ability to be compassionate. Another recall of patient care by a relative in the same Patients Association report spoke of a daughter's gratitude when her father received excellent care. In the account, there is no mention of *care, compassion, nursing skills* or *clinical effectiveness* but rather, the simple acknowledgement that '… they looked after my father as if he was their own relative' (p. 27). The Patients Association expands on the concept of care in expecting nursing care to be '… considerate and thoughtful care' (The Patients Association, 2015, p. 15).

So maybe the essence of nursing practice, the thing that makes nursing and nurses key to quality health care is simply captured in the sentiment that they treat people as they would want their own relative cared for – maybe it really is that simple?

A number of other chapters in this book will mention the global shortage of nurses, increasing pressures on nursing, changing roles and expectations on the profession and constant change as the only certainty in our professional lives. The risk in presenting care and compassion as a focus in a book chapter is that they become seen as academic and abstract ideas rather than the core or essence of our nursing practice. The reality of course is that our own well-being as nurses is absolutely interdependent on the quality of care we can give (Maben *et al.*, 2012).

As this section comes to an end it is important that as nurses we find ways to support and be supported by one another. Chapter 7 provides some very helpful guidance on how to do this. We are reminded and given sobering guidance by the Dalai Lama that:

> For someone to develop genuine compassion towards others, first he or she must have a basis upon which to cultivate compassion and that basis is the

ability to connect to one's own feelings and to care for one's own welfare ...
caring for others requires caring for oneself.

(Dalai Lama, 2003, p. 125)

The final section of this chapter explores cultures of care as the final element
impacting on how our patients experience care and on our own practice.

Cultures of care: Nursing and health services that are human

In 2008, a significant research study was undertaken which involved interviewing
large numbers of NHS staff in 50 NHS trusts and GP practices. The study identified
four elements that those who participated in the study believed had a direct impact
on their ability or motivation to provide safe quality care (Ipsos MORI, 2008).

In identifying these four requirements, the researchers have recognised that an
individual's ability to provide a safe, quality and caring service is enabled or hindered
by the organisational or working culture they are practising in. Earlier in this chapter
we highlighted that individuals needed to maintain personal resilience to be
compassionate; equally important is the need for our work environments to reflect
and demonstrate a culture of caring also. The four key themes identified were:

- the resources to deliver quality care;
- the support needed to do a good job;
- a worthwhile job that offers the chance to develop;
- the opportunity to improve team working.

These four themes require us to consider caring nursing as requiring more than
individual qualities; the 'good' nurse is potentially more than simply a collection of
personal qualities and professional skills and knowledge.

A later research project that was informed through interviews with a range of
nurses working in different care sectors also focused on understanding the factors
that influence the quality of patient care (Kieft et al., 2014). From an analysis of the
researchers' interviews with nurses, seven components were listed as impacting on
the ability to provide good or quality nursing care;

- clinically competent nurses;
- collaborative working relationships;
- autonomous nursing practice;
- adequate staffing;
- control over nursing practice;
- managerial support;
- patient-centred culture.

The seven factors identified reflect many aspects of the earlier Ipsos MORI (2008)
study findings. Important messages from this research study signal the importance

and need for nurses to 'gain autonomy over their own practice in order to improve patient experiences' (p. 2). This claim provides a challenge to nursing and nurses, suggesting that quality nursing care requires organisational systems and confident nursing teams that enable nurses to control their practice. Most importantly is the fascinating statement that 'when patients have positive nursing care, nurses also experience a good and healthy work environment' (Kieft *et al.*, 2014, p. 3).

The case for positive and supportive work environments was also made by Sawbridge and Hewison (2015) when they challenged and made the argument that 'when health professionals are abused and de-humanised by an uncaring system, how can we expect them to show compassion' (p. 194). This claim by Sawbridge and Hewison is not seeking to remove professional responsibility for the care nurses provide but does importantly acknowledge and raise awareness of the impact that the environment nurses work within has on their ability to provide compassionate and caring nursing interventions. Andersson *et al.* (2015) also identified the importance of the context in terms of the provision of nursing care. Following interviews with 21 registered nurses the researchers generated four ways of understanding caring from the nurses' perspective. Caring was described (in ibid., p. 1) as:

- person-centeredness;
- safeguarding the patients' best interests;
- nursing interventions;
- contextually intertwined.

Reflect 2.6

- Take a few minutes to consider the four themes listed above.
- Can you relate these 'requirements' to your current practice placement or work environment?
- Are you able to identify examples of how each of these four aspects have supported you in your practice and/or had a negative impact on your ability to provide good nursing care?

As this chapter concludes it seems that nursing 'care' is an important component of how both nurses and patients understand the interaction that occurs between them. Equally, when thinking about the provision of quality health care services the central role of nursing is identified, with patient satisfaction with nursing care as the strongest influencer of a person's experience of their hospital stay (Laschinger *et al.*, 2005).

While there is clearly value in defining nursing using a care label there may be more beneficial ways of identifying and demonstrating the impact and value of nursing practice. A useful systematic review examined the links between patient experience and clinical safety and effectiveness (Doyle *et al.*, 2015). The review made the important claim that patient experience is positively associated with clinical effectiveness.

Summary

As we conclude this chapter, I hope you have been able to question some 'taken for granted' ideas that you may have had about nursing and nursing care. You have had an opportunity to consider a range of ideas, some of which may have challenged your long-held beliefs or made you think about the use of care which previously you may have given little or no consideration to. In some ways, the debate about *care* can appear academic, when indeed how we describe nursing and what nurses 'do' seems unimportant when we read about or witness examples of poor nursing and the impact this has on an individual's feelings and recovery. However, it is vital that we always question some of these core ideas and beliefs about our nursing practice since this allows us to agree on what are non-negotiable and important aspects of our professional and individual practice as well as helping us to improve how we describe and provide nursing services. Without the ability to clearly describe and understand the core aspects of nursing practice, how can we ever be confident that we will immediately identify when nursing interventions fall below the accepted standard? It is important to recognise the recurring themes in the literature that align care to the specific context of how and where the care is provided. There is also strong recognition of the importance of expert nursing intervention to be able to provide care.

While you may still have difficulty explicitly explaining nursing care, the reality is we are all well able to recognise poor nursing and care. I would encourage you to continue to understand, explain and record the quality of your practice by using a range of strategies such as practice and peer review; use available information and intelligence from nurse sensitive indicator dashboards and feedback from patients and carers through tools such as the friends and family test, complaint reports and patient and carer feedback.

In my opinion, using terms such as 'care' as the only means of defining effective and professional nursing is inadequate, and as we acknowledge the evolving changes in healthcare we must continue to find measurable and meaningful ways of demonstrating how you (the person) and our (the profession) nursing practice influences the patient experience to explain, understand and monitor safe, effective and good nursing.

References

Andersson, E.K., Willman, A., Sjostrom-Strand, A., Borglin, G. (2015) Registered nurses' descriptions of caring: A phenomenographic interview study, *Nursing*, 14(16), pp. 1–10.
Bramley, L., Matiti, M. (2014) How does it really feel to be in my shoes? Patients' experiences of compassion within nursing care and their perceptions of developing compassionate nurses, *Journal of Clinical Nursing*, 23(19/20), pp. 2790–2799.
Dalai Lama (2003) *Transforming the Mind: Teachings on Generating Compassion*. London: Thorsons.

Doyle, C., Lennox, L., Bell, D. (2015) A systematic review of evidence on the links between patient experience and clinical safety and effectiveness, *BMJ Open*. Available from http://bmjopen.bmj.com/content/3/1/e001570.long.

Finfgeld-Connett, D. (2007) Meta-synthesis of caring in nursing, *Journal of Clinical Nursing*, 17(2), pp. 196–204.

Ipsos MORI (2008) *What Matters to Staff in the NHS? Research Study Conducted for Department of Health*. London: Ipsos MORI.

Kieft, R., de Brouwer, B., Franckle, A.L., Delnoij, D. (2014) How nurses and their work environment affect patient experiences of the quality of care: a qualitative study, *BMC Health Services Research*, 14; doi: 10.1186/s12913–015–0788–1.

Kovner, C.T. (1989). Nurse-patient agreement and outcomes after surgery. *Western Journal of Nursing Research*, 11(1), pp. 7–17.

Larrabee, J.H., Bolden, L.V. (2001) Defining patient-perceived quality of nursing care. *Journal of Nursing Care Quality*, 16(1), pp. 34–60.

Laschinger, H.S., McGillis Hall, L., Almost, J. (2005) A psychometric analysis of the patient satisfaction with nursing care quality questionnaire, *Journal of Nursing Care Quality*, 20(3), pp. 220–301.

Lyneham, J., Levett-Jones, T. (2016) Insights into Registered Nurses' professional values through the eyes of graduating students, *Nurse Education in Practice*, 17, pp. 86–90.

Murphy, F., Jones, S., Edwards, M., James, J., Mayer, A. (2009) The impact of nurse education on the caring behaviours of nursing students. *Nurse Education Today*, 29(2) pp. 254–264.

Ó Lúanaigh, P. (2015) Becoming a professional: What is the influence of registered nurses on nursing students' learning in the clinical environment?, *Nurse Education in Practice*, 15(6), pp. 450–456.

Papastavrou, E., Efstathiou, G., Charalambous, A. (2011) Nurses' and patients' perceptions of caring behaviours: Quantitative systematic review of comparative studies, *Journal of Advanced Nursing*, 67(6), pp. 1191–1205.

Phillips, J., Cooper, K., Rosser, E., Scammell, J., Heaslip, V., While, S., Donaldson, I., Jack, E., Hemingway, A., Harding, A. (2015) An exploration of the perceptions of caring held by students entering nursing programmes in the United Kingdom: A longitudinal qualitative study phase 1, *Nurse Education in Practice*, 15(6), pp. 403–408.

Reader, T.W., Gillespie, A. (2013) Patient neglect in healthcare institutions: A systematic review and conceptual model. *BMC Health Services Research*, 13, p. 156.

Richardson, C., Percy, M., Hughes, J. (2015) Nursing therapeutics: Teaching student nurses care, compassion and empathy, *Nurse Education Today*, 35(5), pp. 1–5.

Sawbridge, Y., Hewison, A. (2015) 'Compassion costs nothing' – the elephant in the room?, *Practice Nursing*, 26(4), pp. 194–197.

Stockdale, M., Warelow, P.J. (2000) Is the complexity of care a paradox?, *Journal of Advanced Nursing*, 31(5), pp. 1258–1264.

The Patients Association (2015) *Why our NHS Should Listen and be Human: This is what the public are telling us*. London.

Watson, R., Daryl, I., Lea, A. (1999) A longitudinal study into the perceptions of caring among student nurses using multivariate analysis of the Caring Dimensions Inventory. *Journal of Advanced Nursing*, 30(5), pp. 1080–1089.

Watson, J. (2009) Caring science and human caring theory: Transforming personal and professional practices of nursing and health care, *Journal of Health and Human Services Administration*, 31(4), pp. 466–482.

3

THE CHANGING NATURE OF NURSE EDUCATION

Preparing our future workforce

Elizabeth Rosser

Why this chapter is important

This chapter is important as the face of nurse education is changing apace. Given nurse education is inextricably linked to the workforce, the scope of practice of qualified nurses is increasing significantly, services are being reconfigured beyond recognition and healthcare assistants are taking a more dominant role. Whilst globally there is a shortage of qualified nurses and educators, new career pathways are emerging to accommodate innovative roles such as clinical academic careers. There is of course no crystal ball and successive governments have their own visions of shaping the health service. However, we do know that nurses are the largest workforce of healthcare professionals globally, and the potential for nurse education to influence change is immense.

Chapter trigger question: Is the education preparation of twenty-first century nurses fit for purpose?

Key words: Nurse education, workforce, careers, advanced practice, service reconfiguration, new roles

Introduction

Nursing is experiencing a global shortage of qualified nurses, high student attrition, shortage of quality educators, poor quality of professional work-life balance, high turnover and low morale (Dragon, 2009; Gantz *et al.*, 2012; Flynn & McKeown, 2009; Gabrielle *et al.*, 2008; Aiken *et al.*, 2013). Together these factors combine to have a significant impact on patient care and adversely affect the reputation and morale of the professional nurse. I have been thinking a great deal about these data, not only from a global perspective, which is most worrying but more particularly from a United Kingdom (UK) and specifically England perspective and the implications for nurse education. Reading again the latest English policy documents, the scope of the challenges is huge and so I would particularly like to focus on questions that consider: a) what the future nursing workforce will look like in the next 10–15 years, which of course will impact on the education required; b) the needs of both pre-registration and post-registration nursing education, particularly the need for leadership enhancement; c) the developing role of the healthcare assistant (HCA); and d) the preparation for future educators and researchers in light of the emerging clinical academic careers.

After a brief introduction, setting the scene and considering the need to meet nursing workforce demand, I will explore the work that registered nurses are expected to undertake (see also Chapter 4), although planning future curricula is not as simple as it may seem. In order to understand what nurses will be doing by the end of their programme, we need to look well ahead. It is important to get the best intelligence that we can, to help us in the planning, so involving current students, different healthcare providers and users of the services are essential to ensure a real partnership. We do need to be mindful also of current policy, of the demands of the regulatory body and of course the individual university requirements. We also need to involve other professional groups to assist in the design of the inter-professional agenda and be mindful of the expectations of the assistant role to allow a seamless progression of knowledge and skills development. So, I hope you will engage with me in my deliberations and that it will help you to make sense of the factors currently affecting the profession and the education of nurses specifically.

Background

Nurse education in the UK is distinguished from nursing in most other countries across the globe in that the education system leads to a specialist registration as either an adult nurse, a children's nurse, a mental health or a learning disabilities nurse. Most other countries across Europe and the Western world offer an education that leads to registration as a generalist nurse. The European Union (EU) Directives require all programmes to achieve a minimum of 4,600 hours divided equally between theory and practice and from a UK perspective meet the standards of the UK regulator, the Nursing and Midwifery Council (NMC). Before getting rooted in the minutiae of the various stakeholder needs, with a focus on a specialist qualification at point of registration, is nursing in the UK following a path of self-destruction or is this the pattern for others to follow?

There is clearly no shortage of applicants to nurse education in the UK and, it seems, elsewhere, but with the high level of student attrition, we need to seriously consider whether insufficient work has been done prior to selection of our candidates to prepare them for the programme. Or, perhaps we need to look at our educational programme and how we engage with the new recruits to make them feel they belong. Has our vision become distorted in our direction of specialist travel that students feel they have lost their own direction? Whitehead (2005) certainly seems to think so. He provocatively suggests that there is a deal of overlap of knowledge and skills across the wider healthcare workforce and therefore there is an opportunity to share learning that can be facilitated across their programmes of preparation. This has the prospect of moving us towards a generic health worker with the potential demise of the existing range of healthcare workers including the doctor and the nurse! For sure, some of Whitehead's predictions have become a reality in the UK and other countries with healthcare assistants (HCA) adopting the bulk of the traditional nursing roles and the newly qualified nurses being pushed to advanced practice roles which were previously the remit of the doctor (Kessler *et al.,* 2012). This will be considered in more detail later in this chapter.

In spite of all the demands of the various stakeholders on the preparation of our future nursing workforce, in the UK for example there is no national curriculum for nurse education. Working within the framework of the NMC Standards, each university develops and delivers its own bespoke programme. So I ask myself, is there any consistency in the preparation of the professional nurse in England, or elsewhere in the UK? There are certainly regional variations in terms of patterns of ill health and demographics as well as in the delivery of services. So, perhaps you might wish to consider whether a 'one size fits all' model is not something we should be aiming for at all. We might wish to consider the importance of helping students to develop the transferable skills that will equip them to function in any region of the country or globally for that matter. As I move through the various sections of this chapter I will try to address many of these rhetorical questions and ask you, the reader, to ponder on what it might be like for yourself?

Essentially there are two main areas of focus in educating for effective workforce planning: a) meeting the demand in terms of numbers of qualified staff; and b) the nature of future services.

Meeting the demand

Within the UK, entry into the registered workforce is through either initial nurse education leading to registration or through a return to practice programme for those already qualified nurses returning to the profession following a break.

As already stated, there is a recognised shortage of qualified nurses globally. In England, Addicott *et al.* (2015) acknowledge the failure both locally and nationally to ensure workforce numbers are sufficient to meet current demand, particularly in the areas of mental health, primary care and community nursing. In addition to the escalating agency nursing numbers nationally, UK National Health Service (NHS) Trusts providing hospital and/or community services are still actively recruiting from Europe and elsewhere to meet the demand. This puts additional pressure on the existing workforce to support students as mentors during their education programme, and as their preceptors immediately on qualification. In England alone in 2015/16, Health Education England (HEE) (the education commissioning department of the NHS) allocated £200 million to retrain qualified nurses to return to practice (Willis, 2015), again, putting increased demand on existing staff to support them.

From September 2017, the commissioning and funding of nurse education in England by HEE will cease and healthcare education will move to a similar footing as other university programmes. So, unlike the current system which restricts the number of students accepted on the programme, from 2017, universities will be encouraged to recruit as many students as they can accommodate.

From 2017, nursing students will be subject to the same financial loan system as students on traditional subjects (Gummer, 2015a). In essence, nursing students in England will follow a similar pattern of recruitment and payment as universities in other countries in the Western world and the market will dictate the numbers (albeit that securing sufficient clinical placements for learning will be a constraining factor). The 'boom and bust' situation which existed prior to workforce planning and commissioning is therefore likely to return. Additionally, given that in my own university 65 per cent of our recent student recruits are considered mature, this may have a significant impact on our ability to recruit sufficient numbers to meet even the constraints of our existing commissioned system. As the individual recruits ponders their own personal circumstances, having to pay tuition fees for the first time in the history of English nurse education, they may well have second thoughts. I wonder myself whether this will open up the opportunity for new providers to offer a slimmer, cheaper option. It will surely change the relationship between universities and the commissioners, HEE, who exact considerable monitoring of the NHS contract and a significant workload that other faculties across universities have no experience of.

Reflect 3.1

- What do you think about the concept of a more generic health worker?
- Can you think of any benefits of not having distinct professional groups?

The changing landscape: The nature of future service requirements

At least since the National Health Service Plan (NHS) (2000), successive English governments have hatched their various plans to shape a new leaner NHS where care is delivered in teams around the needs of the service users rather than in professional silos (Addicott et al., 2015). Education for professional nursing practice therefore is required to tailor programmes to prepare nurses who are flexible, adaptable and are able to work inter-professionally. The current system in the UK, preparing nurses in four different specialist fields has attracted considerable criticism (Willis, 2015: Linsley et al., 2008). Those working in Mental Health and Learning Disability nursing in the current specialist preparation are reputed to have insufficient skills in caring for the physical needs of their clients whilst those in adult nursing have insufficient mental health skills, particularly with the escalating numbers of older patients with dementia. With the centrality of primary and community care, there seems to be a need for more 'generalism' to allow for greater cross-boundary working and in particular address improved patient outcomes across physical and mental health services (Addicott *et al.*, 2015).

Necessarily, this will be at a cost to the time spent on developing specialist skills which the services have come to expect. Curiously, in spite of the vision to reduce services in the acute sector in favour of an expanded primary and community care workforce, a number of recent reports such as Francis (2013) on poor-quality care have had a significant impact on the existing workforce. In the transition of re-skilling the acute sector workforce to work effectively in primary care, the acute sector has had to revisit their 'safe staffing' levels to ensure that quality care is retained. Consequently, this has seen a surge in unaffordable temporary staff as well as an unanticipated rise in numbers of acute sector staff over mental health and the community. This has the unintended consequences of impacting seriously on the long-term vision of the NHS, to make the radical changes to achieve its long-term sustainability (Addicott *et al.*, 2015).

Two significant reports in England make compelling reading: NHS (2014) *Five Year Forward View* and the Primary Care Workforce Commission (2015) *The Future of Primary Care*. They each recognise the need for change in the demand, efficiency and funding to sustain the high-quality service currently in existence (Rosser, 2015). Perhaps you could read both of these reports and consider for yourself just what this means for the current and future nursing workforce, as, for sure, a change is required.

Ham *et al.* (2012) acknowledge the changing health patterns experienced across the Western world with people living longer, often with complex long-term conditions. The anticipated changes in public health have now become a reality with the global obesity epidemic, a third of people in the UK drinking alcohol to excess and 20 per cent of adults still smoking (NHS, 2014). This has clear implications for the preparation of the workforce who need to be equipped with the right skills and have the confidence and competence to 'evaluate what they are doing and be empowered to improve the systems in which they are working' (PCWC, 2015, p. 6). To enable change to occur, education in new ways of working is key both for those working towards professional nursing registration as it is for the current qualified workforce requiring to establish a new mindset with new skills and new approaches to their traditional practice.

In the UK, the new standards introduced by the NMC in 2010 require all nursing students to gain experience in community services for one half of their 2,300 hours in placement. Placement opportunities during their initial preparation can inspire and motivate students to embrace the new ways of working enthusiastically and develop early on a confidence and competence to work autonomously; effective mentoring on placement can equip students with the decision-making necessary for the new community practitioner. You might like to reflect on your own experience but many students are also exposed to the contrary.

In an attempt to meet the rising commissioned numbers, traditional placements, often in community nursing homes where the same students once worked as healthcare assistants, can be a demotivator and a reason to leave.

Reflect 3.2

- Given the increasing responsibilities being shouldered by the assistant nursing roles, try and identify what exactly the difference is between nursing assistants and registered nurses.
- It would be beneficial to return to the differences you have identified as your reading progresses through the rest of this book.

In England, it is now acknowledged that mental health presents the largest cause of disability (NHS, 2014), yet it demonstrates one of the greatest areas of inequality in health outcomes. Whilst it is often the adult nursing workforce that is cited as having the greatest staff shortages, the RCN (2014) reports a significant reduction in mental health nurses with requests by NHS providers for temporary agency nurses rising by two-thirds since 2013/14. With such shortages, it seems difficult to argue the need for a return to the generalist approach. However, as previously mentioned, with a future focus on primary and community care, mental health nurses will require to be more adaptable and achieve greater balance in their physical health skills and so have to embrace greater generalist skills as suggested by Willis (2015). Additionally, future services will require greater inter-professional working with a refashioning of opportunities to encourage the wider allied healthcare workforce to make changes, thus permitting nurses to practise and develop to achieve the long-term sustainability envisaged.

So the future of nurse education will depend on the shape of future services. As Imison and Bohmer (2013, p. 4) state, 'it is not possible to separate workforce redesign from work design' and this requires education. Partnership working between education and practice is key to establish the vision and to make it a reality. There is likely to be overlap with a number of other chapters in this book, as the future of nursing education is influenced so heavily by what is expected of nurses as new services evolve.

The nature of pre-qualifying education leading to registered practitioner

The value of history is that we can learn from our mistakes, or at least this is what I propose. Historically, pre-registration nurse education in the UK has been the subject of vigorous debate since 1939 and the Athlone Report, recommending that nurses should have student status. Over the subsequent 70 years, there have been myriad recommendations, many of which were not implemented at the time but have gathered momentum in ultimately achieving graduate status for all those commencing from September 2013 (Willis, 2012, pp. 11–12). This generation of focused debate on the future of nurse education has occurred against a backdrop of most other health and social care professions moving much more speedily towards their own graduate status.

So, in working alongside our health profession colleagues, is the move towards graduate status for nursing a move to improve the quality of care or a move to improve our status as nurses and ultimately the status of ourselves as individual nurses? When considering '*nurses and nursing: the person and the profession*', it is always the individual who initiates and drives change for the profession. However, the individual has been hampered by a strong political force intent on retaining the status quo. The huge cost of withdrawing student nurse labour from the workforce to treat them as students has been prohibitive and it took over 50 years of considerable lobbying when, in 1986, the acceptance of the recommendation to introduce a university diploma qualification paved the way for supernumerary status for all (UKCC, 1986). So, has the education of nurses in institutes of higher education been beneficial to nursing, especially following so many high-profile media reports of poor nursing care e.g. Francis (2013), Berwick (2013) and Keogh (2013)?

Have nurses become 'too clever to care'? There has certainly been vigorous debate in the media and among traditional nurses about its value. However, it was gratifying to see that a more recent independent review of nurse education, Lord Willis (2012) wholly supports the move to an all-graduate profession, dismissing the concern that nurses had become 'too clever to care'. He reported that there were rarely suggestions that other all-graduate healthcare professionals had lost their care and compassion due to the academicisation of their profession, and he could find no evidence to suggest it of nurses.

Perhaps you could give this some thought yourself as to why allied health professionals seem to be immune from any attack on their compassion and why it is so frequently the prerogative of nurses. Given the expanding role of the professional nurse, Willis stated that there was no evidence to suggest that, as nurse education required a more intellectual attainment the less caring and compassionate they had become. Indeed, he reinforced the need for nurses to 'have both intellect and compassion, not one or the other' (Willis, 2012, p. 4). This reinforces the incremental move globally for a graduate workforce, more recently confirmed by Aiken *et al.* (2014) in her large European survey that a graduate workforce improves patient outcomes and reduces hospital mortality.

Willis (2012) did make some noteworthy observations and recommendations for the future of nurse education. He observed the need for service users and their carers to become even more involved in the recruitment of student nurses and in the delivery of their programme to bring the person rather than the condition to the forefront as students learn their craft. Since the publication of Willis's report, this approach has gathered momentum nationally and HEIs have invested heavily in values based-recruitment and values-based curricula. He also recognised the need for nurses to become more challenging of existing practice and to more fully embrace evidence-based care. Indeed, he confirmed the need for research to be more integrated into the pre-qualifying programme with support and encouragement for the next generation academics, acknowledging the need for them to achieve balance in their own integration of clinical and academic work. Importantly he acknowledged that the pre-qualifying programme merely offers a foundation (not the finished product) on which to develop and be supported to grow the skills of the newly qualified nurse. I am sure that you will confirm that this has not always been recognised.

Lord Willis (2015) was further commissioned to review the future education and training of Registered nurses and their assistants and this will be considered later in the chapter. As already noted and with reference to pre-registration education, healthcare within the UK and more particularly in England requires to have a greater public health focus, to empower patients to take responsibility for their own well-being and supported to prevent their ill health. The foundation for this was set in 2006 with the publication of a new direction for community services: *Our Health, Our Care, Our Say* (Department of Health, 2006) and has been reinforced since (PCWC, 2015). So, it is clear, the future workforce needs to think differently, to empower patients as far as possible to take responsibility for their own care, to think prevention and enable integration. This integration needs to be multilayered. Integration needs to occur between health and social care, between nurses and other healthcare professionals, between acute and community care and between physical and mental healthcare. For all this to move forward requires nurse education of today to balance generalist and specialist skills to deal with whatever the future presents.

Students need to develop a more flexible, generic skill set to empower them to work competently and confidently across a range of care settings and build a career that is both rewarding and flexible (Willis, 2015, p. 25). There is no doubt, nursing practice is complex. It occurs within myriad different environments in unpredictable circumstances and often requires the professional to make autonomous decisions about individuals who are experiencing multiple pathology which may affect them physically, psychologically, emotionally and socially. Nurses are individuals themselves and as human beings will instinctively respond to different situations in their own way and must learn to manage their own emotions to focus on the needs of their clients. The management of their own emotions and response to the mundane as well as catastrophic situations needs to be learned and developed over time.

My own observations in asking students nearing completion of their programme to identify any gaps in their preparation for professional practice, repeatedly request more detailed preparation in the core sciences of pharmacology, anatomy and physiology and the like. They rarely request more input on dealing with difficult situations, on further developing their problem-solving and decision-making skills but soon recognise the magnitude of this once they qualify. It is curious to think that the original nursing curriculum at the time of the first registration was three years in duration in the UK, yet over a century later and with all the technological advances, role expansions, research skills, etc., the programme continues as a three-year programme. It is no wonder that Willis (2012) clearly confirms his own observations that the programme merely forms a foundation on which to build professional nursing practice. Knowledge is changing at a pace and I would argue that, in addition to developing their skills of care and compassion, essential requirements for pre-registration nursing curricula are the need for students to learn how to learn independently, how to access new information and be able to analyse its worth; all the skills required of graduates. They need to develop insight into their own scope of practice and acknowledge their limitations yet gain confidence in their own competence to practise and be prepared for their journey of lifelong learning.

Reflect 3.3

• Reflect on your current or past learning experience. Do you believe your nursing programme will or did prepare you well for life as a registered nurse?
• What are the essential skills and knowledge that you consider nurses will need to practise in the next five to ten years?

The role of continuing professional development (CPD) for registered nurses

There seems no doubt that nursing within the UK has borne the brunt of much criticism in recent years both by the media and by a number of high-profile investigations and the focus has inevitably turned to pre-registration education to provide the solutions to all its ills. Whilst there have been a number of reports targeted at the future education of pre-registration nursing (e.g. UKCC, 1986; UKCC, 1999; NMC, 2008; Willis, 2012, 2015), there has been less written about the professional development of registered nurses. We have had to look elsewhere to countries in the Western world which have gained success in the education of a registered nursing workforce, though many countries remain challenged by the global shortage of nurses, the ageing workforce and the need to ensure that as the profession advances, registered nurses need to be equipped with the right skills to address the changing pattern of care (IOM, 2010, p. 5).

As previously acknowledged, globally healthcare systems are challenged with the need to adopt a greater public health focus, a reconfiguring of services and new ways of working, and a re-skilling of the existing workforce must be a key consideration. As already mentioned, the initial Willis Commission (2012) in England recognised that pre-registration education lays a foundation on which to build the lifelong learning of the professional nurse and the need for support immediately on qualification is key to developing their confidence and competence as they grasp the complexity of the role and develop the advanced practice skills and knowledge required of them.

In spite of an increasingly ageing workforce, an ongoing commitment to investing in the existing workforce is essential if they are to embrace the innovations in healthcare, technological advances as well as advanced skills as the profession moves forward. In addition to their day-to-day responsibilities in care, registered nurses are required to support the myriad students in practice, and as such play a significant role in shaping the future workforce. Their motivation to retain their CPD is key, not only for their own skills development but also to nurture the next generation of leaders. Due to the increasing numbers of nursing students in UK nursing, it is rare that qualified nurses are not required to act as mentors to the emerging future workforce. In addition to the newly qualified nurses, healthcare assistants and international recruits need supporting, as do the very large transient workforce of agency nurses. A heavy weight of responsibility rests on the shoulders of the existing workforce, alongside the need to cope with the increasing acuity of care and the ever-changing nature of the services. It is not surprising that the '*person*' often finds the stress of the changing '*professional*' demands overwhelming. Indeed, in a large survey of 201 general and acute hospitals in Europe plus 430 USA hospitals, Aiken *et al.* (2012) found high rates of nursing burnout, job dissatisfaction and intention to leave. This is further supported by Flinkman *et al.* (2010, 2013) who found increasing evidence of nurses leaving the profession globally, within a year of qualification.

So, given that tomorrow's workforce exists today, and the adverse effects of many nurses globally having to work 12-hour shifts (Jennings, 2008), with a dependency on transient agency staff to ensure safe staffing levels, there is little time to engage in CPD within their working day (Willis, 2015). In spite of the move to an all-graduate intake from September 2013, it is estimated that by 2029 over half the current workforce in England will remain as non-graduates (Willis, 2015, p. 50). Given the evidence by Aiken *et al.* (2014) that a graduate workforce offers better patient outcomes and reduced hospital mortality, it is difficult to predict, that without significant investment, both financially and personal cost, how soon an all-graduate workforce in nursing in the UK will be achieved.

Nevertheless, significant investment in the existing nursing workforce is essential to develop their skills and knowledge, as well as support their positive attitude to achieving evidence-based practice and a commitment to their ongoing education as a professional. Their influence on the early socialisation of both student nurses and the newly qualified into a positive acceptance of change will be key to the retention of staff and their willingness to learn. With the recent introduction of the NMC Revalidation (NMC, 2015), all practising nurses will be expected to produce evidence of their ongoing learning. In spite of it being mandatory since 1995, the NMC has lacked confidence in its uptake and brought in changes to the requirements. However, oversight of the implementation of Revalidation will inevitably be costly, in time, money and effort given the 670,000 registrants across the UK. With a remit to improve public protection and as the process becomes embedded, the reader may wish to consider whether this process will achieve its aim of enhancing patient care through feedback and personal reflection, or whether it becomes as the USA system of Multiple Choice Questions part of a regular routine (Rosser, 2015).

Advanced practice

In spite of the move to advance the skills of all qualified registered nurses, in 2010, the Department of Health (2010) stated that all those in advanced practice roles should achieve no less than master's level study. In my opinion, the Department fell well short of requiring a full master's qualification, leaving the baseline requirement up to individual institutions to dictate and individual nurses to achieve. A systematic review undertaken in Canada (Dicenso and Bryant-Lukosius, 2010) identified that patient outcomes improved and the quality of care by clinical nurse specialists and nurse practitioners, who had been educated to master's level with relevant advanced practice competence, delivered care to the same level as that delivered by doctors. Whilst it is disappointing to find that the UK expectations have fallen well short of those in other Western countries, it seems clear that, with the move to a graduate base as the foundation qualification for registered nurses in the UK, it will not be long before completion of a master's programme is mandated for all clinical specialists and nurse practitioners as is the requirement in the USA (NCSBN, 2016).

It is my own view that for those at consultant nurse equivalent, and perhaps in the fullness of time, senior clinical leaders, doctoral level study will be the requirement. It is already a requirement for many nurse academics. Although it is often thought that the USA is ahead of the UK in educational requirements, the Institute of Medicine (2010) in its consideration of the future of nursing, advocated that by 2020, 80 per cent of registered nurses should hold an undergraduate degree and that the number of doctorally qualified nurses should be doubled from 1 per cent to 2 per cent. However, the transition to achieve such ambitious goals for the '*profession*' will impact considerably on the '*person*' who generally has considerable responsibilities within their institution and therefore may find it difficult to return to study.

Additionally, although the '*profession*' may find it an advantage to make master's or doctoral status compulsory, advanced practitioners often have achieved their position due to their leadership in practice and may not see the personal 'added value'.

As the reader, you may have your own views of what is required. From my perspective, what seems to be lacking is a clear career framework for all registered nurses to support a commitment to the ongoing development of nurses. Without a well-educated and highly motivated registered nurse workforce, it would be challenging to achieve a positive learning environment for all learners in practice. Enthusiastic nurses, committed to their education and career development are key to excite the emerging future leaders, able to embrace flexible working, and encourage innovation in service delivery and the development of the future academic and research workforce.

Leadership

Given the high profile of leadership in the plethora of reports on inquiries of the catastrophic failures of the NHS (e.g. Francis, 2013; PHSO, 2011) and indeed evidence of poor-quality care across the globe (Aiken *et al.*, 2012) it would be remiss not to mention the role of education in supporting the development of our future leaders and how leadership can be enhanced. Whilst the catastrophic failures of the Mid Staffordshire NHS Foundation Trust were not restricted to nurses, nurses were often highlighted as key to the coordination and leadership of teams at all levels and as such have been the focus of many of the adverse media comments. One of the key messages arising from the Francis (2013) report was that 'an unhealthy and dangerous culture' (Francis, 2013, p. 1360) existed that linked directly to a lack of leadership: 'It is a truism that organisational culture is informed by the nature of its leadership' (Francis, 2013, p. 1348). Although Francis (2013) suggested that it is not possible to extrapolate this type of culture to all NHS organisations, he intimated that such a culture was widespread due not intentionally to uncaring individuals but, when faced with overwhelming pressures, there was a tendency for individuals to 'shame and blame'.

So, you might ask yourself, how can education help? Often 'culture' and 'leadership' at the organisational level are considered as generic concepts but when challenged to the specific, professional nurses, over other professional groups, are often cited as leaders due to their dominance in the workforce, their role in coordinating care, 24/7 oversight of the care environments and often the leaders of inter-professional teams. From the media perspective, failings of organisational leadership are often targeted at nurses. Nevertheless, it is the '*person*' rather than the '*profession*' who leads and is held accountable for the success of their leadership qualities and so it is the education of the individual that needs to be considered.

As reader, you will have your own thoughts but from my own perspective, education is not about espousing the various theories of leadership, though I have no doubt that reflecting on one's own leadership style helps us to understand how we prioritise, how we make decisions and how we deal with people. More importantly, I believe leadership is about engaging with oneself, and education which helps us understand more about ourselves can help us to think and therefore act differently.

I have been struck by the work of Holroyd and Brown (2011) as they suggest the need to harness 'self' where a sense of leadership comes from within and not by virtue of title or position but of having a sense of 'doing the right thing' in a given situation rather than merely 'doing things right'. Leadership is for every practising nurse whether caring for one patient or an organisation, they need to feel the deep sense of responsibility to take the lead and feel empowered to believe that they really can make a difference to patient care. Nursing leadership has been impeded by a lamentable sense of hierarchy. The hierarchical culture is not one that is evident in the education of nurses but it still prevails in practice. If a sense of self-leadership were to replace the traditional hierarchical culture, I believe that the profession would gain considerable credence. Belief in the '*person*' would encourage belief in the '*profession*'. The future of nurse education needs to consider leadership from day one of the student's preparation, right through to qualification and to retirement to empower nurses to believe in themselves and that they truly can make a difference to people's lives.

Reflect 3.4

- Reflect on the reference to Holroyd and Brown (2011) to '*doing the right thing*' rather than merely '*doing things right*' and how this can be applied to your everyday practice.
- Can you identify colleagues or individuals whom you recognised as always '*doing the right thing*' and what they do that demonstrates this?

Education for the nursing support workforce

Historically, since the acceptance of a diploma-based education for professional nurses in the UK (UKCC, 1986) and the final acceptance of nursing students as having supernumerary status, students ceased to be an integral part of the nursing workforce, reflecting similar approaches in New Zealand, Australia and Canada. This was a radical change to the delivery of healthcare and meant a costly and major increase in the number of assistants, though only about half of the diploma students were replaced in practice when the students returned to study (Kressler *et al.*, 2012). In spite of two independent reviews of the education of the support worker (Willis, 2015; Cavendish, 2013), there has been no uniform and accepted preparation for these three grades of healthcare assistants (Bands 1–3), nor any great clarity in the delegation of work from professional to any one of the assistant grades (Cavendish, 2013). Yet, healthcare assistants in England comprise around a third of the hospital's caring workforce and due to the evolution of care responsibilities, spend more time than registered nurses in direct patient care (Cavendish, 2013). Since the move to an all-graduate intake for registered nurses, some healthcare assistants who aspire to a career in professional nursing can no longer do so due to the raised entry qualifications for a university degree and there is no accepted bridging programme to encourage their ambitions (Cavendish, 2013). Of course there is movement afoot and it is hoped that changes will be imminent but, given the interface with registered nurses, and their own predominance on the frontline, I believe it is necessary to consider healthcare assistants as part of the whole nursing workforce and their education requirements to ensure some continuity of understanding and competence in the essential skills of nursing and ultimately protection of the public.

If we are to consider the '*person*' who will ultimately influence the '*profession*', it is well recognised that due to inconsistent evidence of a recognised education requirement for the nurse assistant role, the '*person*' has often felt 'devalued and overlooked' (Cavendish, 2013, p. 6). If education in part is to assist in the achievement of the delivery of high-quality care, enhance patient safety and contribute to a workforce feeling valued as part of a strong and united team, then the education of the HCA is vital as an essential part of that team. Whilst there are myriad courses, modules and qualifications available to HCAs, it is suggested that without the regulation of the HCA workforce then a mandatory and consistent approach to their education is unlikely to occur as the impact on employers is considerable, not least due to cost (RCN, 2014). Indeed, it would seem that regulation of this workforce would be the trigger to achieve such goals, just as they have been achieved in Belgium, Denmark and France (Griffiths and Robinson, 2010). Given they play such a vital part in the delivery of care in the UK, it is time that investment is made, not only in funding the recommended 'Care Certificate' and for some, the 'Higher Care Certificate' (HEE 2014) but in supporting their clear career structure, their ongoing development and mandatory code of practice. By fully supporting the '*person*', the '*profession*' of nursing will benefit, not least in developing a team where everyone feels valued and respects each other. There is considerable evidence from across Europe, Australia and the USA to support that in addition to a reduction in nurse–patient ratios, it is improved work environments that are associated with increased care quality and patient satisfaction (Aiken *et al.*, 2012).

As the modernisation of the professional nurse has seen the development of specialist and advanced practice roles across the globe, particularly in the UK, Canada, USA, France and Finland, professional nurses have been diverted away from foundational and essential nursing care, entrusting much of the essential care to the HCAs (Kessler *et al.*, 2012). Unlike the previous nursing auxiliary role, HCAs across the country are engaged in advanced skills such as phlebotomy, female catheterisation, cannulation, applying complex dressings, setting up infusion feeds, etc., all tasks traditionally undertaken by professional nurses and even doctors (King's College, 2010). With a requirement for HCAs to be 'appropriately trained' and currently no mandatory assessment of competence, it is the professional nurse who takes the risk of delegating inappropriately and accepting any unintended consequences. In the interest of public safety and the success of robust and well-functioning professional teams, the future of nurse education will depend on a whole-systems approach to adopt a universally recognised training and education for support workers as for the professional workforce.

As the modernisation of careers for professional nurses has developed, so must those of the HCA. If we are to truly consider the '*person*' rather than the entity '*profession*' and develop each individual's potential, then career development is essential. So far, I have just considered NHS Agenda for Change Bands 1–3 but in recent years Band 4 (the level immediately below registered nurse who is likely to hold a more sophisticated qualification than the lower 'bands' but is not registered), assistant practitioner, has been developed by some. I would argue that given the excellent examples that Cavendish (2013) illustrates in her report (with two of the HCAs she met having doctoral degrees), there is much greater scope to develop a more advanced assistant who has a higher level of education preparation than the HCA. Since the demise of the enrolled nurse (an earlier practical nurse who was regulated along with the registered nurse) with the introduction of Project 2000, the UK government has recommended the idea of a new Nursing Associate (Gummer, 2015a). Effectively, there are many similarities between the new Nursing Associate and the previous enrolled nurse. The one difference is that it is proposed that the Nursing Associate will have real career opportunities. By undertaking a Foundation Degree which mirrors the first two years of the registered Nursing programme, there will be opportunities for the Nursing Associate to be able to continue in the future to registration. Investment in their continuing education is also suggested. I would argue that good investment in a higher level assistant role would benefit not only the careers of the HCA, permit an improved skills balance in the workforce but also encourage a greater focus on developing the underpinning knowledge and competence for practice. Offering a two-year Foundation Degree as preparation, would encourage both a sound knowledge for practice but facilitate for some, a staged progression to registered nurse following an additional year (Gummer, 2015b).

So, with evolving changes, '*nurses and nursing*' cannot function without the assistant role and a mandatory and universally accepted training with real career progression. As the reader will acknowledge, a key factor when considering nurse education for the twenty-first century is a whole-systems approach to the delivery of care of which the HCA is a significant and valued partner.

Clinical academic careers and the preparation for future educators and researchers

The future of nurse education would not be complete without considering the nurse educators, researchers and the concept of clinical academic careers. The role of the educator in particular is key to enable the novice practitioner to understand the changing landscape of care, to be excited by the ongoing development of evidence-based practice and help carve out their future career pathway by understanding the interface between clinical practice, education and research. Now well into the technological age, educators, as a section of the nursing workforce, have probably experienced the greatest pace of change, both in terms of their own educational attainment but also what they teach and the way they teach it.

Firmly established in institutes of higher education, the move to the university sector from traditional schools of nursing has not been easy. With a predominant female workforce, nursing has not always been wholeheartedly accepted by all academic colleagues and continues to face challenges of credibility and authority both from their academic colleagues and from senior managers in practice (Ross, 2014). As second career academics, nurses often have well established clinical careers prior to entering teaching and are then required to embark on a retraining programme of a postgraduate teaching qualification and a PhD.

As they become academic leaders, they are then charged with developing their own research profile and developing the research capacity of their colleagues. By virtue of their previous careers, they are often older than their counterparts across the university but are further challenged by their various 'masters' by regularly having to report to nursing's professional regulator, the university quality assurance processes and also the contract managers of the commissioners. As long as the programmes are commissioned, professionally regulated and sit within the university system, this will not change. However, as we move to a change in the model of payment by nursing students in England, a lot rests on the continued recruitment of nurses both from the future workforce perspective but also financially for the university and ultimately security of their own employment. It is at this interface between the university and the NHS where the '*nurse*' is required to use her sophisticated communication and negotiation skills to ensure the sustainability of '*nursing*' within the higher education sector.

So, the future of nurse education is highly dependent on an able academic workforce, well experienced in the art and science of nursing, insightful of the emerging new ways of working, technologically competent, talented researchers and enthusiastic facilitators of learning captivating their students through their innovation. With a six-year part-time PhD to complete before entering the lowest level of academic position after a full clinical career, it is not for the faint-hearted!

Given that the concept of a 'job for life' no longer exists for current school leavers, a flexible career, developing transferable skills as they progress will become the norm, whether the new graduate nurse remains in clinical practice, adopts a clinical research career or moves into education. Nevertheless, it is an exciting prospect that there are educational opportunities for all, and what prevents them from taking these forward is often an individual mindset that rests in the past where 'once a nurse, always a nurse' prevails. Historically, nurses' CPD was once the responsibility of the employer and this is no longer wholly the case. However, where there are pockets of funding to support service development, allied health professionals often compete and so the mindset needs changing and we need to move on positively and with enthusiasm. I am sure the reader will have his or her own views of the way forward but there is a fine line between what is beneficial to the individual '*nurse*' and what is required to enhance the competence of the '*profession*'. Essentially both are important and the educator will influence the next generation workforce in how they motivate them to navigate their path.

Summary

I hope you have enjoyed travelling with me on my journey through the many issues influencing the future of nurse education. Clearly I have only touched on the scope that it has been possible to explore. Nevertheless, I do return to Whitehead's (2005) concept of the generic healthcare worker and wonder if we are nearing our path to self-destruction. Personally I do not believe so. We have an excellent workforce blighted by staff shortages, high turnover and low morale but there is a recognition of this and a mandate to correct it (Willis, 2012, 2015; Addicott *et al.*, 2015; RCN, 2014). The world of healthcare is changing at pace and the vision for service reconfiguration and new ways of working being clearly expressed (PCWC, 2015; NHS, 2014).

So, is the education of twenty-first century nurses fit for purpose? Certainly I have cited support nationally (Willis, 2015) and from across Europe that graduate status benefits patients (Aiken *et al.*, 2014) but whether we in the UK need to move to a more generalist preparation seems more likely. Also I have suggested that the concept of lifelong learning is clearly something that needs embracing from the start of students' careers. I have presented a case for specialist roles to achieve master programme completion and from more advanced practitioners, doctoral status will be the trajectory for most. Empowerment of self in leadership is something that needs harnessing on day one of the students' programme to move away from hierarchical leadership to facilitate change from within.

With HCAs taking such a dominant role in the delivery of healthcare, education of this large workforce needs investment. Moving to regulation underpinned by a code of conduct they need valuing and supporting with a career worth being proud of. Finally, none of this will be possible without the support of the education and research workforce, with students learning about possible career trajectories early on. To raise the position of nurse academics in institutes of higher education nationally and internationally, research and its dissemination need to be encouraged during students' initial training so that they are inspired to write. Nursing, whether clinical, educational or research, needs leaders able to influence culture and enhance patient care and the potential for nurse education to influence this is immense.

References

Addicott, R., Maguire, D., Honeyman, M. & Jabbal, J. (2015) *Workforce Planning in the NHS: Ideas that Change Health Care.* April. London: The Kings Fund.

Aiken, L.H., Sloane, D.M., Bruyneel, L., Van den Heed, K., Griffiths, P., Busse, R., Diomidous, M., Kinnunen, J., Kozka, M., Lesaffre, E., McHugh, M.D., Moreno-Casbas, M.T., Rafferty, A.-M., Schwendimann, R., Scott, P.A., Tishelman, C., van Achterberg, T. & Sermeus, W. (2014) Nurse staffing and education and hospital mortality in nine European countries: a retrospective observational study. Published online 26 February at http://dx.doi.org/10.1016/S0140-6736(13)62631-8/.

Aiken, L.H., Sloane, D.M., Bruyneel, L., Van den Heede, K., & Sermeus, W. (2013) Nurses' reports of working conditions and hospital quality of care in 12 countries in Europe. *International Journal of Nursing Studies*, 50, 143–153.

Aiken, L.H., Sermeus, W., Van den Heede, K., Sloane, D.M., Busse, R., McKee, M., Bruyneel, L., Rafferty, A.M., Griffiths, P., Moreno-Casbas, M.T., Tishelman, C., Scott, A., Brzostek, T., Kinnunen, J., Schwendimann, R., Hienen, M., Zikos, D., & Strømsen Sjetne, I. (2012) Patient safety, satisfaction, and quality of hospital care: cross sectional surveys of nurses and patients in 12 countries in Europe and the United States. *British Medical Journal*, 344: e1717. Published online, 20 March doi: 10.1136/bmj.e1717. Accessed on 5 January 2016 at www.ncbi.nlm.nih.gov/pmc/articles/PMC3308724/.

Berwick, R. (2013) *A Promise to Learn – A commitment to Act: Improving the Safety of Patients in England.* National Advisory Group on the Safety of Patients in England. August. London: Crown Copyright. Accessed on 8 January 2016 at www.gov.uk/

government/uploads/system/uploads/attachment_data/file/226703/Berwick_ Report.pdf/.

Cavendish, C. (2013) *The Cavendish Review: An Independent Review into Healthcare Assistants and Support Workers in the NHS and Social Care Settings.* July. Accessed on 6 January 2016 at www.gov.uk/government/uploads/system/uploads/attachment_data/file/236212/ Cavendish_Review.pdf.

Department of Health (2010) *Advanced Level Nursing: A Position Statement.* 16 November, Department of Health. Accessed on 5 January 2016 at www.gov.uk/government/ uploads/system/uploads/attachment_data/file/215935/dh_121738.pdf/.

Department of Health (2006) *Our Health, Our Care, Our Say: A New Direction for Community Services.* Accessed on 8 January 2016 at www.gov.uk/government/ uploads/system/uploads/attachment_data/file/272238/6737.pdf/.

Dicenso, A. & Bryant-Lukosius, D. (2010) *Clinical Nurse Specialists and Nurse Practitioners in Canada: A Decision Support Synthesis.* Canadian Health Services Research Foundations. Accessed on 5 January 2016 at www.cfhi-fcass.ca/sf-docs/default-source/commissioned-research-reports/Dicenso_EN_Final.pdf?sfvrsn=0/.

Dragon, N. (2009) Nurse education: our students, our future. *Australian Nursing Journal,* 16(7), 22–25.

Flinkman, M., Isopahkala-Bouret, U. & Salanterä, S. (2013) Young registered nurses' intention to leave the profession and professional turnover in early career: a qualitative case study. *International Scholarly Research Notices.* 20 August. doi: 10.1155/2013/916061. Accessed at: www.ncbi.nlm.nih.gov/pmc/articles/PMC3762080/ on 5 January 2016.

Flinkman, M., Leino-Kilpi, H., Salanterä, S. (2010) Nurses' intention to leave the profession: integrative review. *Journal of Advanced Nursing,* 66(7), 1422–1434 [PubMed].

Flynn, M., & McKewn, M. (2009) Nurse staffing levels revisited: a consideration of key Issues in nurse staffing levels and skill mix research. *Journal of Nursing Management,* 17(6), 759–766.

Francis, R. (2013) *The Report of the Mid Staffordshire NHS Foundation Trust Public Inquiry.* London: The Stationery Office.

Gabrielle, S., Jackson, D., & Mannix, J. (2008) Older women nurses: health, ageing concerns and self-care strategies. *Journal of Advanced Nursing,* 61(3), 316–325.

Gantz, N.R., Sherman, R., Jasper, M., Choo, C.G., Herrin-Griffith, D., & Harris, K. (2012) Global nurse leader perspectives on health systems and workforce challenges. *Journal of Nursing Management,* 20, 433–443.

Griffiths, P. & Robinson, S. (2010) *Moving Forward with Healthcare Support Workforce Regulation.* July. Kings College Nursing Research Unit.

Gummer, B. (2015a) *Creating a Modern Nursing Workforce: New Funding Arrangements from August 2017.* Accessed on 7 January 2015 at www.gov.uk/government/speeches/ creating-a-modern-nursing-workforce/.

Gummer, B. (2015b) *Nursing Associate Role Offers New Route to Nursing.* London: Department of Health, 17 December. Accessed on 7 January 2016 at www.gov.uk/governmentin/ news/nursing-associate-role-offers-new-route-into-nursing/.

Ham, C., Dixon, A., & Brooke, B. (2012) *Transforming the Delivery of Health and Social Care: The Case for Fundamental Change.* London: The Kings Fund.

Holroyd, J., & Brown, K. (2011) Self-leadership – a new focus. In: *Leadership and Management Development for Social Work and Social Care.* Bournemouth University: National Centre for Post Qualifying Social Work, 58–66.

Imison, C., Bohmer, R. (2013) *NHS and Social Care Workforce: Meeting Our Needs Now and in the Future? Perspectives.* July. London: The King's Fund. Available at: www.kingsfund.org.

uk/time-to-think-differently/publications/nhs-and-social-care-workforce. Accessed on 4 January 2016.

Institute of Medicine (IOM) (2010) *The Future of Nursing: Focus on Education.* October, Accessed on 5 January 2016 at http://iom.nationalacademies.org/~/media/Files/ Report%20Files/2010/The-Future-of-Nursing/Nursing%20Education%202010%20 Brief.pdf/.

Jennings, B. (2008) Work stress and burnout among nurses: role of the work environment and working conditions. In R.G. Hughes (ed.), *Patient Safety and Quality: An Evidence-Based Handbook for Nurses.* Agency for Healthcare Research and Quality, US Department of Health and Human Services, chapter 26. Accessed on 5 January 2016 at www.ncbi. nlm.nih.gov/books/NBK2668/.

Keogh, B. (2013) *Review into the Quality of Care and Treatment Provided by 14 Hospital Trusts in England.* Accessed on 8 January 2016 at www.nhs.uk/NHSEngland/bruce-keogh-review/Documents/outcomes/keogh-review-final-report.pdf/.

Kessler, I., Heron, P., & Dopson, S. (2012) *The Modernisation of the Nursing Workforce: Valuing the Healthcare Assistant.* Oxford: Oxford University Press. Accessed on 8 January 2016 at www2.rcn.org.uk/__data/assets/pdf_file/0019/332074/NNRU_report_into_ the_regulation_of_HCSWs_July_2010.pdf/.

King's College National Nursing Research Unit (2010) *Moving Forward with Healthcare Support Workforce Regulation.* London.

Linsley, P., Kane, R., McKinnon, J. Spencer, R. & Simpson, T. (2008) Preparing for the future: nurse education ad workforce development. *Quality in Primary Care,* 16, 171–6.

National Council of State Boards of Nursing (NCSBN) (2016) *Advanced Practice Registered Nurses.* Accessed on 5 January 2016 at www.ncsbn.org/aprn.htm Department of Health (2000) The NHS Plan: A Plan for Investment, a plan for reform. HMSO, London.

National Health Service (2014) *Five Year Forward View.* www.england.nhs.uk/wp-content/ uploads/2014/10/5yfv-web.pdf/.

Nursing and Midwifery Council (2015) *Revalidation: What is it and When will it Begin?* Accessed at www.nmc.org.uk/standards/revalidation/ on 5 January 2016/

Nursing and Midwifery Council (2010) *Standards for Pre-registration Nursing Education.* Accessed from: http://standards.nmc-uk.org/PreRegNursing/statutory/Standards/ Pages/Standards.aspx on 5 November 2014.

Parliamentary and Health Services Ombudsman (2011) *Care and Compassion? Report of the Health Service Ombudsman on Ten Investigations into NHS care of older people.* Accessed on 6 January 2016 at www.ombudsman.org.uk/care-and-compassion/home/.

Primary Care Workforce Commission (PCWC) (2015) *The Future of Primary Care: Creating Team for Tomorrow.* Health Education England. July. Accessed at http://hee.nhs.uk/ wp-content/blogs.dir/321/files/2015/07/The-future-of-primary-care.pdf/.

Ross, F. (2014) Nursing in universities: does it matter? *British Journal of Nursing,* 23(7), 375.

Rosser E. (2015) The importance of education for a new primary care workforce. *British Journal of Nursing,* 24(17), 896.

Royal College of Nursing (2014) *Turning Back the clock? RCN Report on Mental Health Services in the UK.* Frontline First. London: Royal College of Nursing. Accessed on 8 January 2016 at www2.rcn.org.uk/__data/assets/pdf_file/0004/600628/004772.pdf/.

United Kingdom Central Council for Nursing, Midwifery and Health Visiting (1986) *Project 2000: A New Preparation for Practice.* London: UKCC. Accessed on 6 January 2016 at www.nmc-uk.org/Documents/Archived%20Publications/UKCC%20Archived%20 Publications/Project%202000%20A%20New%20Preparation%20for%20Practice%20 May%201986.pdf UK Central/.

United Kingdom Central Council for Nursing, Midwifery and Health Visiting (1999) *Making a Difference: Strengthening the Nursing, Midwifery and Health Visiting Contribution to Health and Healthcare.* July. London: Department of Health. Accessed on 8 January 2016 at http://webarchive.nationalarchives.gov.uk/20130107105354/http:/www.dh.gov. uk/prod_consum_dh/groups/dh_digitalassets/@dh/@en/documents/digitalasset/ dh_4074704.pdf/.

Whitehead, D. (2005) Nurse education in the future: will one size fit all? Guest editorial, *Nurse Education Today*, 25, 251–254.

Willis, Lord (2015) *Raising the Bar: Shape of Caring: A Review of the Future Education and Training of Registered Nurses and Care Assistants.* March. London: Health Education England. Accessed on 5 January 2016 at www.hee.nhs.uk/sites/default/files/documents/ 2348-Shape-of-caring-review-FINAL.pdf/.

Willis, Lord (2012) *Quality with Compassion: The Future of Nursing Education. The Report of the Independent Willis Commission on Nursing Education.* London: Royal College of Nursing on behalf of the Willis Commission.

4

THE UNIQUE ROLE OF THE NURSE

The organisation of nursing careers

Kay Norman

Why this chapter is important

Nursing and nurses have changed beyond compare to the historical imagery of a doctor's handmaiden. Nursing has seen the profession grow into a complex and sometimes confusing network of roles which defy its origins. The unique role of the nurse is now extremely varied, incorporating knowledge and skills that advance care delivery, but also help to shape the wider healthcare agenda through management and leadership roles, a political voice, and regulatory processes. However, nursing as a career continues to be shaped by political, economic and social needs.

As more and more 'caring' roles become the responsibility of family, friends, social care and the voluntary sector, is the concept of nursing, and the advancing roles nurses are pursuing, changing the fundamental essence of what it is to be a nurse?

Chapter trigger question: What makes the role of the nurse unique or is nursing an outdated approach to providing healthcare?

Key words: Uniqueness of nursing, advancing roles, organisation of nursing care

Introduction

This chapter explores the influences that are currently affecting nursing, both as a profession and as a role within a healthcare team. It does not aim to define nursing or suggest what nursing 'is' or 'does'; nevertheless it encourages critical debate by questioning whether nursing as a concept is still valid in today's care systems and whether it remains a unique role in the healthcare arena. The variety and complexity of nursing roles, the delegation and acquisition of skills and competencies, and the organisation of 'caring' across boundaries is discussed to highlight current areas for consideration needed to take nursing forward in the twenty-first century. It is hoped you will participate in activities within the reflection sections to examine your own viewpoint and those of your colleagues to share ideas and further develop your thinking to help shape the profession.

Advancing roles – what does nursing hope to achieve?

Nursing has been shaped continually over the past century. In its quest to become a respected, worthwhile and aspirational career, the profession has continued to strive for an encompassing definition and understanding of nursing (Nelson and Gordon, 2006). The difficulties in achieving this are evident, with the traditionally perceived role of the caring doctor's handmaiden conflicting with the image of an intelligent, well-educated, autonomous nursing practitioner.

Michel Foucault (1972) suggests that in order to learn about the present, one needs to write the *history* of the present. However, histories of nursing often constitute a search for origins which identify a thread such as employment or training. This can sometimes lead to seemingly separate, conflicting histories of the origins of nursing, depending on the focus area reviewed. This also suggests that nursing has never been a unified conceptual entity, with an array of differing perceptions concerning the concept of nursing currently held in the discourse (Canam, 2008).

Authors have recommended that nursing should embrace its history and draw upon the history of a professional culture to engender professional pride, leading to a 'collective power' which would help build resilience, critical thinking and a strong identity (McAllister et al., 2009). Nevertheless, nursing roles have developed not only from a professional and personal vision for the nursing profession to become recognised and independent from the traditional medical model, but also through real and perceived social and political needs.

The current public perception of nursing cannot fail to be influenced by media outputs concerning poor standards of care within all care settings, with the UK Francis Report (2013) being seismic in terms of its impact of how nursing is viewed. Yet generations have also been influenced by traditional and stereotypical perceptions of nursing which are difficult to dispel, with some young people currently considering their career options continuing to draw on this historical imagery of nursing (Norman, 2015a). Despite perceptions and perceived misinterpretations of the reality of nursing, the fundamentals of compassionate nursing care must remain, no matter what the nursing role entails. As many patients may not be aware of the changing face of nursing, advanced nursing roles incorporating non-traditional nursing skills may not be recognised or appreciated. Advancing nursing roles can enhance the care a patient receives and ultimately may improve the experience of their care episode. However, are advanced nursing roles returning to a medicalisation of nursing or encouraging the nursing profession to improve knowledge, understanding and skills to deliver the best nursing care possible?

Reflect 4.1

*   Think about your understanding of what advanced level nursing is. You may have worked with or know someone who is an advanced level nurse/practitioner.
*   How does it differ from your current role?
*   Do you feel the role improves patient care?
*   Do you feel an advanced role is something all nurses should pursue or aspire to?
*   Discuss your reflections with a colleague, mentor or clinical supervisor. Compare your views and perceptions.

There has been some inconsistency with the definition and subsequent understanding of advanced nursing practice, with the operationalisation of advanced roles being applied in different ways across varying nations to meet specific needs of populations. In many countries the societal benefits of employing a nurse with advanced skills rather than a medical professional has been an important factor to consider (Lowe *et al.*, 2012). Where medical staff are in short supply, the advanced nurse may offer a suitable alternative in order to ensure appropriate care can be delivered. Political and social need have always determined the availability of healthcare; however, the 'who delivers healthcare' is now an important area to be scrutinised to address the financial needs of healthcare services.

The increase in advanced nursing practice has become a global trend over the past twenty years and therefore nursing is unlikely to return to its origins. As a profession we may not want nursing to regress and therefore should welcome continual improvement and development of the role. There is no denying that advanced nursing practice has resulted in many positive outcomes and benefits to individuals and communities. Sheer *et al.* (2008) in their review of fifty nations utilising advanced nursing roles concludes the factors influencing this were to reduce costs, improve access to care, reduce waiting times, serve the underprivileged and maintain health among specific groups (Sheer *et al.*, 2008, p. 208). However, it is important to reflect on what nursing hopes to achieve in its quest to develop more and more 'technical expertise' and the underlying reasons for doing so, be it financial, societal, status gaining, or politically driven.

The UK Department of Health (DH) (2010) produced a benchmark for advanced level nursing which consists of twenty-eight elements building on the Nursing and Midwifery registration requirements. These are grouped under four themes:

*   clinical/direct care practice;
*   leadership and collaborative practice;

- improving quality and developing practice;
- developing self and others.

The benchmark also suggests that nurses working at an advanced level will have completed Master's level study (including postgraduate certificate/postgraduate diploma level). However, what were once considered as extended roles such as administering intravenous medications are now part of skills and competencies expected from a newly registered nurse. Therefore, what is seen as an advanced nursing role today may be incorporated into initial nurse registration criterion in the future as expectations of nursing roles intensify.

Nurses continue to embrace advancing roles which were once the domain of medical staff. A vast array of nurse-led clinics are available including endoscopy services, aesthetic clinics, primary care interventions, cognitive behavioural therapy, triage services and minor injury/illness centres, all of which are increasing the level of autonomy and responsibility for nurses. It has been confusing for both the nursing profession, other care professionals and most of all the public in deciphering the range of titles used to describe this level of practice. They include specialist practitioner, advanced nurse practitioner, nurse practitioner, clinical nurse specialist, primary care specialist, nurse consultant, etc., with little specific national or international criteria to suggest what skills, competence and knowledge must be achieved in order to use these titles.

As part of the definition of advanced nursing practice the UK Department of Health (DH, 2010) suggest these individuals have the following:

> extensive knowledge in areas such as diagnostics, therapeutics … enhanced skills in areas such as consultation and clinical decision-making … use complex reasoning, critical thinking, reflection and analysis to inform their assessments, clinical judgements and decisions … act as practice leaders … work across professional, organisational, agency and system boundaries to improve services and develop practice …

The above statement suggests that advanced level nursing relates to individual nurses performing a higher level of practice, including leadership. However, it has been suggested that nursing now needs to re-examine the concept of advanced nursing practice to ensure nursing remains 'fit for purpose'. Rolfe (2014) recommends that advancing practice is seen as a 'team' of innovative, experienced professionals working together for patient well-being and service benefits, rather than focusing on individual roles. This would include refocusing on fundamental core nursing values rather than medical and technical skills, and avoiding confusing titles relating to advanced practice. Practice innovation units are promoted, emphasising the process of advanced practice where teams are united by 'a common goal, vision or philosophy … in the desire to make a positive difference to care and disseminate the processes that led to the improvement of care' (Rolfe, 2014, p. 20).

Reflect 4.2

- Take a moment to ask yourself – what is the difference between an advanced nurse practitioner and a physician performing a chest examination as part of a routine appointment to monitor a patient who has asthma?
- Reflect on your answer, considering your perceptions and understanding of each role.
- Discuss this with both nursing and other healthcare colleagues to share viewpoints. Is there a common viewpoint? If not, how do they differ?

Your discussions might have included areas of education and training and depth and breadth of experience. It may have also included concepts of power, status, trust and patient choice. However, the fundamental values, attitudes and skills of nursing that Rolfe (2014) refers to focus on 'how' the episode of care is performed, with the therapeutic relationship being paramount. Whether this is seen as 'advanced' care is debatable, as many would argue this therapeutic relationship is the essence of nursing per se. However, it is important to consider and scrutinise what we perceive as advanced nursing roles and how these differ from other professional roles, how they are being utilised and driven within healthcare environments, and how this will shape the identity of the nursing profession. This will ultimately play a part in claiming the 'uniqueness' of the nurse.

The Future of Nursing report in the US (Institute of Medicine, 2010) focuses on nurses having responsibility for transformational leadership and political awareness to ensure their involvement in decision-making processes for the planning and delivery of healthcare services is optimised (Porter-O'Grady, 2011). Leadership and innovation in nursing remain high on the agenda within the UK, with nurses required to be strategists in developing and acting on ideas for innovation to improve patient care (DH, 2014, 2013). The concept of leadership in nursing has been gathering momentum and is now a fundamental element of pre-registration nursing curricula, alongside post-registration nursing education and development. Leadership is no longer an option in nursing. On becoming a registered nurse, the expectation is that you will lead care delivery, teams of healthcare staff, and manage change. Whether this increased leadership responsibility is a role that nurses feel adequately equipped to do is debatable and unlikely to be a consideration in applicants' decision-making to enter nursing.

The image of the nursing profession is powerful in influencing current and future generations' perceived career trajectories in terms of societal worth and the 'type' of candidate it recruits (Norman, 2015a). As nursing roles become more specialised, involve higher-level study, promote leadership and management opportunities, the profession may afford higher social status through salary increases and potential development pathways. This may encourage an alternative recruitment strategy with those who have previously dismissed nursing as a low paid, menial, vocational job with no prospects, now considering the opportunities that nursing could bring. Will the focus on traditional values of nursing stand up to scrutiny in an increasing world where registered nurses are leaders and managers of care rather than deliverers of care? It is this balance of compassion, kindness, advocacy and caring, along with critical decision-making, leadership, reflexiveness, autonomy, and skills and competence that may continue to promote nursing as unique.

New roles are emerging that mirror advanced nursing roles, in particular within the technical competence and traditional medical skills employed. These include physician assistants who have similar educational programmes to advanced nursing practice programmes and have similar roles. The philosophy of the two roles was initially seen as different, with a 'nursing vs medical' debate. It will be interesting to see how the future philosophy of nursing will develop in needing to include advanced 'medical' roles, or whether these will become standard 'nursing' roles.

Debates around what nursing should aspire to will continue, with many adopting rose-tinted spectacles to argue for the 'good old days'. The concept of nursing will need to continually change to adapt to the fluctuating needs of populations, communities, individuals, services and healthcare environments, with the blurring of healthcare roles seen as essential to encourage collaborative and integrated care. It is this blurring of healthcare roles which may ultimately determine the uniqueness of the nurse.

How nursing care is organised – do nurses have a voice?

Collaborative working, multi-disciplinary/inter-disciplinary working, partnership working and integrated care are not new concepts, with much literature from the 1980s and 1990s promoting the benefits of healthcare professionals having a real understanding of each other's roles in order to work together to improve care delivery, reduce repetition and promote cost-effectiveness (Baggs et al., 1988; Schull et al., 1992; Leathard, 1994). This theme continues within current healthcare organisations across many nations and is promoted as an essential organised delivery system. The expansion of services included as part of integrated healthcare systems which were outside the traditional healthcare arena, such as social care, have introduced additional complexities. The Kings Fund report (Goodwin et al., 2013) suggests that integrated care will improve outcomes for patients and populations by increasing coordination of services to ensure continuous and seamless care, reduce fragmentation and achieve greater efficiency.

Nursing has always needed to change its services to meet political demands. The shift away from hospital-based care to community-based care saw challenges in how nursing care was delivered, with much tribalism seen in areas where staff expertise and skills were being threatened. Integrated care brings new challenges in the organisation of service delivery with nursing needing to adapt to new political landscapes. Ham and Walsh (2013) insist that integrated care must consist of whole systems working but acknowledge there is no 'best way' of integrating care. They suggest that emphasis should be on discovery rather than design when developing policy and practice. It is unclear how nurses will demonstrate their involvement in new policy and practice and whether their voice will be heard in the competition from a multitude of stakeholders to be part of decision-making processes. As discussed previously, many applicants to the nursing profession do not have leadership or influencing experience, nor do they consider these as essential skills they will need in a future nursing career. For nursing to continue to shape its own identity, it has been argued that it needs to have a strong political voice with champions of nursing not only promoting the fundamental values of nursing, but also advocating for patients, communities and populations in decisions relating to healthcare delivery.

Reflect 4.3

- Reflect on an example where *you have influenced* decision-making at a local or higher level. This could be within your own team, healthcare organisation, or at a national level.
- What were the outcomes of your experience, both positive and negative?
- What would be needed in order for you to feel empowered to influence decision-making on a macro level?
- Discuss your thoughts with a colleague, mentor or clinical supervisor.

Traditional images of nursing may influence others' thinking in terms of nurses' abilities to lead, challenge and influence strategy. It is not every nurse who wants, or aspires to embrace this type of role, although it is seen as essential if nursing wants to have a voice that is recognised as influential, expert, and essential to decision-making strategies. With a range of health and social care professions now involved in shaping and developing integrated care services, can nursing afford to let other disciplines incorporate a nursing perspective and be directed in how to deliver care, or will nursing as a profession improve its standing and status in the healthcare arena and be counted as a strong voice to be listened to?

Ham and Walsh (2013, pp. 3–7) consider sixteen points needed at a local level to develop integrated care at scale and pace. These are:

- Find common cause with partners and be prepared to share sovereignty.
- Develop a shared narrative to explain why integrated care matters.
- Develop a persuasive vision to describe what integrated care will achieve.
- Establish shared leadership.
- Create time and space to develop understanding and new ways of working.
- Identify services and user groups where the potential benefits from integrated care are greatest.
- Build integrated care from the bottom up as well as the top down.
- Pool resources to enable commissioners and integrated teams to use resources flexibly.
- Innovate in the use of commissioning, contracting and payment mechanisms and use of the independent sector.
- Recognise that there is no 'best way' of integrating care.

- Support and empower users to take more control of their health and well-being.
- Share information about users with the support of appropriate information governance.
- Use the workforce effectively and be open to innovations in skill-mix and staff substitution.
- Set specific objectives and measure and evaluate progress towards these objectives.
- Be realistic about the costs of integrated care.
- Act on lessons learned together as part of a coherent strategy.

Reflect 4.4

- Reflect on the bullet points above.
- What are your thoughts on the current or potential opportunity for implementation of integrated care in your area of care delivery?
- What role do you think you could play in successful implementation of integrated care going forward?
- Discuss this with a colleague, mentor or clinical supervisor.

Nurses have multiple roles in a variety of care environments. Chapter 1 has examined some of the tensions that have arisen from a historical and popular media perspective and some of the reasoning for the status of nursing as a profession today. In many areas of nursing, care is still directed by medical staff and in other areas, nurses are independent and direct care accordingly. How the organisation and mobilisation of nursing care is determined relies on various factors including political drivers, cost, demographics, population needs, service needs, healthcare staff recruitment and required expertise.

A huge change in the UK relating to public health nursing has seen health visitors and school nurses now being designated to local authorities rather than remaining within healthcare organisations. Private healthcare providers bid for contracts to deliver care services and employ nurses as managers/directors of care. Increasing pressure on hospital services has resulted in political drivers to deliver more care in communities, drawing on voluntary sectors to arrange and deliver some aspects of care which were once the domain of nursing. How nursing care is organised can have an effect on both patient outcomes and also nurses' own perceptions of their professional and clinical roles.

As nurses are increasingly required to be directors of care in some care environments rather than at 'the bedside', rationing of nurse time is evident due to staff shortages and organisational failures. In the light of reports highlighting inadequate care and missed care opportunities (Francis, 2013), the decision by 'nurses' in how they ration their time is under scrutiny. Literature suggests that rationing can be seen as an end product of clinical decision making and critical judgment when nursing resources are too scarce to provide all the necessary care to all patients. Nurses are then forced to ration their attention across patients, minimize or omit certain duties, thereby increasing the risk of adverse patient outcomes.

(Papastavrou *et al.*, 2014, p. 316)

This can be seen as an important variable to consider when organising nursing care and can be influenced by teamwork, the practice environment and the leadership of the organisation.

Aiken *et al.*'s (2012) cross-sectional survey of nurses and patients across 488 hospitals over 12 countries of Europe and 688 in the US reinforces the suggestion that improved working environments and reduced rates of patients-to-nurse ratios are associated with improved outcomes, increase in care quality and safety, and improvement in patient satisfaction. Results of this study demonstrate the majority of nurses across the countries surveyed could identify a 'good' hospital which they would recommend as a good working environment. The study also suggests that merely increasing staff resources does not improve care quality alone; it appears that the working environment is paramount to recruit and retain a committed nursing workforce to instil quality care. These results are not generalisable within all care environments; however, the principles of embedding an organisational culture that values staff, promotes opportunities for development and instils the values of the nursing profession can be seen to be essential in achieving the best possible outcomes for both patients and staff (Norman, 2015b).

Reflect 4.5

- How is the area of care delivery organised where you are currently studying or working?
- Do you feel you need to 'ration' your care at times? If so, how does this make you feel and what impact do you feel it has on patient outcomes?
- Consider what makes a good working environment and how do you see your role in this process?
- Discuss your thoughts with a colleague, mentor or clinical supervisor.

Entering into a first clinical placement as a student nurse can be both exciting and daunting. Many prior perceptions of what a nurse does and what the nursing profession is are dispelled as experience is gained in varying aspects of care. These experiences will affect the socialisation into nursing and will hopefully be positive. The mentor, preceptor, clinical supervisor and peers will all influence how we will embrace the values and attitudes needed to practise as a qualified nurse. Thomas *et al.* (2015) reiterate the importance of these influences and how positive socialisation will encourage nurses to develop confidence, challenge poor practice and nurture high standards of care. Therefore, active mentorship/preceptorship through positive

role-modelling is vital to reduce negative attitudes and to ensure nursing values are promoted. In organising care delivery, effective mentorship of all staff from nursing students to advanced specialists can help reduce conflict, encourage team working and inspire staff to innovate goals for the delivery of care. Below is a list of ways in which you and your colleagues can help foster positive professional socialisation within your area of care delivery. You may wish to discuss these points with colleagues at a future team meeting. This is not an exhaustive list, so you and your colleagues may identify additional points to include (Norman, 2015b, p. 35):

- Acknowledging own and others areas of knowledge, competence and expertise.
- Being committed to self-development and continuing professional development.
- Valuing and encouraging team contributions in the planning and delivery of care.
- Instilling the importance of collaborative working with practice and wider multi-professional teams.
- Displaying motivation and enthusiasm for a learning and continuous improvement culture.
- Taking an interest and encouraging others' ideas to improve care.
- Encouraging reflection.
- Planning time to discuss and address issues arising and helping others to solve problems.
- Having the confidence to identify and challenge areas of performance with staff to develop ongoing improvement.
- Using methods of learning such as social media and e-learning to discuss professional socialisation as a way of complementing formal and informal learning.
- Enlisting the help of colleagues who can act as positive role models for staff and who display the values and standards of the profession and leadership attributes.
- Contributing to a welcoming, supportive culture where self-esteem and confidence are nurtured.
- Being clear, concise, constructive and honest when evaluating performance and care delivery.
- Being consistent and fair in feedback approaches.
- Asking for feedback on your own performance.
- Engaging in peer review.
- Reflecting and developing personal action plans as appropriate.

When nurses feel valued, inspired, supported and encouraged, they will feel confident to challenge assumptions, traditions and poor practice, suggest new ways of working and help develop innovative practices, act as role models for others, and ultimately have a voice in shaping quality care. Is it this voice in promoting professional competence, aligning all nurses to embrace and display the profession's common values that makes nursing unique, or is this common to other healthcare professions who care for individuals, communities and populations?

Levels of care – can anyone be a nurse?

The focus of this chapter is not to provide factual information on role descriptions of nurses or healthcare professionals, but to encourage critical understanding of nursing practice and question how nursing identity is shaped, perceived and viewed by nurses and the profession. Nurses have been tribalistic in their attempts to hold onto tasks and services they feel only nurses can provide which has also mirrored medical staff attitudes and behaviours when relinquishing some of their traditional roles to nurses. However, numerous healthcare roles are now planning and implementing care delivery, crossing boundaries of traditional professions and taking on a variety of care skills and competencies to meet a variety of needs. Unregistered professionals are routinely delivering traditional nursing care across a variety of settings. Patients' basic care needs have not changed, although it could be argued that multiple care conditions have made care management more complex. *Who* meets these needs has changed significantly.

Again the question of whether nursing is unique is called into question. Law and Aranda (2010, p. 283) suggest that we are entering a 'post-nurse' era where nursing needs to be 'de-constructed to reimagine and rethink concepts such as nursing, professionalism, caring and care work'. What nursing 'is' will be defined in a multitude of ways depending on who is defining the concept and will be influenced by ideology, power base, and self-interest. The need for a flexible, efficient, low-cost workforce in healthcare is paramount across the globe, in particular with the growing concept of integrated healthcare models. In many areas, 'registered' nurses delegate tasks to other care workers, but this relies on those delegating the task to be clear, accountable, confident and knowledgeable about the person's ability to perform the task, and ensure they evaluate the care episode.

A UK study by Hasson *et al.* (2013) suggests that student nurses do not understand the hierarchy of nursing care and have difficulty in understanding the skills and competencies of healthcare assistants and support workers in order to delegate tasks safely. Many unregistered care workers have a range of skills and competencies which are not standardised and therefore may prove difficult to draw upon when planning care delivery until the individual's expertise is known, observed and evaluated. However, with the introduction of educational programmes specifically tailored for healthcare support workers, successful completion of required competencies provide additional evidence of abilities. There is no question that healthcare support workers play an integral role in achieving the best possible outcomes for patient care and are an important part of the healthcare team. A particular strength is the personal relationship that healthcare assistants build with patients through their role in providing personal care at the bedside or at home over a specific time period, a role that many nurses now delegate. Lovatt *et al.* (2015) highlight the emotional support that healthcare assistants provide to patients and their family, offering a reassuring presence and listening to their needs. Despite concerns raised in the UK relating to unregulated care and calls to regulate healthcare assistants (Francis, 2013; Willis, 2015) it may be the lack of rigidity of this role and the lack of identified role definition that gives scope to delivering practical care and 'doing what needs to be done' (McPherson *et al.*, 2014).

In the UK following the 'Shape of Caring' review (Willis, 2015), the concept of nursing associates is being considered to bridge the gap between healthcare support worker and registered nurse (Health Education England, 2016). This role is similar to the generalist support role seen in Canada, the US and Australia and should not be seen as an assistant practitioner role who are experienced support staff working in a particular area of clinical practice or speciality. Whether this role will be 'registered' is yet to be decided and is said to be 'driven by the gap in intermediary skills that can provide high quality frontline care to patients so that nurses can focus on leading, managing and designing high quality patient interventions and solutions' (HEE, 2016). Does this suggest that nurses will continue to be removed from the delivery of care? Eley *et al.* (2012) research concludes that individuals who enter the nursing profession do so with a fundamental reason – to have the opportunity to 'care'. It can be argued that leading and developing services in healthcare must incorporate an element of caring but may be judged as somewhat detached from the reality of 'personally providing' care for individuals.

Reflect 4.5

- Reflect on your current role as a student nurse or registered nurse and that of an unregistered care worker. What are the differences and how do both roles influence care delivery in your area of practice?
- How do you see both roles developing in the future of care delivery?
- Discuss your thoughts with colleagues, mentor or clinical supervisor.

Members of the public have expectations of what care will be provided in particular circumstances and environments, who will provide that care and how that care will be delivered, although these expectations may vary in the light of their own experiences and influences from others. It is important for nurses to analyse patient satisfaction rates and understand their expectations for particular episodes of care in order to plan and implement care appropriately and in partnership. As patient satisfaction surveys do not solely concentrate on clinical outcomes but on 'care' received, it is important that expectations are known early as they do not always mirror the actual care received and may be idealistic in nature. Expectations that are listened to and acknowledged but also discussed in terms of what realistically can be offered will improve satisfaction rates (Reck, 2013). This needs to include detail of who will deliver the care, why and how this will be delivered and evaluated. If patients have full awareness of these factors they are more likely to accept varying healthcare staff performing roles that do not always fit their expectations. It is surprising therefore that a recent international study (Topaz *et al.*, 2016) concludes that only 12 per cent of the 536 nurses surveyed stated that they ask patients about their expectations and levels of satisfaction. The study suggests that healthcare providers need to structure discussion and training for staff in how to address expectations in order to increase satisfaction. This may also go some way to address the confusion members of the public feel with different levels of care, accountabilities and the roles of various caregivers and providers. With a multitude of 'uniforms' and titles adding to the confusion, it may be difficult to establish the necessity for the nurse to remain a unique concept, with generic terms for care giving seen as more appropriate for all types and levels of care. The public need to have an awareness and understanding of the care being received and develop an equal relationship with those providing care, although relinquishing control to patients may prove difficult to embed within care teams.

Control of care has an interesting power base on both macro and micro levels. From governments, large healthcare provider organisations, public health organisations, professional bodies, localised care teams and the individual nurse, the control of care should surely be in partnership with the patient. How patients make decisions regarding their involvement in the planning of care delivery and the interventions they will accept from service providers is not new to healthcare, although it has taken many years to be embraced and accepted. The concept of people-centred care has been adopted globally although the operationalisation of this concept has been successful to greater and lesser degrees. Some have relied on only involving patients as a mechanism for feedback, others have involved patients in policy decision-making. With access to Internet sources and information readily available, the public are increasingly aware of their healthcare choices and how to influence their care delivery (Juhnke and Muhlbacker, 2013). Consequently, how do nurses involve patients in their care decisions and are they happy to relinquish control?

Reflect 4.6

- How do you share decision-making with patients in your area of practice and what methods do you and your colleagues use to ensure this is appropriate for both the patient and the service?
- Is this something that is routinely part of the philosophy of care within your team or practice area? If not, how could this be incorporated?
- Discuss your thoughts with colleagues, a mentor/preceptor or clinical supervisor.

The education of nurses has long been debated, with current thinking implying graduate nurses will be prepared for the complex roles needed in the current healthcare arena. The academic level of a nurse relating to perceptions of what nursing is continues to be questioned, with the influence of media reports seen as contributing to the stereotypical and traditional imagery of nursing. The 'too posh to wash' and 'too clever to care' phrases have added to the media discourse (Gillett, 2012). Despite this, evidence suggests that degree-level nursing across the globe improves patient outcomes. The critical thinking and higher-level decision-making through solution-focused planning and delivery of care is seen to improve the quality of care and the way in which it is delivered and evaluated (Blegen *et al.*, 2013). The return to a 'golden age' of nursing as advocated by some is based on nostalgia, which is unhelpful in moving nursing forward to achieve a realistic vision of nursing for the future, whatever that may be (Girvin, 2015).

Studies have shown that newly qualified nurses feel their educational programmes have not fully prepared them for the nursing role of the twenty-first century. The model of providing a period of professional development for newly qualified nurses through preceptorship or mentorship is promoted as bridging the student–nurse gap and encouraging positive professional socialisation. Pennbrant *et al.* (2013) identified sub-processes evident within recently qualified nurses who were in the process of mastering the professional role over their first four years of registration (Figure 4.1). Influencing factors also emerged from the data analysis which were viewed as important in terms of professional development as a nurse.

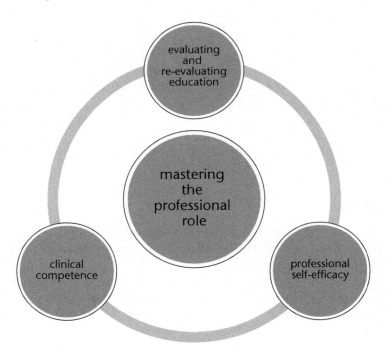

FIGURE 4.1 Mastering the professional role

Influencing factors affecting mastery of the professional role

co-workers – attitudes, support and understanding;

family and friends – stable relationships, resources (financial, support);

patients and significant others – positive and negative encounters effect on perception of own professional competence;

management of new nurses – manager influence through supportive environment and appropriate induction period;

healthcare organisation – clarifying the nursing role, workload, restructures, opportunities for development;

social values and norms – societal/media perceptions and imagery of nursing, held in low regard.

As nursing goes forward in this era of integrated healthcare and constant change, educational opportunities are needed to develop thinking, attitudes and skills throughout the pre-qualifying stages of nursing and beyond, recognising that nothing stands still and no one can know everything. Nursing must shape its own identity and challenge preconceptions of what nursing 'is' and 'does' as there appears to be no true definition that encompasses all.

Reflect 4.7

- What is your vision for nursing over the next five years?
- Reflect on your experiences of nursing so far in your career and write your own definition of what nursing is. How does this reflect the views of your colleagues? Are there common themes?
- Discuss these with your mentor/clinical supervisor.

Education providers will continue to market programmes of study that reflect current healthcare and government drivers in line with professional regulatory body standards. They will also provide alternative courses which address the educational and developmental needs of service providers in respect to the healthcare workforce, whether that be healthcare support worker roles, apprenticeships or new generic care roles in the future. The required educational attainment within professions is linked to status in terms of the social and economic benefits that status will provide. It will be interesting to see how educational providers influence potential recruitment to various care and nursing educational programmes and how links between courses will be promoted to assure progression for career pathways. A generic care programme that incorporates all caring roles within an inter-professional learning model may be too simplistic to propose in the light of the above discussions. However, for nursing to remain unique, the profession must be prepared to define itself.

Family members, voluntary sector services, and charities are also taking on traditional caring and nursing roles, with many becoming expert in their understanding of conditions and treatment needed to ensure patient needs are met. In addition, public health workers are adopting roles to promote health across communities, patient experts are recruited to give advice to others, and Internet sources are readily available, it could be argued that the uniqueness of nursing is favouring the more technical, advanced roles as discussed above.

Summary

This chapter has questioned the uniqueness of nursing, exploring influences on how nursing is defined and accepted by both the profession and the public. As a nurse of thirty years, I often reflect on changes within the nursing profession and the somewhat cyclical nature of nursing practice resulting from various government drivers. Nostalgia is not always a bad thing and as discussed above, it is important to learn from history to inform the future. However, for the profession to adapt to change and influence how it is shaped going forwards, it needs to discontinue its search for one whole-encompassing definition and aim, as this will ultimately prove impossible in a world where nursing roles are so varied, complex, and blurred with other healthcare professionals. The uniqueness of nursing can be argued from various standpoints depending on philosophical positions and the vision you have for the role and the profession. This chapter did not propose a vision of nursing but has introduced you to some areas needing critical debate for you to discuss with your colleagues within and outside the nursing profession. I hope you will think critically and reflect on your experiences to date, ultimately taking the opportunities available to you to ensure your voice is heard to take nursing forward … whatever that will be …

References

Aiken L., Sermeus W., Van Den Heed K., Sloane D.M. and McKee M. (2012) Patient safety, satisfaction and quality of hospital care: cross sectional surveys of nurses and patients in 12 countries in Europe and the United States. *BMJ*, Vol. 344, pp. 1–14.

Baggs J.G. and Schmitt M.H. (1988) Collaboration between nurses and physicians. *Journal of Nursing Scholarship*, Vol. 20(3), pp. 145–149.

Blegen M.A., Goode C.J., Park S.H., Vaughn T. and Spetz J. (2013) Baccalaureate education in nursing and patient outcomes. *Journal of Nursing Administration*, Vol. 43(2), pp. 89–94.

Canam C.J. (2008) The link between nursing discourses and nursing science: implications for a knowledge based discourse for nursing practice. *Journal of Advanced Nursing Science*, Vol. 31(4), pp. 296–307.

Department of Health (DH) (2010) *Advanced Level Nursing: A Position Statement*. DH. London.

Department of Health (DH) (2013) *Patients First and Foremost: The Initial Government Response to the Report of the Mid Staffordshire NHS Foundation Trust Public Enquiry*. DH. London.

Department of Health (DH) (2014) *Department of Health Corporate Plan 2013 to 2014*. DH. London.

Eley D., Eley R., Bertello M. and Rogers-Clark C. (2012) Why did I become a nurse? Personality traits and reasons for entering nursing. *Journal of Advanced Nursing*, Vol. 68(7), pp. 1546–1555.

Foucault M. (1972) *The Birth of the Clinic: Archaeology of Medical Perception*. New York: Vintage Books.

Francis R. (2013) *Report of the Mid Staffordshire NHS Foundation Trust Public Inquiry*. The Stationery Office, London.

Gillett K. (2012) A critical discourse analysis of British national newspaper representations of the academic level of nurse education: too clever for our own good? *Nursing Inquiry*, Vol. 19(4), pp. 297–307.

Girvin J. (2015) Editorial: The public understanding of nursing – time for a step change? *Journal of Clinical Nursing*, Vol. 24, pp. 3341–3342.

Goodwin N., Smith J., Davies A., Perry C., Rosen R., Dixon A., Dixon J. and Ham C. (2013) *A Report to the Department of Health and the NHS Future Forum. Integrated Care for Patients and Populations: Improving Outcomes by Working Together*. The Kings Fund. London.

Ham C. and Walsh C. (2013) *Lessons from Experience: Making Integrated Care Happen at Pace and Scale*. Kings Fund. London.

Hasson F., McKenna H.P. and Keeney S. (2013) Perceptions of the unregistered healthcare worker's role in pre-registration student nurses' clinical training. *Journal of Advanced Nursing*. Vol. 69(7), pp. 1618–1629.

Health Education England (HEE) (2016) *Consultation on the Role of the Nursing Associate*. Accessed 2 February 2016. Available at www.hee.nhs.uk/sites/default/files/documents/Response%20to%20Nursing%20Associate%20consultation%2026%20May%202016.pdf/.

Humphries R. (2015) Integrated health and social care in England – progress and prospects. *Health Policy*, Vol. 119, pp. 856–859.

Institute of Medicine (IOM) (2010) *The Future of Nursing: Leading Change, Advancing Health*. IOM. USA.

Juhnke C. and Muhlbacher A. (2013) Patient-centredness in integrated healthcare delivery systems – needs, expectations and priorities for organised healthcare systems. *International Journal of Integrated Care*, Vol. 13, pp. 1–14.

Kaambwa B., Lancsar E., McCaffrey N., Chen G., Gill L. (2015) Investigating consumers' and informal carers' views and preferences for consumer directed care: a discrete choice experiment. *Social Science and Medicine*, Vol. 140, pp. 81–94.

Law K. and Aranda K. (2010) The shifting foundations of nursing. *Nurse Education Today*, Vol. 30, pp. 544–547.

Leathard A. (ed.) (1994) *Going Inter-Professional: Working Together for Health and Welfare*. London: Routledge.

Lovatt M., Nanton V., Roberts J., Ingleton C., Noble B. *et al.* (2015) The provision of emotional labour by health care assistants caring for dying patients in the community: a qualitative study into the experiences of healthcare assistants and bereaved family carers. *International Journal of Nursing Studies*, Vol. 52, pp. 271–279.

Lowe G., Plummer V., O'Brien A.P. and Boyd L. (2012) Time to clarify – the value of advanced practice nursing roles in health care. *Journal of Advanced Nursing*, Vol. 68(3), pp. 677–685.

McAllister M., John T. and Gray M. (2009) In my day: using lessons from history, ritual and our elders to build professional identity. *Nurse Education in Practice*, Vol. 9, pp. 277–283.

McPherson K.M., Kayes N.K., Moloczij N. and Cummins C. (2014) Improving the interface between informal carers and formal health and social care services: a qualitative study. *International Journal of Nursing Studies*, Vol. 51(3), pp. 418–429.

Nelson G.R. and Gordon S. (2006) The rhetoric of rupture: nursing as a practice with history? *Nursing Outlook*, Vol. 52(5), pp. 255–261.

Norman K. (2015a) The image of community nursing: implications for future student recruitment. *British Journal of Community Nursing*, Vol. 20(1), pp. 352–357.

Norman K. (2015b) How mentors can influence values, behaviours and attitudes of nursing staff through positive professional socialisation. *Nursing Management*, Vol. 22(8), pp. 32–37.

Papastavrou E., Andreou P., Tsangari H., Schubert M., and De Geest S. (2014) Rationing of nursing care within professional environmental constraints: a correlational study. *Clinical Nursing Research*, Vol. 23(3), pp. 314–335.

Papastavrou E., Efstathiou G., Tsangari H., Karlou C., Patiraki E. and Jarosova D. (2015) Patients' decisional control over care: a cross-national comparison from both the patients' and nurses' points of view. *Scandinavian Journal of Caring Science*, pp. 1–11.

Pennbrant S., Nilsson M.S., Ohlen J. and Rudman A. (2013) Mastering the professional role as a newly graduated registered nurse. *Nurse Education Today*, Vol. 33, pp. 739–745.

Porter-O'Grady, T. (2011) Future of nursing special: leadership at all levels. *Nursing Management*, Vol. 42(5), pp. 32–37.

Reck, D. (2013) Can and should nurses be aware of patients' expectations for their nursing care? *Nursing Administration Quarterly*, Vol. 37(2), pp. 109–115.

Rolfe, G. (2014) Advanced nursing practice 2: a new vision for advanced nursing practice. *Nursing Times*, Vol. 110(28), pp. 18–21.

Schull, D., Tosch P. and Wood M. (1992) Clinical nurse specialists and collaborative care managers. *Nursing Management*, Vol. 23(3), pp. 30–33.

Sheer B., Kam F. and Wong Y. (2008) The development of advanced nursing practice globally. *Journal of Nursing Scholarship*, Vol. 40(3), pp. 204–211.

Thomas J., Jinks A. and Jack B. (2015) Finessing incivility: the professional socialisation experiences of student nurses first clinical placement, a grounded theory. *Nurse Education Today*, available online at doi: 10.1016/j.nedt.2015.08.022.

Topaz M., Lisby M., Morrison C., Levtzion-Korach O., Hockey P., Salzberg C.A (2016) Nurses' perspectives on patient satisfaction and expectations: an international cross-sectional multicenter study with implications for evidence-based practice. *Worldviews on Evidence-Based Nursing*, pp. 1–12.

Willis G. (2015) *Raising the Bar: Shape of Caring: A Review of the Future Education and Training of Registered Nurses and Care Assistants*. Health Education England, London.

PART II

Developing your nursing practice

5

NURSING REGULATION

Being a professional

Maureen Morgan and Robert Parry

Why this chapter is important

Nursing as a profession is subject to regulatory legislation in the UK and in many other countries. It is crucial that nurses understand the purpose and meaning of being a regulated professional, the requirements of codes of professional standards of practice and behaviour and the relationship between compliance and protection of the public. Though some nurses may confuse the role of the regulator with that of professional bodies, and fail to see its relevance, we invite them to consider how regulation and registration underpins the status of the profession and confirms the trust of those who place themselves or their families into its care.

Chapter trigger question: Can professional nursing regulation really ensure safe standards of patient care?

Key words: professional codes, conduct, professionalism, registration, regulation, revalidation

---

Introduction

This chapter discusses the registration and regulation of nursing. We consider what it means to be a professional nurse in modern times, and how public trust in the profession is maintained and enhanced.

We examine the purpose of regulation, discuss external control and professional self-determination. We review the concept of professionalism, the impact on professional regulation of societal changes, consumerism and the emergence of a less deferential society. We describe how a professional regulatory system can be future-proofed to encourage lifelong learning for nurses and ensure better protection of the public.

We use the United Kingdom (UK) as our prime case study as it has a long-standing, well-developed process for regulating nurses as well as being the country of residence and practice of its authors.

In so doing, we give due consideration to the future of professional regulation and the challenges faced by nurses and the nursing profession in the wake of far-reaching reports into major system failures in healthcare and health care systems. Most recently, the Francis Inquiry (2013) raised questions about the way in which employers and health regulatory systems should work together. We explore the contribution regulation makes to standards of patient care and safety and ask whether regulation is, of itself, sufficient.

Purpose of regulation

Professional regulation exists to protect the public. It underpins the natural trust the public has in health professionals, with formal assurance that this is not misplaced. It does so primarily, by (UK Government, Department of Health, 2007):

- setting and promoting standards for admission to a register and for remaining on it;
- keeping a register of those who meet standards and checking that registrants continue to meet standards;
- administering procedures for dealing with those whose right to remain on the register is called into question;
- ensuring high standards of education.

Historically in the UK, calls for the regulation of nursing via statutory registration began in the 1850s; however, regulation of nurses was not implemented until 1919. Differences in opinion between nurses and hospital administrators about how, or indeed whether, this should be done hindered progress.

Florence Nightingale herself supported neither group and was opposed to any registration for nurses, believing the essential qualities of the nurse could neither be taught, examined or regulated! The founder of modern nursing would be severely out of step with the current zeitgeist.

Later, two voluntary registers existed: the Hospital Association's administrative list and the newly formed British Nursing Association, now the Royal British Nursing Association, which sought to:

> unite all British nurses in membership of a recognised profession and to provide for their registration on terms, satisfactory to physicians and surgeons, as evidence of their having received systematic training.

Nurses fought hard for the professional status conferred by statutory registration, and viewed their work as complementary to, but different from, medicine. They recognised the need to align with medicine and to gain credence for their knowledge and skills, as one professional to another, but distanced professional nursing from the image held by many of a lay service provided by women of good character, acting under the direction of a doctor.

Influenced by the aftermath of the First World War, a nurse registration private member's bill was passed into law, and the General Nursing Council was established. Today the GNC has been superseded by the Nursing and Midwifery Council (NMC). It was not until 1951 that male nurses in the UK were admitted to the nursing register.

Reflect 6.1

* Are you able to identify the professional regulatory body responsible for nursing where you live?
* How does your regulatory body define nursing practice and professionalism and what is their role in ensuring safe nursing practice?
* Reflect on the expectations your nursing regulatory body has on nurses and how it influences your nursing identity and everyday practice.

International approaches to nurse regulation

How nurses are regulated varies across the globe. Systems may be run on a national, state or regional basis. Responsibilities range from government ministries, nursing organisations or independent statutory bodies. In many systems, especially in the developed world, responsibility belongs to the profession: professional or self-regulation. Some regulators consider one basic level of register entry is a sufficient threshold for public protection. Others require nurses practising at advanced level to register higher, master's or doctorate qualifications. The last is the case in the USA and Canada.

Several regulators define the duties, responsibilities and tasks of nurses and define differences between those practising at primary registration and advanced levels. Others operate a more flexible system to prevent regulation from hindering the development and expansion of nursing roles needed to meet the demands of rapidly modernising health care. In the UK, the only 'advanced' duty that is regulated is that of prescribing medicines.

Many countries protect the title nurse, while in some like the UK, a nurse can be a descriptor of many roles such as caring for small children or for sick animals; with the nomenclature 'registered nurse' reserved for those regulated by the NMC.

In 2013 the International Council of Nurses issued a position statement setting out thirteen principles for effective regulation. They included the need to take account of multiple interests, achieve representational balance and professional 'optimacy'. They stated the overriding purpose of statutory regulation of nursing is that of service to and protection of the public. They called for regulatory standards to be based on clear definitions of professional scope and accountability through to professional 'ultimacy', meaning that standards should 'promote the fullest development of the professional commensurate with its potential social contribution' (ICN, 2013).

The latter has gained traction in recent years in many countries, as they strive to contain the ever-rising costs of health care by optimising the use of all of the workforce: nurses take on work once the province of doctors, and in turn pass over aspects of fundamental care to largely unregulated health care assistants.

Self-regulation: Balancing interests of profession, the public and governments

Historically self-regulation has been a hallmark of health care professions. Here the professions themselves set standards for initial education and restrict access to the register to those who meet the required level of competence. The original Hippocratic oath governing medicine was rooted in the notion of a moral community, based on ethics, principles and values, and obligated to protect the interests of the patient, above their own. The concept of trust between health professionals and patients generated the belief that they would act in the interests of their patients and were logical guardians of standards. Furthermore, professionals alone had the knowledge and experience to judge the competence of their peers, and protect the public from harm.

While prominent in medicine, self-regulation has not been viewed in the same way in nursing. A 2002 World Health Organization report suggested the practice of nursing had long been influenced by a range of people: politicians, doctors, lawyers and civil servants to name a few, each of whom sought to control the way nurses practise. The WHO noted that frequently, in ensuing debates, the voice of nurses themselves was absent (WHO, 2002). This statement by the WHO implies, in the past at least, regulation could be seen as something *done* to nurses, in its benign forms to ensure patients are safe in their care, or in less favourable systems, to *restrict* their work from impinging on the province of others.

The College of Registered Nurses of Manitoba in Canada in their 2011 fact sheet describes professional self-regulation as acknowledging,

> that a profession itself is in the best position to regulate its members because their specialised body of knowledge makes external regulation difficult and impractical. Registered nurses understand registered nursing better than anyone else so it simply makes good sense to have professionals regulate themselves as long as they do so in the public interest.

The College of Registered Nurses of Manitoba in Canada recognise conflicts of interest may arise wherein the profession may guard its own interest rather than that of patients, in which case the college arbitrates.

Professional self-regulation was the norm in the UK until well into the 1980s and consecutive UK governments were content that regulation could largely be left to the professionals. The politicians assumed that provided different interests or strands of the profession were adequately represented, they could be trusted to carry out regulatory affairs without interference (Davies & Beach, 2000). A number of key events challenged this prevailing approach. Changes within the global economy coupled with risings costs of health care prompted UK governments to begin to see public services as a drain on the national purse. In the National Health Service general managers were brought in to bring a more businesslike agenda, to control costs, and importantly, with a remit to challenge professional practice to improve efficiency and ensure value for money (Griffiths, 1983).

Some on the right of the political spectrum saw health and other professionals as self-interested monopolies that hindered the operation of the market.

Unease with leaving professionals to govern themselves heightened following well-publicised scandals about poor care, primarily but not entirely involving the medical profession. Regulators began to be viewed as acting more in the interests of the professions than those of the public, which brought the whole question of self-regulation into focus (Kennedy, 2001).

Societal changes also exerted their own pressure to bear on how professionals are regulated, and how transparently accountable they are for the safety of the public. Growing emphasis on consumer choice, coupled with a dramatic increase in sources of information available for patients, and a decline in deference to professions, meant people were starting to question public services and expect more of them.

In the UK, the National Consumer Council turned its attention to the health professions' regulatory bodies, asking what protection they were providing for the public. They collected information on how regulation worked, what powers regulators had and what guarantee they offered to the public. Their subsequent report listed fourteen principles for public protection, notably that there should be substantial representation for the lay public on regulatory bodies with clear criteria for their appointment (NCC, 1999). This has been accepted as a necessary condition in the UK, to which we return later.

Common to all regulatory systems is that nurses should practise in accordance with a code of conduct or ethics. While nursing does not have an internationally accepted model like the Hippocratic oath, most codes set out rules for practice that uphold the safety of the public. In 2012 the ICN updated its code, stating that nurses have four fundamental responsibilities: to promote health, to prevent illness, to restore to health and to alleviate suffering. They state the need for nursing is universal and inherent in its practice is respect for human rights (ICN, 2012).

Reflect 6.2

* Think about the four ICN fundamental responsibilities and your nursing practice.

- Can you identify and write down examples from our own practice that reflect each of the four ICN fundamental responsibilities?
- Are there any of the four which are more prominent in your daily work or ones that you can provide examples for? If so, can you explain why?

The UK code of professional conduct

In the UK, the Nursing and Midwifery Council (NMC) is responsible for registering over 680,000 nurses and midwives. In 2015 the NMC published a new professional code which set out the professional standards that registered nurses and midwives must uphold called *The Code: Professional Standards of practice and behaviour for nurses and midwives*.

Table 5.1 identifies the four themes and **Table 5.2** details the twenty-five subthemes contained in the NMC code.

The NMC code (2015) encourages registrants to use it to guide their daily practice, proposing they read it regularly. It states registrants must treat people with compassion, ensure their needs are assessed, and exercise candour if errors or harm occur.

Given the set of duties, competences, attitudes and behaviours required by nurses from the NMC code it may be argued that compliance with the code would mean a nurse should have an untroubled professional career?

It can be seen this updated code places considerable emphasis on the duty of nurses to uphold the rights of the individual and to raise concerns promptly. Nurses are also required to be honest with patients and their relatives about adverse incidences, the so-called 'duty of candour'.

The code clearly spells out what nurses, joining or renewing registration, are obligating themselves to uphold. It also makes plain to all – nurses, patients and the public alike – what good nursing practice looks like, and describes what makes a professional nurse.

The code plays a crucial role for the NMC in the registration, fitness to practise and revalidation of nurses and midwives. Elements of the NMC code (2015) are explored further under the subheading professionalism.

TABLE 5.1 The NMC code's four main themes

- Prioritise people
- Practice effectively
- Preserve safety
- Promote professionalism and trust

TABLE 5.2 The NMC code's twenty-five subthemes

Prioritise people
- Treat people as individuals and uphold their dignity
- Listen to people and respond to their preferences and concerns
- Make sure that people's physical, social and psychological needs are assessed and responded to
- Act in the best interest of people at all times
- Respect people's right to privacy and confidentiality

Practice effectively
- Always practice in line with the best available evidence
- Communicate clearly
- Work cooperatively
- Share your skills, knowledge and experience for the benefit of people receiving care and your colleagues
- Keep clear and accurate records relevant to your practice
- Be accountable for your decisions to delegate tasks and duties to other people
- Have in place an indemnity which provides appropriate cover for any practice you take on as a nurse or midwife in the United Kingdom

Preserve safety
- Recognise and work within the limits of your competence
- Be open and candid with all service users about all aspects of care and treatment, including when any mistakes or harm have taken place
- Always offer help if an emergency arises in your practice setting or anywhere else
- Act without delay if you believe that there is a risk to patient safety or public protection
- Raise concerns immediately if you believe a person is vulnerable or at risk and needs extra support and protection
- Advise on, prescribe, supply, dispense or administer medicines within the limits of your training and competence, the law, our guidance and other relevant policies, guidance and regulations
- Be aware of, and reduce as far as possible, any potential for harm associated with your practice

Promote professionalism and trust
- Uphold the reputation of your profession at all times
- Uphold your position as a registered nurse or midwife
- Fulfil all registration requirements
- Cooperate with all investigations and audits
- Respond to any complaints against you professionally
- Provide leadership to make sure people's well-being is protected and to improve their experiences of the healthcare system

The scope of professional practice

The scope of professional nursing practice, meaning the range of activities and interventions of nurses, is dynamic. Practice must respond to rapid societal, technological, political and financial changes impacting on the contribution made by nurses. These include rising demands for healthcare, the need to contain costs and to manage technical advances in medicine. Earlier in Chapter 4 the impact of changing demands in how health services are provided also identified how nursing scopes of practice have changed to reflect these developments and how this has driven new nursing roles.

This flexibility requires nurse regulators to devise and operate systems that support their prime duty of protecting the public, but do not inhibit the profession's ability to respond to the demands of modern health care. The ICN's 2013 position statement on standards for regulation (ibid.) described this as enabling *professional ultimacy*, i.e. the fullest development of the profession commensurate with its potential social contribution.

Kennedy *et al.* (2015) undertook a review and comparison of nursing and midwifery regulatory and professional bodies' scopes of practice and associated decision-making frameworks, and found two main approaches to the regulation exist internationally. The first is policy- and regulation-driven and behaviour-oriented. The second is based on notions of autonomous decision-making, professionalism and accountability. The two are not mutually exclusive, having similar elements but with different emphases. Both lack explicit recognition of the aesthetic aspects of care and patient choice, which is a fundamental principle of evidence-based practice. As Kennedy *et al.* (ibid.) conclude, nursing organisations, regulatory authorities and nurses must recognise that differing scopes of practice and the associated responsibility for decision-making, provides a very public statement about the status of nursing within its jurisdiction. In the UK, the scope of nursing practice is bounded only by the skills, knowledge and competence of each nurse, underpinned by agreement with her or his employer. While this places responsibility on the nurses to ensure they are practising safely, it has allowed them to develop new skills, enhance their role, increase job satisfaction and career prospects. It has also enabled the National Health Service to cope with rapidly rising demand for a highly technical skilled workforce. Most importantly, however, is the recognition that regardless of how pressing the need, nurses must still practise within the NMC's regulatory requirements and must not work beyond their scope of practice even if asked to do so by an employer.

Professionalism and nursing

Codes of conduct, principles and ethics required by nurse regulators stem from a belief about the attributes and behaviours that constitute the professional nurse. As it is accepted that such characteristics can be defined, taught and observed nursing practice must embody professionalism.

Professionalism, though, can be a complex issue. For many nurses across the world and for the ICN Code of Ethics (2012), being a professional incorporates behaviours, skills, values and competence, coupled with empathy, compassion and altruism. Nurses must put aside their own interests, political, cultural and religious beliefs, while caring for patients. Requirements are set out in a set of rules or code, non-adherence to which can result in a range of sanctions, the most serious of which is suspension or curtailment of the right to practise. It is vital, therefore, that nurses understand what professionalism means of itself, and in the context of their own jurisdiction and working environment.

Morrow *et al.* (2011) when researching healthcare professions, identified that 'Professionalism ... was not seen as a static well-defined concept, but rather constructed in specific interactions. Consequently, definitions of professionalism are fluid, changing dynamically with changing context' (p. 22). From the perspective of patients and service users, professionalism appears to incorporate a range of attributes and characteristics that include technical competence, appearance, image, confidence level, empathy, compassion, understanding, patience, manners, verbal and non-verbal communication, an anti-discriminatory and non-judgemental attitude, and appropriate physical contact. In the UK, absence of, or inconsistency in, the projection and manifestation of these characteristics underpins many of the complaints patients, service users and carers make about care (Parliamentary and Health Service Ombudsman, 2011).

Two of the countries within the UK – Scotland and Wales – explored their own definitions of professionalism. The Scottish government concurred with others that professionalism is complex, multifaceted and difficult to define, which is unsurprising given the notion that it is fluid, dynamic and changes according to context (ibid.). They recommend changing the emphasis from negative behaviours to reinforcing positive ones (ibid.). Morgan *et al.* in their Delphi study into professionalism (2014), for the chief nursing officer in Wales, claimed they achieved a sufficiently high level of consensus to enable a definition of what constituted professionalism in nursing in Wales. They defined professionalism as:

> the personal qualities found in individuals' attitudes and behaviours with resultant outcome of constancy in personal integrity, humility, caring and striving to build therapeutic relationships, challenging and empowering others while taking accountability for actions, own learning and delivering up-to-date, evidence-based quality patient and family centred care.
>
> (Ibid., p. 32)

Interestingly, this definition reflects the central tenet of this textbook and the intertwined nature of the person and the profession.

Stern (2006) developed four principles when considering the notion of professionalism (please see Table 5.3: Stern's Principles). While helpful, each of the principles would be subject to individual, social and cultural interpretation. Stern's principle of 'excellence' could imply notions of standards, ethics, values; whereas

TABLE 5.3 Stern's Principles and contextual definition of professionalism

Stern's principle	Contextualised definition
Excellence	Demonstrating practice that is distinctive, meritorious and of high quality
Accountability	Demonstrating an ethos of being answerable for all actions and omissions, whether to service users, peers, employers, standard-setting/regulatory bodies or oneself
Humanism	Demonstrating humanity in everyday practice
Altruism	Demonstrating regard for service users and colleagues and ensuring that self-interest does not influence actions or omissions

'accountability', patient–nurse relationships; equality, self-regulation; 'humanism'; respect, empathy, compassionate care; and 'altruism' may imply always acting in the best interest.

Stern claims that inherent in professionalism are internal drivers that include personal values, attributes and a sense of personal responsibility. The UK Royal College of Physicians (2005) study noted that professionalism is influenced by how practitioners behave towards one another and towards patients. It also reflects that organisational values are supported by external drivers such as environmental and cultural influences, engaged leadership and facilitation of learning, and through feedback from patients, carers, service users and colleagues.

Schön's (1983) classic text on the 'reflective practitioner' noted activities associated with reflective practice are key influences on professionalism and with regular reflection on practice being recognised as a way of developing and improving performance. Here, there is an assumption that practitioners who regularly reflect on their practice are more likely to be receptive to change or new developments. Furthermore, they are more likely to be responsive to feedback and more willing to adapt and change their practices and behaviours.

The UK nursing regulator, the NMC, includes standards for how professionals must behave to users and colleagues. It describes the responsibilities of registrants and also places a duty on employers to ensure staff can uphold the code, as part of providing quality, safe services expected by patients and the system regulators. Examples are detailed in Tables 5.1 and 5.2 in this chapter. The *prioritise people theme* states that nurses and midwives must put the interests of people needing their services first, make care and safety their primary concern, ensure people's dignity is preserved and their needs are recognised, assessed and responded to. They must ensure people are treated with respect, their rights are upheld and discriminatory attitudes and behaviour are challenged. This includes treating people with kindness and 'compassion', and recognising when they are anxious or in distress.

The code theme, *promote professionalism and trust*, requires nurses and midwives to uphold the reputation of their profession, and demonstrate a personal commitment to the code's standards. They must show integrity and leadership that others can aspire to and which generates trust and confidence in the profession. This includes:

*   maintaining objectivity and clear professional boundaries with patients, former patients, families and carers;
*   not exploiting vulnerability or causing distress;
*   refraining from expressing personal beliefs in an inappropriate way;
*   ensuring complaints do not prejudice care, but are used for reflection and learning.

As professionalism is at the heart of nursing practice, students entering the profession must be made aware of what it means, and what is expected of them, at the beginning of their career. Their registered nursing colleagues also have an obligation to act as role models for them, as a vital step in helping to shape student nurses' professional identity (Ó Lúanaigh, 2015).

Though the part played by professional regulators in determining how nurses work, nursing may not feature highly in the public's mind, it is obvious that people do have firm views about what makes a good nurse. They expect their nurses to provide excellent care, listen to them and serve their best interests at all times. In short: to embody professionalism.

Revalidation: Maintaining standards, competency and lifelong learning

A major UK government review in 2007, prompted by a highly publicised case involving a doctor convicted of murdering his patients proved to be the final call to action and sounded the death knell of exclusively self-regulation for health professionals. The subsequent White Paper set out new conditions for regulating health professionals, wherein the requirements of government, the public and the professions would each be recognised and balanced. As a result, in the UK, professional regulators like the NMC must now have an equal number of lay members to registrants on their governing councils. This aimed to dispel the perception that regulators are overly sympathetic to professionals.

> Professional regulation needs to sustain the confidence of both the public and the professions through demonstrable impartiality. Regulators need to be independent of government, the professionals themselves, employers, educators and all the other interest groups involved in healthcare.
>
> (UK Government, Department of Health, 2007)

Importantly, the review insisted professional regulation should be as much about sustaining, improving and assuring the professional standards of the overwhelming majority of health professionals as it is about identifying and addressing poor practice or poor behaviour. This turned the NMC's attention to how they could ensure lifelong competence to practice and how the register could be used to encourage continual learning throughout each nurse's career.

An early NMC mechanism of self-declaration of competence introduced in 1989 was radically updated in 2016 to better conform to the new requirements. Known as revalidation, the system aims to ensure nurses' practice remains evidence-based and safe throughout their careers. Every three years those on the register must demonstrate knowledge of, and adherence to, the NMC code. They must show they have completed the required number of practice hours, provide written evidence that they keep abreast of modern techniques and that they have developed new skills and competencies, as required by their field of practice. Nurses wishing to re-register must also provide evidence that they reflect on their own practice and consider how effective they are and how well they meet patients' needs. Another person, usually but not necessarily their line manager, must confirm written accounts as relevant and appropriate to their practice. Revalidation is not intended to be an assessment of a nurse's fitness to practise nor a way of raising fitness to practise concerns. Instead, it aims to embed the standards described in the code into everyday practice and to make reflection a key component of nurses' work. Not only does the NMC anticipate nurses are more likely to stay up to date, however long their career, they also see it as a means to strengthen public confidence in the profession as a whole.

Regulation in practice: Does regulation make patients safer?

Nursing is a profession in demand across the world, especially in Western countries experiencing ageing demographics, and this trend appears to be quickening. In recognition of the global nature of healthcare, the movement of populations, and in response to employers, regulators are attempting to harmonise nursing standards across borders. The European Union (EU) has been involved in the Recognition of Professional Qualifications Directive, which allows professionals to have their qualifications awarded in one member state recognised in another. This enables them to pursue their profession anywhere in the European Economic Area, and Switzerland, and is proving a vital strategy in helping manage over-supply and shortages of the nursing workforce across twenty-eight countries.

We have shown there is considerable consensus among researchers and regulators about the factors that characterise a professional nurse, bound by standards of behaviour, attitudes, ethics and codes. We have also seen that professionalism is complex and governed by context and specific interactions. Many factors come into play, not least the expectations of patients and the public that vary from country to country, as will the policies of governments.

For example, in recent years, UK health policy has stressed the value of patients as partners in their care, the imperative of offering choice and has raised the importance of how patients experience their care as a key measure of performance. Nurses are held accountable for their practice and are expected to advocate for their patients as necessary. For some nurses across the world, used to a more hierarchical system, this may not chime with the context in which they learned their profession. In such instances receiving countries and employers need to pay close attention to helping nurses adapt, so they can become confident and capable, socialised into the prevailing culture and able to practise within the professional code and standards expected. It is not enough to simply make sure nurses from overseas are clinically competent. They must be helped to understand what may be unspoken, but is nevertheless a key expectation of professional nurses within the receiving jurisdiction.

Fitness to practice

Regulators have robust legal powers to take action against those who do not adhere to their standards, including removal or suspension from the register and restrictions on practice. Though in the UK at least, only a small minority of nurses are affected (the NMC *Annual Fitness to Practice Report 2014–15* details 0.7 per cent of the 686,782 on the register) it has a profound effect on both the individuals involved and in levels of confidence in the nursing profession.

Wherever they practise – hospitals, communities, education or management, at fundamental or advanced levels – nurses are expected to conform to the highest levels of professionalism.

Indeed, nurses expect this of themselves and their colleagues. In the UK and many countries, they remain one of the public's most trusted and respected workers. It becomes therefore even more shocking and distressing when reports of unprofessional behaviour by nurses are reported in the media. Such behaviour can span an increasing variety of forms, some of which involve 'inappropriate' use of social media, while others may be an expression of less deferential youth to previous societal norms. That these events, deplorable though they are, are considered headline news, perhaps reflects that by and large, education, clarity of ethics, standards and codes, do guide and inform the practice of the majority of nurses most of the time. This is not, though, the whole story. A notorious event in the UK involving nursing malpractice and callous treatment of patients has had far-reaching effects. The subsequent investigation described extensive system failures in care, and noted that 'unprofessional behaviour' of nurses exists alongside low morale and job satisfaction (Francis Report, 2013).

Our expectation of professionalism must therefore take account of other factors such as morale, pride, values and passion, and how leaders of organisations succeed or fail in their responsibility to generate these traits in their workforce.

Does regulation keep patients safer?

While professional regulation is a necessary component of patient safety, is it sufficient?

Regulators take action when individuals fail to uphold standards, but they can only ever be third in line in defence of safety and quality. The professionals form the first line themselves: how they understand their interaction with their patients and how they utilise their knowledge, skills and competencies, their attitudes and behaviours and the ethical basis of their work. The NMC guides behaviours in some detail but it's up to individual nurses to apply it in practice. Recruits to nursing overwhelmingly come into the profession with the intention of making things better. So how can even a small number of them, as reported by Francis be capable of neglectful and uncaring behaviour? Campling and Ballatt quote Raymond Tallis, retired professor of geriatric medicine, as citing the appalling nature of some of the jobs carried out each day by health care staff, and the harrowing contact with emotional distress and disturbance they witness, as a possible factor (Campling and Ballatt, 2011).

Another writer claimed that the majority of healthcare staff suffer from anxiety on and off throughout their career (Firth-Cozens, 2003). For some this may affect their ability to empathise fully with their patients. This makes employers themselves the crucial second line of defence in supporting high-quality, safe care. Employers have a critical role in promoting an organisational culture where staff are appreciated, their work valued and where the reality of their work is recognised. In such an environment staff can be helped to acknowledge and manage their feelings, and everyone has the support of an open and honest culture.

> It is really very simple: the safer people feel in their role, the more they will be able to look with curiosity at their own attitudes and prejudices and be more open to the emotional experience of their patients.
>
> (Ballatt and Campling, 2011)

We have described the first, second and third levels of defence but there is another important player: system regulators. System regulators such as the UK's Care Quality Commission (CQC) have a crucial contribution to make. The CQC is able to take an organisation-wide view of what it is like to be a patient and what it is like to be a member of staff. It seeks answers to five questions during their inspections of organisations: is it safe, is it effective, is it caring, is it responsive and is it well-led? The answers to these questions have a clear impact on the context and environment in which nurses practise, the care they are able to provide for patients. Professional regulators are encouraged to share information with system regulators so that working conditions that may be causal factors underpinning poor or sub-standard practice can be identified. They can then demand that action is taken so that nurses and others can uphold their code of conduct. Professional regulators and system regulators working together can present a strong force for high-quality and safe care for patients.

Summary

Across the world, the delivery of healthcare today is highly political with greater financial controls, performance and outcome measurements and public scrutiny, sitting alongside, and potentially in conflict with, professional values. The overarching requirements to improve quality, not least the experience patients have, improve safety and avoid waste, are dominating healthcare services.

How nurses can meet and sustain high-quality care for patients in the high pressure, highly technical and highly performance–managed environment that characterises much of our health care system, depends on balancing the requirements of regulators, governments, organisations and patients themselves with the ability of the nurses to articulate what is needed for the profession to thrive. They must be able to influence policy, not just within the boardroom, but make their voice heard from wherever and whatever level they are practising.

The desire for professionalism must come from nurses themselves and they must also be willing to work with their regulators to ensure codes are brought to life. Though nurses have sought professional regulation and the status this conferred, in the UK the role of its regulatory body the NMC is today not necessarily understood by its practitioners. Nurses tend to confuse the function of the regulatory body with those of professional associations such as the Royal College of Nursing (RCN) in the UK.

Some see regulation as a bureaucratic, judgemental system of scrutiny out to punish hard-working nurses for minor misdemeanours, or take action against those unfortunate enough to have been caught up in circumstances they see as beyond their control, such as understaffing and lack of resources. Nurses must take ownership of the concept of the professional nurse and work with the regulator so they are able to convey to governments, the public, organisations and other professionals, exactly what makes a modern nurse, what value is added through their work, and how the practice of nursing is so much more than the sum of its tasks.

References

Ballatt J, Campling B (2011) *Intelligent Kindness: Reforming the Culture of Healthcare*. London: RCPsych Publications.

College of Registered Nurses of Manitoba (2011) *Self-Regulation Fact Sheet*. www.crnm. mb.ca/uploads/document/document_file_193.pdf?t=1442260574/ (accessed 2 April 2016).

Davies C, Beach A (2000) *Interpreting Professional Self-Regulation: A History of the United Kingdom Central Council for Nursing, Midwifery and Health Visiting*. London: Routledge.

Firth-Cozens J (2003) Doctors, their well-being and their stress. *BMJ*. 326, 670–671.

Francis Report (2013) *Mid Staffordshire NHS Foundation Trust Public Inquiry*. http://bit. ly/1bbgTtO (accessed March 2016).

GMC and NMC (2015) *Openness and Honesty: When Things Go Wrong: The Professional Duty of Candour*. www.nmc.org.uk/standards/guidance/the-professional-duty-of-candour/ (accessed 2 April 2016).

Griffiths R (1983) *NHS Management Inquiry*. London: Department of Health.

International Council of Nurses (2012) *Codes of Ethics for Nurses.* Revised edition. www.icn.ch/who-we-are/code-of-ethics-for-nurses/ (accessed 2 April 2016).

International Council of Nurses (2013) *Position Statement Nursing Regulation.* www.icn.ch/images/stories/documents/publications/position_statements/B04_Nsg_Regulation.pdf/ (accessed 2 April 2016).

Kennedy C, O'Reilly P, Fealy G, Casey M, Brady A-M, McNamara M, Prizeman G, Rohde D, Hegarty J (2015) Comparative analysis of nursing and midwifery regulatory and professional bodies' scope of practice and associated decision-making frameworks: a discussion paper. *Journal of Advanced Nursing.* Vol. 71(8), 1797–1811.

Kennedy I (2001) *The Report of Public Inquiry into Children's Heart Surgery at the Bristol Royal Infirmary 1984–1995: Learning from Bristol.* London: HMSO.

Morgan J, Hopkins W, Acreman S, Jewell K, Garword L, Candy E (2014) What does professionalism look like? Attitudes and behaviours derived from a Delphi study. *Nursing Management.* Vol. 21(7), 28–40.

Morrow G, Burford B, Rothwell C, Carter M, McLachlan J, Illing J (2011) *Professionalism and Conscientiousness in Healthcare Professionals. Final Report for Study 1 – Perceptions of Professionalism.* Durham: Medical Education Research Group, School of Medicine and Health, Durham University, p. 22.

National Consumer Council (NCC) (1999) *Models of Self-regulation – An Overview of Models in Business and the Professions.* London: National Consumer Council.

NMC (2014/15) *Annual Fitness to Practise Reports.* www.nmc.org.uk/about-us/reports-and-accounts/fitness-to-practise-annual-report/ (accessed 2 April 2016).

NMC (2015) *The Code: Professional Standards of Practice and Behaviours for Nurses and Midwives.* www.nmc.org.uk/standards/code/read-the-code-online/ (accessed 2 April 2016).

Ó Lúanaigh P (2015) Becoming a professional: What is the influence of registered nurses on nursing students' learning in the clinical environment? *Nurse Education in Practice.* 15(6), pp. 450–456.

Parliamentary and Health Service Ombudsman (2011) *Care and Compassion? Report of the Health Service Ombudsman on Ten Investigations into NHS Care of Older People.* www.ombudsman.org.uk/__data/assets/pdf_file/0016/7216/Care-and-Compassion-PHSO0114web.pdf/ (accessed 2 April 2016).

Royal College of Physicians (2005) *Doctors in Society: Medical Professionalism in a Changing World. Report of a Working Party of the Royal College of Physicians of London.* www.rcplondon.ac.uk (accessed 2 April 2016).

Schön D (1983) *The Reflective Practitioner: How Professionals Think in Action.* New York: Basic Books.

Scottish Government (2012) *Professionalism in Nursing, Midwifery and the Allied Health Professions in Scotland: A Report to the Coordinating Council for the NMANP Contribution to the Healthcare Quality Strategy for NHS Scotland.* Edinburgh: Scottish Government.

Stern DT (2006) *Measuring Medical Professionalism.* Oxford: Oxford University Press.

UK Government Department of Health Trust Assurance & Safety, 2007.

World Health Organization (2002) *Nursing and Midwifery: A Guide to Professional Nursing.* http://applications.emro.who.int/dsaf/dsa189.pdf/ (accessed 2 April 2016).

6

NURSES INFLUENCING HEALTHCARE

Leading as a professional

Lisa Bayliss-Pratt and Liz Fenton

Why this chapter is important

This section of the book will challenge you to consider the role of nurses as both leaders and influencers of health and care services. It provides an opportunity to reflect on the concept of effective nursing leadership and consider and develop your opinions on the notion of nurses as key influencers of service provision. You will also have the opportunity to consider and reflect on your own leadership style and start to think about how you lead and influence within your own role.

Chapter trigger question: Are nurses serious contenders as leaders and influencers of health services?

Key words: leadership, influence, nurses as leaders

Introduction

The health and care system globally has an exciting future, but if that potential is to be fully realised, decision-making must be aligned to a shared long-term vision for high-quality care that is centred on people and their communities and within which nurses are placed at the front and centre of this service provision.

As an example of an approach to redefining health services, in 2014, NHS England published the *Five Year Forward View* (NHSE, 2014), developed with partner organisations that both deliver and oversee health and care services. This document set out the shared vision that will enable health and care services in England to collectively address and close the gaps in health and well-being, care and quality and funding and efficiency. This vision is based around new and innovative models of care, and reflects a desire to address the challenges in sustainable service provision experienced by health economies around the world as detailed in Chapter 10.

The collaborative approach to producing the *Five Year Forward View* brought together system leaders in partnership, and ensured that the principles of, and approaches to, developing new care delivery models were aligned, and are clearly owned across health and care services in England.

The *Five Year Forward View* challenges all care providers in England to think very differently about how health and care might best be delivered. Rather than invent or re-invent new organisational structures, systems or titles, the commitment is rather to better work across the traditional cultural and organisational divisions – placing people and their communities at the forefront of care and in doing so enable transformation.

The *Five Year Forward* strategy contains a clearly stated vision to make better use of the wealth of skills, knowledge and talent that is within the health and care workforce and in particular the nursing workforce, to improve timely and coordinated access to safe, high-quality care. The approach advocated in this strategic document reflects the points made earlier in Chapter 4 of this book.

From a UK perspective, the nursing profession represents the largest percentage of the health and care workforce (King's Fund, 2014). Approximately 630,000 registered nurses are on the professional register of the Nursing and Midwifery Council in the UK, of whom approximately 323,000 work within National Health Service (NHS) hospitals and community settings. A further 60,000 registered nurses work across diverse social care settings. There are more registered nurses and midwives on the Nursing and Midwifery Council (NMC) professional register, than in any other country. As a professional body and trade union, the Royal College of Nursing (RCN) has the largest memberships of registered nurses in the world.

Nursing as a profession has a history of powerful and influential leadership – often in challenging times and against the odds. Florence Nightingale influenced and shaped the development of nursing across Europe whilst in the United States, Clarissa Howe Barton, the pioneering nurse, founded the American Red Cross. Yet, despite this strong history, as other chapters have discussed, in 2013 powerful patient stories related as part of the Francis Inquiry spoke of a lack of empathy, privacy and dignity and poor communication. These moving accounts of the care experience that form the basis of the Francis Report recounted that the very fundamentals of the artistry in nursing were absent, and as a result the public's confidence in the nursing profession was rightly rocked.

Nurses have a profound effect on people's lives 'at times of basic human need when care and compassion are what matter most' and frequently when individuals are at their most vulnerable (NHS Constitution, 2015). Nursing has evolved enormously since the profession's inception: changing from a role that was largely fulfilled by nuns into the vibrant and varied profession it is today. Nursing has and must always be about providing care for patients and support to their families, but these duties can take place within a variety of specialities and settings – it is this that has enabled the diversity within the profession that has evolved over the last 50 years (nursingschoolhub.com).

So, although the notion of nurses and nursing has been around since the beginning of time, nursing today is considered one of the most important professions within the health and care system (nursingschoolhub.com). This does, however, challenge us to consider whether nurses can and do have the level of influence and control across health and care systems that their numbers within the workforce would suggest. A recent report from the All Party Parliamentary Group on Global Health (2016) highlights that by the very nature of the role a great deal of nursing is invisible – taking place either behind closed doors or curtains – and recommends that the collective impact, capability and potential of the nursing profession needs to be better understood.

Nurses can bring and apply their knowledge and skills that are key to unlocking system-wide health and care transformation. Without the leadership and influence of the nursing workforce, it is hard to believe how the advancements made within the medical and the allied health professions – not to mention the advancements in the delivery of healthcare – could have been achieved to the extent that they have today. Some examples include:

1. Advances in surgical and anaesthetic techniques that have enabled thousands of patients to be treated as 'day cases' with services led and delivered by nurses.
2. Personalised Medicine that uses information about a person's genes, proteins and environment to prevent, diagnose and treat disease.

Case Study – developing leaders and innovators

The Older Person's Nurse Fellowship (OPNF) was created by Health Education England in partnership with the Florence Nightingale Faculty of Nursing and Midwifery, King's College, London in 2014 in the wake of a number of critical national reports into the care of older people (Francis Report, 2013; CQC, 2014). The philosophy of the programme is to better enable senior nurses working at the frontline of care delivery to fulfil their potential as leaders and innovators in the care of older people. The principles are to support an already expert group of nurses to reach their full potential as leaders and role models and skilled collaborators working with older people and their families and in doing so prepare them to work across traditional organisational and sector boundaries shaping local, national and international older person's care policy and strategy. For more information on this fellowship please visit: www.kcl.ac.uk/nursing/.

Effective nursing leadership: Positive care outcomes

As we consider the role of nursing within a health and care system that is fit for the future, we must recognise the need for the profession to continue to evolve if we are to meet the joint challenges of the changing demographics and care needs. At the same time, we must acknowledge that citizens will always need and deserve care that is locally delivered and is responsive to their individual needs.

Francis (2013), Berwick (2013) and Keogh (2013) each made the direct association between effective leadership and positive care outcomes, but as we consider the role of nurses as system leaders and influencers, both now and in the future, we must first consider what makes an effective leader. Forbes (2012) described the ten qualities that define a great leader as being:

- **Honesty** – setting the standard you expect and want to see.
- **Delegation** – and build trust in those around you.
- **Communication** – clearly articulating your vision.
- **Confidence** – your team will take their cues from you.
- **Commitment** – and led by example.
- **Positive attitude** – which will motive others.
- **Creativity** – exploring a variety of options.
- **Intuition** – learn to trust yourself.
- **Inspire** – and express appreciation to others for their part.
- **Approach** – recognising that people respond to different styles.

6.1 Reflect

- First, think about someone in a leadership role that you admire.
- Now consider what it is about their actions that you think makes them a good leader.
- What skills and attributes do they demonstrate that makes them effective?
- Did any of their qualities mirror any of the ten qualities suggested by Forbes (2012)?

The foundations of nursing leadership

The nursing profession in England was thrust into turmoil when Sir Robert Francis (Francis, 2013) published his damning report following the inquiry into the failings at Mid Staffordshire NHS Foundation Trust in the UK. Such was and continues to be the impact of this report that many authors within this book have highlighted this inquiry. Against this backdrop, a review of the education and training of registered nurses and care assistants was led on behalf of Health Education England by Lord Willis of Knaresborough. *Raising the Bar: Shape of Caring* (Willis, 2015) tells us that nurses must be confident and feel empowered if they are to lead and advocate on behalf of the public and the profession and in doing so effectively 'raise the bar' (Willis, 2015).

Our collective ambition as nurses must be to ensure that we maximise the impact of our significant numbers and of our connectivity across all aspects of health and care. In doing so we can enable the profession itself and the professionals within it to effectively lead and influence not only within their local communities and communities of practice but also at a national and international level. Doing so will enable us to evidence nursing's unique and essential contribution and best improve both the quality and experience of care.

Nurses can lead and influence on a variety of levels and within a variety of contexts – be they using their nursing skills and knowledge in research, education, direct care delivery or in roles such as Chief Nurse or Director of Nursing. Yet are nurses and the nursing profession itself seen as pioneering enablers? Jones *et al.* (2016) discussed the increased scrutiny under which Executive Nurses have found themselves as a result of recent failings in care and quality, noting that while these nurses provide critical advice and support to boards, it often remains the case that these vital roles are not fully understood, with some boards *still* challenging the need for nursing to have a voice at executive level. Yet we know many counties now set the expectation that organisations will appoint an Executive Nurse as part of their accreditation quality standards (Centre for Healthcare Improvement, 2012).

Nursing and care remains under scrutiny and at times subject to widespread criticism as a result of serious failures in care such as occurred at Mid Staffordshire. Nursing leadership in these contexts is often defined as being weak or absent. Nurses, however, have risen to the challenge of effecting the necessary change and to deliver the vision set out in *Compassion in Practice* (NHS Commissioning Board, 2012), in order to begin to rebuild the public's confidence in the profession in England. *Compassion in Practice*, a vision and strategy for nursing, underpinned by the six Cs of care, compassion, competence, communication, courage and commitment, emphasises the value of nursing in providing the holistic care that supports well-being, treatment, recovery and care at end of life and provides a useful example of how clarity around the nurse's role and associated nursing leadership can address challenges to the autonomy of nursing practice (Bylone, 2010).

6.2 Reflect

- Take some time to think about the six Cs – care, compassion, competence, communication, courage and commitment.
- How have these ways of being informed or influenced your practice and that within your team?
- Do or could the six Cs help to inform and shape your nursing practice?
- Are the six Cs useful in developing a foundation as an effective nursing leader?

Creating your nursing leadership identity

Leaders in nursing are challenged with affecting the delicate balance between the need to innovate, develop care strategy and ensure sustainable services whilst at the same time managing the immediate demands of capacity and ensuring safe, effective care. This requires the skill of adaptability. The most effective leaders are able to adapt to the individual or group they are working with; this leadership approach was described by Hersey (1985) as situational leadership. Situational leaders draw on a suite of skills and tools to realise their creativity to engage and motivate others with their vision and in doing so enabling talent at all levels to be identified and have the maximum impact.

We need to take time to reflect on our ways of being with those we provide care for and consider how we may use those same skills to connect with colleagues and embrace the concept of collective leadership as opposed to command and control as the optimum foundation to establishing a culture of compassion.

Leadership is ultimately about relationships, and for nurses to be truly impactful across a system requires us to have motivation, resources and influence (Trofino, 1993). Root (2016) helpfully listed the ten qualities credible leaders required (please see Box 6.1). The qualities suggested by Root (2016) were supported when Robert Francis QC argued for strong, principled and caring leadership to come to the fore to ensure quality of care and enable lessons to be learnt when things go wrong. We must as leaders also focus on improving the work experiences of our colleagues who deliver are whilst addressing the current financial challenge facing health services around the world.

Identifying the talent and developing nurses as leaders needs to start from day one of entry into a career in nursing and care. Health Education England undertook a research project that explored the leadership development components within the pre-registration curricula of three higher education institutes. This provided evidence that whilst leadership development could be found throughout all the curricula reviewed, it was often an implicit component rather than explicit one within those programmes. In order to affect a change, the recommendations in Box 6.2 were made.

BOX 6.1 TEN WAYS TO BUILD CREDIBILITY AS A LEADER

- Honesty
- Education
- Competence
- Action
- Focus
- Accountability
- Loyalty
- Trust
- Respect
- Strength of character

(Root, 2016)

BOX 6.2 RECOMMENDATIONS FOR LEADERSHIP DEVELOPMENT WITHIN THE NURSING CURRICULUM

1. Branding of leadership – with overt use of leadership terminology.
2. Responsibility to lead reinforced as part of students' development.
3. Utilising the experience of service users in the delivery of the curriculum.
4. Adoption of overarching inter-professional learning approaches.
5. Personal profiling – encourage learners' self-assessment of their leadership skills.
6. Ensure leadership behaviours are assessed in practice.

(Jones *et al.*, 2015)

6.3 Reflect

• Consider your own pre-registration nursing programme for a moment.
• Was/is there a focus on identifying and developing your leadership and influencing skills within that programme?
• Would you consider that the skills and knowledge relating to leadership were explicit within your programme?

Nurses can and do lead and influence at local, regional and national levels – from advocating for patients to the reconfiguring of services and formulation of national policy. As a profession we recognise nursing as being so much more than a series of tasks and we need to gain this recognition on a wider level. It is, however, not enough for nurses merely to be a part of the process – health care is complex and none are better placed than nurses to lead it. This leads us to consider the need for a shift in our leadership approach towards a collective model in which everyone takes the responsibility for the success of an organisation as a whole, rather than a focus on their own jobs (Kings Fund, 2014).

Chapter 3 of this book explores the notion of clinical academic careers for nurses and considers the important role of these nurses in influencing and motivating the next generation within the profession. We need to enable the growth of the careers of the clinical academic workforce who build our evidence base and develop care practice – without these brilliant nurses our practices would have remained the stuff of myth and old wives' tales. Their leadership roles combine research and evidence-based practice that improve services and inspire others to achieve excellence.

Yet are nurses and the nursing profession seen as pioneering enablers, or are we viewed as passive bystanders who merely react and respond to the latest developments?

We put people at the centre of all that we do and are frequently the one consistent care provider or navigator throughout the life course – from pre-conception to the end of life. We have the ability to develop empowering partnerships and through these partnerships, nurses are able to develop care in the context of the values, preferences, goals and beliefs of those with whom we work. We must consider how we harness these same skills to be recognised and valued as leaders and innovators.

6.4 Reflect

- Take a moment to consider a recent care conversation you have had with a patient or their family.
- How did you tailor your approach to them in order to be respectful of that individual and their circumstances?
- On reflection did you make any conscious or subconscious assessments that informed your approach on that occasion?
- Now consider how these 'soft skills' may be utilised by leaders to enable them to influence care and services.
- Can you identify leaders around you that use these skills to enable them in their roles?

Should nurses simply accept the criticism that they are 'too posh to wash' or 'too clever to care', a phenomenon experienced by many nurses as we moved to become an all-graduate profession and pre-registration nursing education shifted from being hospital-based to a full university delivery system in the UK and many other countries around the world? It seems extraordinary that some may still hold the belief that nurses are too well-educated – a criticism we would never hear levelled at our medical or allied health professional colleagues. If we are to address the negative perceptions of the nursing profession then the ability to actively seek out and build the evidence for best care, to solve problems with knowledge and to work as an equal from board to point of care are all prerequisites. This requires a focus on the development of collective leadership capability, not just the development of individuals and the embedding of that leadership development within the organisational context (Kings Fund, 2014).

The ability to exert influence is an essential and powerful leadership tool for nurses (Starbucker, 2010), but one that first requires the commitment of time towards building relationships both within and between teams, committing the necessary time to listen, interact and be open.

The concept of collective leadership – as opposed to traditional command-and-control structures – provides an excellent basis on which to build a caring culture (Central Office of Information). Collective leadership requires the courage to distribute and allocate leadership power to wherever the expertise, capability and motivation sit within our organisations. All nurses need to be empowered with the confidence to challenge when appropriate and to exercise their Duty of Candour whenever they believe the standard of care is compromised.

Collective leadership to support patient care

Chapter 2 of this book asks us to consider if you need to be caring in order to be a good nurse. Although all compassionate leaders are by definition caring, it is nonetheless necessary for leaders to enable the courage within the profession to distribute authority to wherever the expertise, capability and motivation sit – this is the essence of collective leadership (Kings Fund, 2014). Collective leadership builds a social network in which individuals are empowered to act and be creative, which is not the case within our more traditional hierarchical management structures. Collective leadership also establishes the key pillars of trust and belief that were explored in Chapter 2 that, to be impactful at the level of direct care, need to be role modelled by nursing leaders.

Individually, nurses must be open and honest – known as the Duty of Candour. When things go wrong in care, nurses need to step forward and, as leaders, ensure that incidents and near misses are reported and lessons learned (NMC, 2015). To fully enact our statutory Duty of Candour requires compassionate leadership to create the culture that enables colleagues to feel empowered and able to be open when things do go wrong and to challenge where they are concerned about the quality of care or services.

To ensure sustainable services we need to attract, retain and re-attract nurses into the profession, and use our collective energies to rebuild and revise the image of nursing. You will recall the public image and perception of nurses being explored in Chapter 1 – if we are to truly lead as a profession and exert our influence across health and care it is important to effect the required transition in the eyes of the public from administering angel to a professional nurse. Jones *et al.* (2015) drew our attention to the four generations currently working within healthcare and highlighted the generational typologies with leaders urged to 'Mind the (generational) Gap' – to better understand their needs and motivations. As leaders this reminds us that we must focus upon building and supporting our nursing and care teams, establishing a sense of 'family at work', developing a supportive environment, and establishing a culture of compassion.

As we develop new roles and ways of working, with activities previously being undertaken by registered nurses being taken on by those in support roles, leaders need to maximise the opportunity to further develop the role of our graduate workforce; raising the bar for those nurses. Figure 6.1 shows us how nurses may advance their careers, enabling them to take their rightful place as serious contenders in influencing and leading health service planning and delivery. By supporting nurses to work at the top of their scope of practice we will build for them more meaningful roles and attractive career pathways which will in turn improve outcomes and experiences for patients.

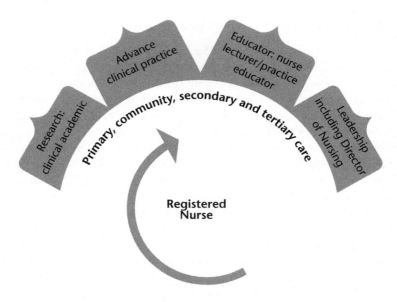

Progression into advance nursing careers

FIGURE 6.1 Key enablers to becoming serious contenders (HEE response to *Raising the Bar: Shape of Caring*, 2016)

6.5 Reflect

- First, think about the roles and interventions that today we describe as working at an advanced level of practice.
- Consider how, in your areas of nursing, these roles may have changed or developed over the last five to ten years.
- Now try looking to the future – do you think that today's advanced practice will become 'business as usual' for nurses in the future?

Leadership is a key skill for nurses, wherever they work and at all levels of the career trajectory, and is not something just restricted to those with more traditional direct managerial responsibility. To truly advocate for patients and their families, all healthcare professionals need the tools and the confidence to be able to lead, whether that be a group of patients, students or other colleagues within the context of a multidisciplinary team.

Leadership and enterprise often combine to create conditions within which innovation can thrive: an example of this is the development and expansion of nurse-led clinics and care pathways. Many registered nurses already own and run care homes supporting elderly people, while a growing minority are setting up innovative organisations such as social enterprises, and tendering for services in community health. We have also witnessed examples of enterprise in general practice, with an increasing number of practice nurses becoming practice partners and leading their own nurse-led general practices.

Our future registered nurses must be confident and effective as leaders, agents of change and champions of care, with a powerful voice at all levels of the healthcare system. To support this, senior management staff must be accountable for championing care and quality throughout their organisations, from point of care to the executive management board.

Nurses as compassionate leaders: Can you be compassionate and credible?

The increasing level of vulnerability associated with complex needs and an ageing population requires a particular focus on compassionate care. Chapter 2 challenges you to think about just what we mean by care and asks if this is simply shorthand to describe the whole range of nursing interventions. With the increase of graduates entering the workforce and more registered nurses undertaking roles that include more advanced practice and clinical decision-making skills, expectations of the role are changing. Nurses must be educated to deliver excellent standards of evidence-based clinical care themselves; they must be developed to think critically in order to make decisions while also delegating many fundamental aspects of care to others who are sufficiently trained and who operate under their supervision.

There are, however, strong feelings, both within and without the nursing profession, as regards the current and future role of registered nurses, and the range of skills that they will need. In the future, registered nurses will continue to be considered as expert clinicians, change agents, entrepreneurs, champions and leaders of multi-professional teams. Any debate on the future role of the nursing profession must focus upon the best interests of patients and the public, ensuring in England for example that registered nurses and care assistants are adhering to the '6Cs' – the values and behaviours outlined by the English Chief Nursing Officer's *Compassion in Practice* report (care, compassion, commitment, courage, competence and communication) (NHS England, 2012) and in Health Education England's values-based recruitment framework (Health Education England, 2014).

Effective leadership is nonetheless key to building the culture of care within organisations and systems. Consciously or unconsciously, nursing leaders set the tone through what they say and do. The challenge for us is in better understanding how best to develop and sustain a culture that supports those that work within an organisation to deliver high-quality care and that enables them always to put the service users, families and carers first. This requires our colleagues to be nurtured and supported in the work environment in order that they might give of their best – this culture of care and compassion must recognise the emotional labour of nursing (Sawbridge, 2013).

Registered nurses need to feel valued throughout their career and should understand that, like other professions such as medicine, there is commitment to them as essential and valuable members of the team. As registered nurses assume responsibility for multi-agency assessment and care roles, as well as the responsibilities for leading and managing inter-professional teams, it is important that their education and training is inter-professional wherever possible. Each team will need to determine the methods and models that best reflect the particular needs of their client group and their carers. The leadership and care coordination role should be assigned to the most appropriate person to lead and deliver optimal care for each patient, as well as to recognise educational training and its application in context.

The past is to learn from and not to live in ...

Leading a person-centred culture of learning and improvement in which nurses are supported to innovate and challenge will 'raise the bar' (Willis, 2015) and enable that ambition to become reality. This will require us as nurses to lead a paradigm shift in the professional workforce and challenge the very premise of nursing, changing conversations with patients and families from asking 'What's the matter?' to a focus on 'What matters to you?'

Nurse leaders can and do play a leading role in enabling high-quality services (Ó Lúanaigh and Hughes, 2016) and possess the skills and knowledge that can enable the development of both the artistry and science within the profession and in turn produce positive outcomes for patients, their families and organisations. However, with that comes significant responsibility. The context for health and care workforce transformation is challenging and never has the quality of the education and learning for the nursing workforce been more important than it is today. We have an army of talented individuals out there, and it is clear that they need to be nurtured and developed by strong, empowering and empowered nurse leadership if we are to truly influence and deliver health services that are really fit for the future. Considering the generational differences amongst practitioners will enable us to play to the strengths and capitalise on the key characteristics that will enable those nurses to play a major role in the future (Jones et al., 2015).

Summary

In this chapter we have begun to explore the concept of nursing leadership and influence. We recognise that high-profile nurses such as Florence Nightingale and Mary Seacole are still held up as role models for the profession today. Yet whilst nurses may form the largest number of professionals with our health and care workforce we do not yet have the strength of voice that such numbers would suggest. Identifying and nurturing leadership skills is critical from the point of entry to the profession and throughout the career pathway if we are truly to achieve the often articulated ambition of nurses leading across services and at every level. We can evidence that motivated and empowered nurses have a positive impact on the outcomes for patients and families in their care and therefore we must be alert to the continuing challenge to nursing leadership and influence and clearly articulate the value of our contribution to care quality and service transformation.

References

All Party Parliamentary Group on Global Health (2016) *Triple Impact: How Developing Nursing Will Improve Health, Promote Gender Equality and Support Economic Growth.* London: APPG.

Berwick, D. (2013) *A Promise to Learn – A Commitment to Act: Improving the Safety of Patients in England.* London: Department of Health.

Bylone, M. (2010) 'Appropriate staffing: more than just numbers'. *AACN Advanced Critical Care,* 21(1), 21–23.

Care Quality Commission (2014) *The State of Health Care and Adult Social Care in England 2013/14.* London: HMSO.

Central Office of Information (2010) *Front Line Care: The Future of Nursing and Midwifery in England. Report of the Prime Minister's Commission on the Future of Nursing and Midwifery in England 2010.* Available at: http://webarchive.nationalarchives.gov.uk/20100331110400/http://cnm.independent.gov.uk/wp-content/uploads/2010/03/front_line_care.pdf/.

Centre for Healthcare Improvement, Queensland Health (2012) *Model Governance Framework for Quality and Safety in Local Hospitals and Hospital Networks.* Available at hhtp://qheps.healthqld.gov.au/schsd/docs/dist./,lhhn-mgf.pd/.

Forbes (2012) *Top 10 Qualities that Make a Great Leader.* Available at www.forbes.com/.

Francis, R. (2013) *Report of the Mid Staffordshire NHS Foundation Trust Public Inquiry.* London: The Stationery Office.

Health Education England (2014) *National Values-Based Recruitment Framework.* Available at: http://hee.nhs.uk/workprogrammes/values-based-recruitment/national-vbr-framework/

Health Education England (2016) *Raising the Bar: Shape of Caring. Health Education England's Response.* London: HMSO.

Hersey, P. (1985) *The Situational Leader.* New York: Warner Books.

Jones, A., Lankshear, A. and Kelly, D. (2016) *Giving Voice to Quality and Safety Matters at Board Level: A Qualitative Study of the Experiences of Executive Nurses Working in England and Wales.* Available at hht://dx.doi.org/10.1016/j.ijnurstu.2016.04.007/.

Jones, K., Warren, A., Davies, A. (2015) *Mind the Gap: Exploring the Needs of Early Career Nurses and Midwives in the Workplace.* Health Education West Midlands.

Keogh, B. (2013) *Review into the Quality of Care and Treatment Provided by 14 Hospital Trusts in England: Overview Report.* London: NHS England.

Kings Fund (2014) *Developing Collective Leadership for Healthcare.* London: Kings Fund.

Maben, J., Peccei, R., Adams, M., Robert, G., Richardson, A., Murrells, T. and Morrow, E. (2012a) *Exploring the Relationship between Patients' Experiences of Care and the Influence of Staff Motivation, Affect and Wellbeing.* London: National Institute for Health Research Service Delivery and Organisation Programme. Available at: www.netscc.ac.uk/hsdr/files/project/SDO_FR_08-1819-213_V01.pdf/.

Maben, J., Adams, M., Peccei, R., Murrells, T., Robert, G. (2012b) '"Poppets and parcels": the links between staff experience of work and acutely ill older peoples' experience of hospital care'. *International Journal of Older People Nursing,* vol. 7, no. 2, pp. 83–94.

Mannion, R., Davies, H., Konteh, F., Jung, T., Scott, T., Bower, P., Whalley, D., McNally, R. and McMurray, R. (2008) *Measuring and Assessing Organisational Culture in the NHS (OC1).* London: National Co-ordinating Centre for the National Institute for Health Research Service Delivery and Organisation Programme (NCCSDO).

Mannion, R., Davies, H., Marshall, M. (2005) 'Cultural characteristics of "high" and "low" performing hospitals'. *Journal of Health Organisation and Management,* vol. 19, no. 6, pp. 431–439.

Massie, S. (2016) *Compassionate Leadership in Health and Social Care*. London: The Kings Fund.

NHS Constitution for England (2015) Available at: www.gov.uk/government/uploads/system/uploads/attachment_data/file/480482/NHS_Constitution_WEB.pdf/.

NHS Commissioning Board (2012) *Compassion in Practice: Nursing, Midwifery and Care Staff, Our Vision and Strategy*. London: NHS.

NHS England (2014) *Five Year Forward View*. London: NHS.

Nursing and Midwifery Council and General Medical Council (NMC) (2015) *Guidance on the Professional Duty of candour*. Available at www.gmc-uk.org/DoC_guidance_englsih.pdf_61618688.pdf/.

Ó Lúanaigh, P. and Hughes, F. (2016) 'The nurse executive role in quality and high performing health services'. *Journal of Nursing Management*, vol. 24, no. 2, pp. 132–136.

Root, G.N. (2016) *Ten Ways to Build Credibility as a Leader*. Available at http://smallbusiness.chron.com/ten-ways-build-credibility-leader-20954.html/.

Sawbridge, Y. and Hewison, A. (2013) *Thinking about the Emotional Labour of Nursing – Supporting Nurses to Care*. University of Birmingham.

Schippers, M.C., West, M.A. and Dawson, J.F. (2013) 'Team reflexivity and innovation: the moderating role of team context'. *Journal of Management*, vol. 41, no. 3, pp. 769–788.

Starbucker, T. (2010) *Building Influence in the Workplace: It Has to be Personal*. Internet blog deniseleeyohn.com/bites/tag/terry-starbucker/.

Trofino, J. (1993) 'Transformational Leadership in an age of chaos'. *Nursing Administration Quarterly*, vol. 17, no. 1, pp. 17–24.

West, M., Eckert, R., Steward, K. and Pasmore, B. (2014) *Developing Collective Leadership for Health Care*. London: Kings Fund.

Willis, G.P. (2015) *Raising the Bar. Shape of Caring: A Review of the Future Education and Training of Registered Nurses and Care Assistants*. London: Health Education England. Available at www.kingsfund.org.uk/sites/files/kf/field/field_publication_file/Workforce-planning-NHS-Kings-Fund-Apr-15.pdf/.

7

CREATING YOUR PROFESSIONAL IDENTITY

Becoming the nurse you want to be

Mike Cook

Why this chapter is important

Given the many challenges that most nurses experience, most of which have been explored in this book, do you feel equipped to respond to the complex, ethically demanding and personally challenging situations that you have already encountered or will continue to encounter? Perhaps you have natural abilities that mean others seek you out as a sounding board? Perhaps you feel equipped to answer most questions based on your experience? Either way, this chapter is intended to stimulate deeper thinking about supporting yourself and others to become the nurse you or they want to be.

Chapter trigger question: Can nurses really practise effectively without ongoing investment and effort to support one another through coaching and mentorship?

Key words: Coaching, mentorship, action learning

Introduction

In Chapter 3 the case was made for lifelong learning from the start of a student's career. As such a great deal of learning can occur in the workplace while doing the job, tapping into the learning opportunities that occur in practice is critical to your development. This chapter provides three effective ways to enable you to improve the care that you and others deliver. These are Coaching, Mentoring and Action Learning.

Reflect 7.1

* Imagine you have been pondering a particular dilemma such as speaking to a colleague about an aspect of their behaviour that concerns you.
* Having considered many possibilities, you decide to share your thoughts with a friend or colleague.

  (*At this point you are really looking for an opportunity to share your thoughts with someone you respect. You are not necessarily looking for answers.*)
* How do you think you would respond to being asked such a question?
* How do you think your friends and colleagues would respond?

Of course several things can happen at this point. Having disclosed your thoughts, your friend or colleague may immediately launch into providing solutions and answers usually based on their experiences and insights. They don't take time to learn how the dilemma impacts on you or what you would like to achieve. They don't explore any other options or find out a little more about the reality of the situation from your perspective, nor do they find a way of finding out what support you may need to commit to some form of action.

Or they may explore the dilemma with you and take time to explore the issue a little further. Depending on your approach to life or needs at the time one may seem better than the other. Providing solutions is a common approach. Of course why would you have asked for their view in the first place if not for their solutions? The more exploratory approach places you in control of the outcome and reflects principles of coaching.

Reflect 7.2

* Imagine needing to learn new skills or knowledge as a qualified nurse with no access to lecturing staff or a structured learning programme. How might you go about achieving this?
* You may have thought about needing access to new environments, opportunities to talk with more experienced colleagues. How will you achieve these?
* Think about leading a change in your care setting. How will you gain the support of others to achieve the change?

Gaining access to new learning or leading a change may be helped by a mentor. Mentoring amongst nursing has a specific meaning, usually associated with making judgements on learners. However, in other professional environments the word *mentor* means something quite different. This chapter will introduce you to a different way of thinking about mentors, especially if your experience has so far been based on others making judgements about your progression and performance.

Reflect 7.3

- Consider dealing with a really difficult situation, one that you have tried to resolve but keep coming across difficulties. What might you do in this situation?
- This can be a difficult situation to be in and can be emotionally tiring to deal with as an individual.

In Reflect 7.3, you may have considered a range of options: possibly one that you may not have thought about is 'action learning'. This approach is being used with more frequency amongst more experienced nurses and other healthcare professionals. Action learning entails working with a group of colleagues to explore and generate new insights to issues using probing questions in a mutually supportive environment. Action learning is introduced in this chapter as another developmental approach that you may wish to consider.

Of course not all issues are suitable for coaching, mentoring or action learning. In some situations, clinical supervision will be appropriate or counselling may be a more suitable option. Neither of these is explored in this chapter but more about clinical supervision can be found by reading Freeman's article (2005), and most universities and healthcare environments offer counselling, usually through an occupational health department. It is, however, important not to confuse coaching, mentoring or action learning with counselling. The British Association for Counselling and Psychotherapy describe counselling as an 'umbrella term that cover a range of talking therapies … delivered by trained practitioners who work with people over a short or long term to help them bring about effective change or enhance their wellbeing' (BACP, 2013). One of the key aspects of this definition is 'enhancing wellbeing'; this is very much about personal mental health as opposed to workplace performance.

This chapter provides an overview of coaching, mentoring and action learning sets as ways of engaging with the nursing world and learning in a slightly different way. The ideas presented in this chapter are not new. Many books, articles, YouTube clips and podcasts have been presented based on coaching, mentoring and action learning. Some of these resources are provided in the references and may prove useful – others you will discover for yourself – so please share with others you work with the resources you find helpful. Of course these approaches are also suitable to all other areas of life; becoming an effective facilitator or coach to support others can be used in all areas of your life.

Defining and understanding coaching, mentoring and action learning

Clarifying the difference between coaching, mentoring, action learning and counselling is helpful in deciding when to use each of the approaches. The following definitions are helpful in describing the differences between coaching, mentoring and counselling.

Coaching

Coaching facilitates learning, mentoring gives advice, action learning is a group that meet regularly to support one another in their learning in order to take purposeful action on work issues whilst counselling has a therapeutic goal (CIPD, 2004).

A useful definition that I believe encapsulates coaching is from Jenny Rogers (2012, p. 7).

> Coaching is a partnership of equals whose aim is to achieve speedy, increased and sustainable effectiveness through focused learning in every aspects of the client's life. Coaching raises self-awareness and identifies choices. Working to the client's agenda, the coach and client have the sole aim of closing the gaps between potential and performance.

Quite a long definition, but it contains some important points about coaching. Each reader will select their own important points; here are mine:

- Coaching is a partnership of equals.
- Coaching identifies choices.
- Drawing on the work of one of the most influential writers on coaching, James Galway (1974), Rogers refers to potential and performance.

I find the following equation important when I am coaching or teaching coaching.

Potential minus **Interference** is equal to **Performance**

In essence, as interference reduces then more of the potential is available and so performance can increase.

Reflect 7.4

- Write down some of the things you can identify that may have interfered with your performance (at anything) in the past.
- Looking at your list do any of the following appear?
  - Trying to impress
  - Aiming for perfection
  - Fear of failure
  - Fear of hurting someone
  - Trying too hard
  - Anger or frustration
  - Boredom.

It would be natural for your list to contain some of these factors along with others not mentioned above.

The role of the coach is to help the person being coached to identify what the interference is and to explore options to reduce this interference. Coaching is non-judgemental: the aim is to help identify the interference, not to judge the interference.

This chapter provides an outline of some coaching principles and is intended to develop your interest in coaching as a way of working with others and introduce some of the key skills. Many coaching conversations are short, happen spontaneously and can be very helpful. So the principles outlined here can be used for short spontaneous conversation, such as when a colleague or friend makes a seemingly simple comment such as *I am fed up* (five minutes) or longer, more structured and planned conversations arising from comments such as *I really need a career change* (three one-hour-long sessions).

Mentorship

According to Clutterbuck and Ragins (2002) mentoring is 'support, assistance, advocacy or guidance given by one person to another in order to achieve an objective or several objectives over a period of time'. It is also viewed as an integrated approach to advising, coaching and nurturing, focused on creating a viable relationship to enhance individual career, personal, professional growth and development (Adams, 1998).

These definitions illustrate the apparent confusion that exists in distinguishing differences between the concepts of mentoring and coaching. Some writers appear to use the terms interchangeably, whereas others embrace coaching as a category of mentoring. Fleden *et al.* (2009) helpfully suggest that coaching is defined as directly concerned with the immediate improvement of performance and skills by a form of tutoring or instruction. Mentoring is one step removed and is concerned with the longer-term acquisition of skills in a developing career. Mentoring is not about telling, giving solutions, criticising mistakes, giving advice or jumping in to handle solutions without being asked; a mentor is the person who guides another to success.

Action learning

Action learning is a group activity that is underpinned by some coaching principles. It is a group of between four and seven people who meet regularly to support one another in their learning in order to take purposeful action on work issues.

An introduction to coaching

This section introduces the benefits and some key principles of coaching. The skills outlined can be used in mentoring and action learning. Coaching, when performed well, is probably one of the most effective development tools that can enable effective change for individuals. Coaching has an intensity that other forms of learning don't reach (ILM, 2010). In healthcare, West (2013) has undertaken significant work to redirect attention to the 'people' aspects of leadership and as a result executive coaching activity is increasing in healthcare. Gallwey (2000) describes coaching as 'unlocking people's potential to maximize their performance'. This emphasises coaching as a technique that helps people learn rather than teaching them. Research evidence indicates that learning through coaching is far more effective than that of learning gained from telling or showing Beaumont, (2002). Coaching has been defined as the provision of support and guidance for people to use their existing knowledge and skills more effectively (Bentley, 1995) and is concerned with the immediate improvement of performance and development of skills (Goldsmith *et al.*, 2000; Whitmore, 2003). Performance coaching is an acknowledged approach to the development of human capital resources. Buck (2003) provides research evidence to suggest that a coaching training programme for managers can be successful in changing behaviour and improving employee perceptions about how they are managed.

Kopelman (1997) suggests that coaching may be used to overcome the problems associated with the transfer of the learning process. That is, coaches can provide problem-focused training and encouragement for people being coached (coachee) to be proactive. It is a goal-focused process that requires action so the coachee can move forward (Hanson, 2003). A coachee can be helped to focus on personal skills (e.g. goal setting, planning and initiation), interpersonal skills (e.g. communication, conflict resolution and team development), and system changes necessary for leadership development. Essentially, it is about providing a structure and time for reflection to help the individual gain awareness, with the aim of continuous improvement (Law, 2008). The purposes of coaching may be diverse, but can include transitions from one role or state to another, shifts in role or career, dealing with organisational changes, resolution of issues and problems, and skills development. Faced with a complex leadership situation, members of a team I worked with implemented a team leadership coaching programme. This was delivered jointly with trust staff experienced in leadership coaching, myself as an experienced coach and an independent training organisation (The Performance Coach) that have undertaken significant coaching development work in healthcare settings. The key premise of the programme was that unlocking the potential of team leaders and their team members could generate positive change. Twenty-six staff attended a series of coaching development sessions. The results were then evaluated and in all cases improved performance and transformations in care delivery occurred across the patch. The following quotation encapsulates the experiences of many from the course.

> This course is not 'just another' leadership course. The coaching skills gained on the programme are not only empowering but also enable you to develop the personal skills needed to manage the challenges of the ever changing pressures leading services in the NHS. The coaching techniques have been

used to improve integrated working, empower and motivate staff and improve performance. The service is evolving from efficient to effective with the patient experience at the heart of what we do.

(Course participant, 2013)

Improving the coaching skills of an increased number of staff can support benefits for both staff and patients. Staff with coaching skills have the ability to enhance their leadership effectiveness. Coaching development can help staff to progress from 'Essential' to 'Exemplary' across the nine dimensions of the NHS Leadership Academy, *Healthcare Leadership Model* (NHS, 2013). Given the significance of 'integrated working' coaching also supports the local government *Living Leadership* aspirations for leadership (2014). Care organisations are clearly identifying characteristics that the twenty-first century leaders require. This involves a change in mindset, attitude and behaviour, and coaching is a powerful tool to bring about these changes.

Health coaching for behaviour change

Coaching techniques are also being used by healthcare practitioners with people requiring care and support. Health practitioners that are skilled in coaching techniques are discovering improved health outcomes for patients that want to and can engage with coaching techniques.

Reflect 7.5

- From your experience of nursing so far which of the following approaches may begin a constructive dialogue to helping a patient from stopping smoking?
  - *Approach one*: Health care professional says to the patient – "You must stop smoking" or ...
  - *Approach two*: "What is in the way of you stopping smoking?"

Reflect 7.6

- What do you think would be the impact of asking similar questions or making statements in different ways?

Table 7.1, extracted from an evaluation report conducted by Health Education England in the East of England in 2014, captures the key benefits of health coaching. A compelling case for more development in health coaching has been generated. The following extract from one allied health professional (AHP) that attended a coaching training session clearly supports this investment.

As AHPs in the community dealing with long term conditions, health coaching was presented as a credible way to be more effective with service

TABLE 7.1 Reported patient and financial benefits of health coaching

Patient benefits	*Financial benefits*
More effective consultations tailored to the patients' needs, expectations and readiness to change	Reducing inappropriate patient activities
Improved health by supporting patients to make healthier choices	Reducing patient demand, e.g. from stopping smoking and weight reduction
Changes to patient expectations, motivation and confidence to self-manage	Reducing patient attendance by supporting self-care
Setting more effective and realistic goals based on patient priorities	Reduces patient follow up rates
Improved compliance with prescribed medication routines	Reduction in pharmacy costs (e.g. dispensing the medications) and medication wastage (e.g. patients that have the medications at home, but never use them)
Creating shared responsibility between patients and healthcare providers	Reduce demand from patients as they understand what they need to do to improve their health
Improved health outcomes for patients	Reduced patient need as patients' health improves

Adapted from HEE EoE (2014) *Health Coaching for Behaviour Change.*

users and to be more efficient – particularly in terms of being able to see more new patients by reducing the need for follow ups and promoting self–care so that our interventions coincide with when we are needed rather than when we had scheduled a review. It also seemed to fit well with other training that has been undertaken recently – including behaviour change, clinical reasoning and leadership skills – without forgetting clinical skills.

In a study comparing managers' successes on project work, following either coach training or conventional management development approaches such as classroom teaching, there was a 22.4 per cent increase in productivity after management training but 88 per cent increase after coach training (Olivero *et al.*, 1997).

Reflect 7.7

• What are your views on the following statement?

> I am convinced that developing more staff with coaching skills will generate a significant change for both patients and staff.

- What impact does this statement have on your desire to learn more about coaching? If it encourages you to learn more – then why is this?
- If it dissuades you and in fact puts you off from wanting to learn more – then why is this?
- As you have considered your own views to the statement – what are you learning about yourself?
- How do you think your colleagues would react?

What does coaching look like?

In my experience coaching is as much about the mindset of the coach as it is about the skills required. Personally, at the start of each coaching session, that I undertake as the coach, I remind myself that whilst I may sometimes have some insight into the issue being discussed it is not my experience. I therefore need to listen effectively to tune into the perspective of the person that has sought coaching.

It is not possible in this short chapter to outline all of the techniques or approaches to coaching. I will therefore provide an outline of some of the models and skills that I find effective. They can be used in a variety of ways and provide a framework for an effective coaching conversation. I hope this stimulates you to try some of the techniques and explore coaching in more depth.

Coaching is based on a trusting relationship between coach and coachee (the person being coached). As Figure 7.1 shows, building rapport helps to build trust and the more rapport and trust that can be fostered then the more effective the coaching. Referring to Figure 7.1 you will note the reference to data and facts under the transactional area of the model. This recognises that a transactional conversation may discuss, for instance, the number of staff in the area and the types of work undertaken. This part of the conversation can be important to establish trust and rapport at the start of the relationship. Developing an effective transactional relationship can then help you develop a deeper conversation, one that enables the coachee to explore issues of a more sensitive nature leading to new insights. This is a 'transformational' conversation. Context is also important as this helps to sensitise both the coach and the coachee to the culture in which they are operating and the organisational norms that may be present. Understanding the context can help the coach ask meaningful questions that enable the coachee to develop new insights.

Building on this model, high rapport can enable an effective coach to challenge the person they are coaching. Challenge is an important skill for coaching and requires sensitivity to get the level of challenge right. Challenge is about asking the right questions at the right time. More will be said about questions later in this chapter. Figure 7.2 indicates that rapport enables the coach to challenge the coachee to increase the amount of challenge. However, a word of caution on two fronts.

High rapport without any real challenge can lead to a comfortable conversation that may feel pleasant, but it is unlikely to lead to increased awareness, new insights or generate effective actions. Increasing the challenge when one has not generated

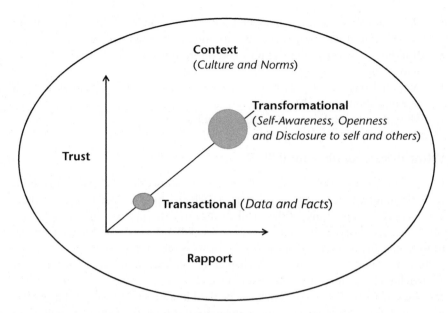

FIGURE 7.1 The impact of rapport and trust within the coaching relationship

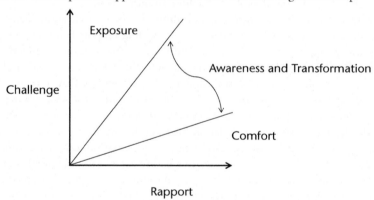

FIGURE 7.2 Generating an environment that enables appropriate challenge

an effective rapport can lead to 'exposure'. This is where the coachee begins to explore issues that may generate strong emotional responses and the coachee may not be ready to deal with some of the more intense issues that they are facing. So as can be seen coaching does have its pitfalls. A good coach will be aware of some of these pitfalls and as with most human interaction it is not always possible to know what is going to happen.

Skill one is about generating a relationship in which a coaching conversation can occur. Look at Figures 7.1 and 7.2 again. What skills do you have already that can be used to build the right relationship? What do you need to improve and how will you do this?

Before looking at some effective questions, please consider how a coach can at least check their intent. It is useful to use six questions to self-check how useful a question or challenge may be.

- Is it **T**imely?
- Will it leave **R**esponsibility?
- Will the question raise **A**wareness?
- Will it leave **C**hoice?
- Is the **R**elationship strong enough to withstand the intervention?
- Is there sufficient trust in my intention?

During a formal coaching session whilst listening intently and formulating questions it is useful to have the above questions in your mind. I use the mnemonic **TRACR** as a reminder to the above list. Skill two is to ensure that your intentions are sound during a coaching conversation. For instance, with the stopping smoking question it may not be timely to ask this question as a person is about to go to the operating theatre, whilst is may actually meet the other four criteria.

Many books use the headings **TGROW** to help shape a coaching conversation.

T – Topic – What do you want to talk about?
G – Goal – What do you want from this conversation?
R – Reality – What is happening now?
O – Options – What could you do?
W – Will – What will you do?

Each of these headings helps to provide some shape. Importantly, note that each of the headings refers to the actions of the person being coached. In more detail:

- Topic – by exploring the topic the coach is enabling the person to understand the context, the parameters of the conversation, relevance of the issues, build rapport and to help provide new insights as to what will be talked about.
- Goal – the purpose of goal is to help the coachee provide a statement that captures what they would like as an outcome for the conversation.
- Reality – this heading is about raising awareness, perspective and responsibility by exploring, challenging and confirming the current situation.
- Options – this is the time to explore options that create multiple possibilities to achieve the goal and to recognise where new and additional choices can be made.
- Will – is an expression of commitment to action arising from the coaching conversation. The coachee is able to confirm and commit to what they can take forward in terms of a plan of action that best achieves their goal within their individual context.

It is important that the TGROW model is not a sequence to be followed, but are points in a coaching conversation. When you are initially trying out this model, you may find that you use the model in quite a linear way. It can be effective, but can feel a little forced for the person being coached.

The next area to explore is effective coaching questions. Several authors (Downey, 2003; Rogers, 2012; Whitmore, 2009) point out the importance of effective questions as a key to being a good coach.

The most effective questions in coaching have a number of common features:

- They raise awareness by provoking thinking and challenge.
- They demand truthful answers by helping to stop rambling or waffling.
- They are short.
- They go beyond asking for information by asking for discovery.
- They encourage the person to take responsibility for themselves.
- They stick closely to the person's agenda.
- They lead to learning for the person.
- They are more likely to begin with the words 'what' or 'how'.

My own coaching training provided by 'The Performance Coach' company provided some very useful questions that I tend to use time and time again. These are generally:

- Content free
- Short
- They do not include the word 'I'.

They have a natural progression moving from the problem, to goal, naming options and then committing to action. Rogers (2012) has generated a list that can be used in many situations. They help avoid giving advice by not using words like Have, Would, Could, Was. Leading by the coach, for instance, 'So would you agree that … '.

Creating a defensive atmosphere by avoiding the use of the word 'why'? The word *why* may seems like a very useful question and when I am supporting people to undertake research projects it is a common question that I use. I use it as a way of enabling the person to defend their decisions about method or sample size for instance. Please note that whilst supervising research I am asking the person to 'defend' their choice. I have a view on what is right. During a coaching conversation I have no view on what is right or wrong. I have to be as neutral as possible to provide the space for an effective coaching conversation.

Jenny Rogers' (2012) coaching questions are:

- What's the issue?
- What makes it an issue now?
- Who owns this issue or problem?

- How important is it on a scale of one to ten?
- How much energy do you have for a solution on a scale of one to ten?
- Implications: what are the implications of doing nothing (or of letting things carry on as they are)?
- What have you tried already?
- Imagine this issue being solved. What would you hear and feel?
- What's standing in the way of that ideal outcome?
- What is your own responsibility for what has been happening?
- What early signs are there that things are getting better/going all right?
- Imagine that you are at most resourceful. What do you need to say to yourself about this issue?
- What are the options for action here?
- What criteria will you use to judge the options?
- Which option seems the best one against those criteria?
- So what is the next/first step?
- When will you take it?

Naturally these questions need to be adapted to your own individual vocabulary and preferences. Having tried them a few times in a number of coaching conversations I can vouch for their effectiveness. Jenny Rogers (2012) articulates why these questions are so powerful in her book *Coaching skills*. If you want to learn more about the underpinning rationale for the above questions it would be a good book to read.

Reflect 7.8

Consider any opportunities that may have arisen in the last few weeks when a coaching approach may have been useful either for you to be coached or for you to coach someone else.

- What was the situation?
- What happened?
- How could coaching have been useful?
- How will you spot any future coaching opportunities?

Reflect 7.9

- To gain more confidence with coaching, try out Jenny Rogers' coaching question and see how it works for you.
- Explore how the model feels to use, share the idea with a trusted friend and have a go.
- Each has about ten minutes to be either the coach or the coachee.

- Each picks a real but not too challenging topic to talk about, this becomes the topic.
- Then as the coach listens to what is being said and using the above questions move through the topic.
- Of course you may have to improvise at certain points, but do at least try to follow the order of the questions and have fun trying it out with a friend.
- With your friend try to work out why this series of questions works.
- To help, you may wish to look at the questions with the TGROW model.

You may have noted how short the questions are. I am always surprised how little I need to know about the person's context to have an effective coaching session. None of the questions above require an exploration of the context. Instead of thinking about these questions in the context of a friend or colleague, read them again in the context of a patient that has just said they want to stop smoking. It may not necessarily be a long conversation and may have positive results. Note that the questions are short, places the responsibility for action with the person being coached and asks them to make a commitment. The other point that I have come to value is asking the person to say what they would hear and feel if the issue was solved. This question can help to reveal the goal and moves them from focusing on the symptoms of the problem to fixing the problem. It is important to ask the right questions, but so long as your intent is to help the person you are working with to find their own solutions then you can be confident that you are on the right path.

Mentoring

As mentioned in the introduction, I am using the word *mentor* in a different way to that it is frequently used in nursing programmes. In this context I am using the word mentor as defined by Bozeman and Feeney (2007). Mentoring is:

> a process for the informal transmission of knowledge, social capital, and the psychosocial support perceived by the recipient as relevant to work, career, or professional development; mentoring entails informal communication, usually face-to-face and during a sustained period of time, between a person who is perceived to have greater relevant knowledge, wisdom, or experience (the mentor) and a person who is perceived to have less (the protégé or mentee).

Having a mentor can be regarded as a valuable development opportunity and can play a crucial role in early career and business success. Mentors can be very useful when you are keen to learn more about the world that you are working in. To learn more you may need access to new environments, opportunities to talk with more experienced colleagues or you may want an opportunity to lead a change in your care setting. Gaining access to these opportunities may be helped by a mentor. So this is quite different to a mentor that is usually associated with making judgements on learners.

Reflect 7.10

- Think about your nursing career in about three to five years' time.
- What do you want to have achieved – either in terms of promotion or developing your clinical skills?
- Who do you know working in these areas currently?
- Do you know how they got there?
- What key questions would you want to ask them if you could?
- Can you think of anyone that would be really helpful to help you develop?

If you have thought about these questions, then you may have decided that you need someone to help you in your quest. So how do you find a mentor?

From my experience the best mentors are ones that you choose yourself. Some organisations now allocate mentors to new members of an organisation. In my experience they are selected quite randomly based on the capacity to take on a new person or they work in the same unit. Seldom do they have any training for the mentor role and seldom are they asked about the mentee they are to be allocated. This does not seem a good starting point for an effective mentoring relationship. This is not to say that I am advocating not having an allocated mentor, but just to be aware of the background to the selection of your mentor and work hard to get the most out of the opportunity. However, a person that you approach to be a mentor based on their position in the organisation, their interests that align to your own or their positive personality may be a good starting point. When you are talking with people that you professionally admire try asking them who influenced them most. Most will be able to tell you of someone that they worked with or met that was important to them. They may not use the word mentor, but they may talk about them providing an opportunity to meet someone or explore a new area of work. The maxim 'it's not what you know but who you know' is relevant and in many places important. So how do you find a mentor? A simple answer is to just keep your eyes and ears open and be ready to take an opportunity that may present itself. Once you meet someone that you think may be a good mentor then ask them some relevant questions. Maybe even offer to help with a project that they are working on. Don't be offended if they reject your offer or do not want to engage with you. There may be a wide variety of reasons. But you may be nicely surprised as well. Sometimes it is useful to seek new environments and opportunities to meet a wider circle of people. In many professional environments this is called networking and in some environments is big business in itself. Networking can be as simple as attending your local healthcare organisation events. Some of the healthcare provider meetings are in public and anyone can attend. Healthcare organisation websites can be a source of great information. Some organisations have research forums, or events aimed at clinical specialisms. Personally I have found attending conferences and professional forums a vital way of meeting people that I sometimes work with in the future or introduce me to an opportunity that I did not know existed.

LinkedIn is a business networking social media platform that can broaden your reach internationally. Networking is simply using opportunities to meet people that may have interests similar to your own. As a more detailed explanation is beyond the scope of this chapter then a most useful resource for a more thorough explanation is the Businessballs website (http://www.businessballs.com/business-networking.htm).

Mentoring is important to yourself. Chao *et al.* (1992) found that mentees in mentoring relationships received more career-related advice and had better career outcomes. As your career progresses it is also important to the wider organisation you work within. DeLong *et al.* (2008) identified that effective mentoring is critical to the long-term future of organisations. As people exercise their rights to relocate to seek greater fulfilment in both work and personal life, mentoring can help organisations retain and recruit the best people. Imagine being responsible for employing specialist nurses and you need two new staff and the expertise may not be available amongst your staff at present. Of course you can advertise and hope for the best. But most effective people know who the experts are and can at least tap into their expertise about their own wider network and knowledge about who may be looking for a new opportunity.

Also do not underestimate how mentoring also provides a two-way learning relationship. For example, mentoring can have a 'boomerang' effect, as ideas are exchanged (Dickinson *et al.*, 2009). In healthcare this is critical. Staff in new roles need to learn the ways of working and the more experienced staff acting as mentors need to learn how new generations of professionals are thinking and learning or trends in clinical care. One good example in this context is the use of social media such as Twitter to share and shape ideas and generate relationships.

Action learning sets

Reg Revans,[1] often referred to as the father of action learning, said 'action learning takes so long to describe because it is so simple'.

I have been using action learning sets with a variety of groups to deepen their understanding of particular issues and generate solutions to problems. This has included postgraduate students to support their research skills, general practitioners dealing with recruitment and retention problems and senior clinicians that are exploring complex research questions.

Reflect 7.11

- Make notes about the circumstances when you learned most effectively.
- Whilst everyone is different many adults, and for some reason in my experience nurses, learn best when they decide what it is they want to learn and when the learning is closely linked to practical issues or problems of immediate concern to them.

- People learn from their peers, from people for whom they have regard or when an appropriate degree of personal risk is present.

I use action learning with several groups and having been a participant in other action learning sets I recognise that some participants find the experience frustrating. This has led me to modify action learning and trying other approaches incorporating elements from coaching.

For example, I lead some clinical research action learning sets and encourage others in the set to share their research experience during the session. This leads to a more rapid learning exchange. It could of course be argued that this is not pure action learning, but is an adapted form of learning. Either way it certainly helps busy clinical practitioners engage with their projects effectively. The key here is to make sure that any experiences from the group are shared towards the end of the session.

Understanding action learning sets (ALS)

ALS are a group of between four and seven people, who meet regularly to support one another in their learning in order to take purposeful action on work issues. A professional set facilitator, who enables the set members to ask searching questions and the problem holder to reflect on the actions to be taken, facilitates the meetings. For more details you may wish to read Weinstein (2002). The power of the set comes from the type of questions used and the gift of time for reflection. If you are more interested in how creating powerful time to think in the work setting can be then I would recommend reading *Time to Think* by Nancy Kline (2002). Time granted and dedicated listening to the other set members can generate new insights for the problem holder. The set members also consider the process: was it effective, what questions worked well and what emotions had to be considered?

So, what does this process look like during an ALS session? Action learning identifies that people may well already have enough knowledge and what they need are new ways of applying what is already known to new situations. The emphasis is on reflecting, deciding to experiment with new action, taking action and, having moved on to a different place, starting the cycle again.

In effect, individual set members present a problem, have their thinking provoked by the questions of fellow set members, are given time to reflect, go away and take appropriate actions and then at the next session tell the set what happened.

Problems are the focus of the set: unlike puzzles, problems have no one right solution – rather, they have many different solutions and the presenter of the problem has a choice as to the course of action to be taken.

Reflect 7.12

- What issues could you take to an action learning set now if you had access to one?
- What would make you feel secure in the set?

Ground rules

Learning happens at a number of different levels and it can be an uncomfortable process. It is therefore vital that the set is a place where members feel safe enough to express themselves and say, 'I don't know'. To make this work, set members agree the ground rules. These vary from group to group. Two that I have found critical are that the set starts and finishes at the agreed times. This is important for busy practitioners that may have clinical commitments. The second is that the meeting content is entirely private. 'What is said in the set, stays in the set'. In clinical learning sets it is important to maintain patient confidentiality, so it is important to ensure that no patient identifier information is used.

The acronym **RECIPE** covers some of the main points:

- **R**esponsibility for oneself.
- **E**xperience-led, i.e. the problems presented are real problems.
- **C**onfidentiality – the only thing taken out of the set is the learning.
- '**I**' language is used.
- **P**rocess is addressed, as well as content. Attention is given to feelings, relationships and feedback.
- **E**quality of opportunity is ensured.
- Why does it work?

Because action learning initiates a dialogue, this gives each person space to focus on themselves and what they are grappling with at work. The constant emphasis is on learning and how it is achieved, building on the asking of questions and listening, followed by reflection, free from time pressure. It does not rely on the giving of advice or the offer of ready-made solutions.

Reflect 7.13

- From your own experience of learning in groups make a list of the key skills that you think are required to be an effective set member?

  I would be surprised if your list did not include some of the following points:
  - *Rapport and relationship skills*: These are needed to enable members to be open and to trust each other.
  - *Listening skills*: Set members need to listen not only to what is said but also the meaning behind what is being said and to ambiguities. They also need to be comfortable with silence in order to fully allow time for reflection.
  - *Questioning skills*: Open questions are usually most useful – i.e. they cannot be answered with 'yes' or 'no'. It is worth reading the questions section that was presented earlier in this chapter in the coaching section and see if any of these can be adapted.

Questions are a critical part of action learning and like coaching adapting the questions to the person being supported is critical. Some of the main types of questions are:

- Pure inquiry – to help the client clarify the situation, the options, the way forward.
- Challenging questions – to help the client achieve insight.
- Catalytic questions – to trigger new ideas.
- Cathartic questions – on those few occasions when it may help to release the emotions associated with the problem.

It benefits set members to use a common model to channel the questions so they have a cumulative impact. An example of a simple questioning framework is as follows and you will note that this is adapted from coaching:

- Goal – What do you want to achieve?
- Reality – Where are you now?
- Options – What could you do and what else could you do?
- What next – What action will you take? By when will you report back?

What is the role of the facilitator?

Most action learning sets have a facilitator that helps the set focus on the process for the group. Sometimes this is a completely independent person or sometimes it is a member of the set that fulfils this role in rotation with others.

The facilitator's role is to introduce set members to action learning and to manage the process during the set. The facilitator enables everyone in the set to participate, ensures that the questions build up coherently to be of most use to the presenter of the problem and checks the usefulness of the process at each step, with the participants. Many sets are self-led and each person in the set takes turns in facilitating.

Reflect 7.13

- What skills do you think an effective facilitator needs?
- You may have identified the same or similar skills as follows:
  - Self-management – staying with the process and not getting sucked into the issue is important. I find my role generally is to remind people to ask open questions.
  - Knowledge of and ability to work with group dynamics.
  - High order listening skills.
  - Familiarity with problem solving models.
  - Ability to time interventions and keep them to a minimum.
  - Emotional Intelligence – e.g. being aware of what is happening and how you and others may be feeling in the room. For more on emotional

intelligence you may wish to read the work of Daniel Goleman (1996, 2000) or refer to the link.[2]

Learning sets – process

The following outline provides a structured process and each session takes about 25 minutes. Each set tends to adopt slightly different approaches to suit their own style. The action learning sets that I facilitate vary from 20 minutes to more intense problems that may take 50 minutes. Some writers are quite strict about timings but I find flexibility helps the dynamics of the set. Just like coaching rapport, trust and challenge are important elements of an effective set.

Each person takes a turn at being the presenter or 'client' with the others acting as 'consultants'. The timings below are only approximates although some facilitators are more rigid than I am. These timings indicate the proportion of time allocated to the client episode.

1.   (Eight minutes) Client sets out the problem.
2.   (Two minutes) Set members ask any clarifying questions.
3.   (Fifteen minutes) Set members ask open, exploratory questions.
4.   (Six minutes) Set members develop an explanation of what's going on, with thoughts and ideas of dealing with the issues or behaving differently (the client listens).
5.   (Four minutes) Client summarises how they are thinking and feeling about the problem and outlines actions to take forward.
6.   (Five minutes) Set members offer feedback on what was observed.

Being flexible as a facilitator is critical to an effective set. I use a range of techniques to engage a set and this will depend on the situation being explored and the mood of the set. One of the useful tools that I have used at times is a series of thought-provoking and stimulating pictures. These can be used in a myriad of ways, but are always used to reveal to a group, things that they already know about, but may not have applied to the problem under scrutiny before. To be effective, action learning sets are best when they are appropriately and sensitively applied to the needs of the set members.

Reflect 7.14

- Find some friends or colleagues to try working as an action learning set.
- It is preferable to work with real-world examples that members of the set have, rather than inventing something.
- Have fun trying this out, share the model openly and experiment with different approaches.

- I have never tried an online action learning set, but I can see that being effective for groups, so long as the 'chat' can be kept private and rules of privacy and confidentiality are agreed.

Summary

Comparing coaching with mentoring a study by Flelden *et al.* (2009) found that both coaching and mentoring have significant benefits in terms of professional and personal development. In summary they suggest that coaching may be most effective at the beginning of a cycle of career progression (e.g. promotion), rather than as means to further career progression. It therefore appears important to use the right tools at the right part of the career cycle.

Common to both mentoring and coaching are the following pitfalls:

- The aspect of 'challenge' may be forfeited at the expense of rapport. Both parties may enjoy their discussions but the lack of challenge means that nothing is really being achieved.
- Time factors can be a barrier. The activity is abandoned in the face of more urgent, if less important, demands on time (Sutherland, 2005).
- If confidentiality is breached or perceived to be breached by either party this generates a loss of trust and hence both rapport and challenge suffer.
- A lack of commitment from either side, a lack of clarity of the purpose or roles and boundaries not being respected can lead to frustrating experiences for all.

Action learning seems to blend elements of coaching and mentoring. All three are designed to enable people to grow and develop and become the people that they want to be. As you progress and develop your professional role and identity I hope you will have the opportunity to try and make use of some or all of the strategies presented in this chapter.

Notes

1 See Reg talking about Action Learning: https://www.youtube.com/watch?v=2bJ9RXkYPSU/.
2 http://www.businessballs.com/eq.htm/.

References

Adams, H.G. (1998) *The Mentorship Briefing Guide: Handbook for Establishing and Implementing a Mentoring Programme.* Notre Dame, IN: GEM Consortium.

BACP (2013) *What is Counselling?* Available at http://www.bacp.co.uk/crs/Training/whatiscounselling.php/.

Beaumont, S. (2002) Coaching for business success. *Selection and Development Review*, 18(2), 7–10.

Bentley, T. (1995) Performance coaching. *Training Officer*, 31(2), 36–38.

Bozeman, B. and Feeney, M.K. (2007) Toward a useful theory of mentoring: A conceptual analysis and critique. *Administrative and Society*, 39(6), 719–739.

Buck, F. (2003) Performance coaching – spin or win? An evaluation of the effectiveness of a coaching training programme in a retail organisation. *Selection and Development Review*, 19, 19–23.

Chao, G.T., Walz, P.M. and Gardner, P.D. (1992) Formal and informal mentorships: A comparison on mentoring functions and contrast with non-mentored counterparts. *Personnel Psychology*, 45, 620–636.

Chartered Institute of Personnel and Development (2004) *Coaching and Buying Coaching Services*. London: CIPD.

Clutterbuck, D. and Ragins, B.R. (2002) *Mentoring and Diversity: An International Perspective*. Oxford: Butterworth and Heinmann.

DeLong, T., Gabarro, J. and Lees, R. (2008) Why mentoring matters in a hypercompetitive world. *Harvard Business Review*, 86(1), 115–121.

Dickinson, K., Jankot, T. and Gracon, H. (2009) *Sun Mentoring: 1996–2009*. Sun Microsystems. Available at http://research.sun.com/techrep/2009/smli_tr-2009-185.pdf/. Accessed 3 September.

Downey, M. (2003) *Effective Coaching*. Mason, OH: Thomson and Texere.

Fielden, S.L., Davidson, M.J. and Sutherland, J. (2009) Innovations in coaching and mentoring: Implications for nurse leadership development. *Health Services Management Research*, 22(2), 92–99.

Freeman, C. (2005) *Clinical Supervision Guidelines for Registered Nurses*. Birkenhead and Wallasey Primary Care Trust. Available at http://www.supervisionandcoaching.com/pdf/page2/CS%20Guidelines%20(Birkenhead%20&%20Wallasey%20PCT%20-%20UK%202005).pdf / Accessed October 2016.

Gallwey, W.T. (2000) *The Inner Game of Work*. New York: Random House.

Goldsmith, M., Lyons, L. and Freas, A. (2000) *Coaching for Leadership: How the World's Greatest Coaches Help Leaders Lead*. San Francisco: Jossey-Bass.

Goleman, D. (2000) Leadership that gets results. *Harvard Business Review*, March–April, 82–83.

Goleman, D. (1996) *Emotional Intelligence: Why It Can Matter more than IQ*. London: Bloomsbury.

Hanson, K. (2003) The Hanson coaching model: Towards a new framework. *The Occup Psychol; Special Issue Coaching Psychol*, 49, 20–24.

ILM (2010) *The Pursuit of Happiness: Positivity and Performance among UK Managers*. Available at: https://www.i-l-m.com/~/media/ILM%20Website/Downloads/Insight/Reports_from_ILM_website/research_positivity_and_performance%20pdf.ashx/.

Kline, N. (2002) *Time to Think*. Beccles: Octopus Books.

Kopelman, R.E. (1997) 100 days to better service in health care. *Training and Development*, 51, 84–85.

Law, H. (2008) Diversity coaching. *People and Organisations at Work*, 8, 6–7.

Leadership Centre for Local Government (2014) *Living Leadership*. Available at http://www.localleadership.gov.uk/images/living_leadership.pdf/ (accessed November 2014).

NHS EoE (2014) *Health Coaching for Behaviour Change*. Available at https://eoeleadership.hee.nhs.uk/Evaluation (accessed April 2016).

NHS Leadership Academy (2013) *The Healthcare Leadership Model*. Available at: http://www.leadershipacademy.nhs.uk/resources/healthcare-leadership-model/structure-healthcare-leadership-model/ (accessed November 2014).

Olivero, G., Bane, K.D. and Kopelman, R.E. (1997) Executive coaching as a transfer training tool: Effects on productivity in a public agency. *Public Personnel Management*, 26, 461–469.

Rogers, J. (2012) *Coaching Skills: A Handbook*. New York: McGraw-Hill.

Sutherland, V.J. (2005) *Nurse Leadership Development: Innovations in Mentoring and Coaching – The Way Forward*. London: NHS Leadership Centre.

Turnbull, S. (2013) *The twenty-first century Leader*. The Leadership Trust. Available from http://www.leadership.org.uk/files/uploads/77.pdf (accessed March 2013).

Weinstein, K. (2002) *Action Learning: A Practical Guide*. Aldershot: Gower.

West, M. (2013) *Developing Cultures of High Quality Care*. Available at http://www.kingsfund.org.uk/audio-video/michael-west-developing-cultures-high-quality-care (accessed November 2014).

Whitmore, J. (2009) *Coaching for Performance: Growing People, Performance and Purpose*, 3rd edn. London: Nicholas Brealey.

PART III

Contexts of health care and nursing

8

HEALTH LITERACY AND THE NURSE–PATIENT PARTNERSHIP

Jacquie Kidd

Why this chapter is important

Patients and families are not passive recipients of our expertise, although we often treat them that way as we selectively share our expertise in ways that are designed to create compliance with health care and treatment plans. However, the 'information explosion' that has emerged from the Internet and social media is frustrating our efforts to retain our privileged position of 'the expert' in our nursing role through the sharing or withholding of knowledge.

In this chapter you are challenged to consider whether the expert nursing role has any relevance in a world where information is so readily available.

Chapter trigger question: Do well-informed health consumers still need registered nurses?

Key words: Health literacy, health information, demands, non–compliance, nurse–patient partnership

---

Introduction

The milieu in which nursing occurs is changing rapidly with the onset of new technology and new ways of engaging with information. This change is evident in everyday practices such as digital patient records, bedside access to online information to support clinical decision-making, and telemedicine. There is a growing body of nursing knowledge about the growth of information technology, its effect on the nursing role, and strategies for how nurses can maximise the positive impact of technology and information on patient care (Huston, 2013; Alexander *et al.*, 2016).

Similarly, while information about patients, health problems, and treatments is more readily available for nurses than ever before, patients and their families also have relatively easy access to significant amounts of in-depth and varied information about health and illness. Patients who want to be well-informed about their health and illness can now visit websites that record individual experiences of their particular illness; advocacy groups who have a particular agenda about health issues; online 'medical' gurus who dispense (frequently questionable) generic advice without assessing the patient; international medical specialists who offer remote care via videoconferencing and email; open access journal papers providing highly specialised reviews or research reports; or even an entire specialist textbook downloadable at a single click. There is obviously a huge variation in the quality of the information on offer, so there is concern among health professionals about how the patient and family go about sifting through and drawing conclusions about the value of what they find.

One aspect of nursing that has not changed, and hopefully never will, is the central importance of the nurse–patient relationship. How and when patients receive and understand information, their ability or willingness to act on it, and the confidence to analyse information and adapt it to their own contexts all fall within a nurse's influence in the nurse–patient relationship. Historically known in nursing contexts as *health education* and *health promotion*, a more complex understanding of the need for information and how it is used has been developed in the last two decades under the umbrella of 'health literacy'. Low health literacy is implicated in poor health outcomes across the full range of conditions and socioeconomic statuses (Johnson, 2014), and includes gaps in preventative health behaviours, delayed diagnosis through non-recognition of early symptoms and limited participation in screening programmes, non-attendance at health services, and lack of effective disease management (Dewalt *et al.*, 2004).

Achieving high levels of health literacy in patient populations is a laudable goal for nurses. Having well-informed patients and families who fully participate in a health partnership with their nurses, understand and adhere to treatment decisions, and proactively manage their health and illness would appear to be a nursing version of utopia. Yet achieving health literacy is not quite as simple as it seems. There are multiple ways of understanding health literacy, as well as difficulties and challenges from the patient, family, nursing and organisational perspectives, and even some doubt about whether it is desirable for every patient, every time. There is also concern about whether, in trying to advance health literacy for patients and families, we are in fact attempting to make the patient into a mini doctor and take unreasonable levels of responsibility for their own health and illnesses (Rubinelli *et al.*, 2009).

It is important that nurses take the time to consider how we want to engage with this abundance of information and technology, and all the different ways the drive towards health literacy can impact on patients and families.

Understanding health literacy: It's not so simple!

Health literacy first emerged in the 1970s, and was focused on the idea that people needed to be competent in literacy and numeracy in order to read and understand written health information (Batterham *et al.*, 2016). For example, literacy and numeracy are required to make sense of these medication instructions: *Take one or two tablets up to three times a day, as needed for pain. Do not exceed 200mg per day.* However, even when the patient understands the instructions, the next step is to act on them. In this scenario the action of taking the tablets will probably take place as the patient wants to reduce their pain level. However, if the instructions related to a medication that does not have an immediate benefit, such as the latter doses of an antibiotic or a statin, we can acknowledge that the patients may understand the instructions perfectly, but for some reason they decide they will not follow through. Thus there is more to developing health literacy than having an individual patient understand and follow a set of medical instructions.

By the 1990s the concept of health literacy had become more varied, ranging from the original simple definition that focused on having the individual understand and comply with medical instructions to a more nuanced understanding of it as 'the cognitive and social skills which determine the motivation and ability of individuals to gain access to, understand and use information in ways which promote and maintain good health' (Nutbeam, 1998). Within the updated definition the patient's ability to read instructions and understand basic mathematics remained important, but their motivation and social skills were included to make sense of how patients decided whether to adapt their behaviour in response to health instructions or information. In this definition patients were viewed as having choices, but those choices were constrained by their cognitive and social skill levels.

Nutbeam (2000) expanded on his first definition of health literacy to highlight three interconnected components: functional, interactive, and critical. In broad terms, functional health literacy is the ability of the patient to receive factual information and act on it, as shown in the scenario above. This simple definition remains the most common way for health professionals to measure health literacy in patients, but it lacks any contextual understanding and can easily lead to a situation where the patient is blamed (and chastised) for not complying with medical instructions.

Interactive health literacy refers to the patient being more independent in seeking out information, figuring out how it applies to their situation or illness, and applying their knowledge. Examples of interactive health literacy include going to a primary care doctor with a new problem and jointly making a plan to manage the problem then acting on it, or searching out natural preventatives or remedies for a minor illness. Interactive health literacy is also evident in inpatient settings when patients question their healthcare team in order to improve their own knowledge of their diagnosis and treatment, and discuss the risks and benefits of treatments. The implication in this definition of interactive health literacy, although not one that is often explored, is that the patient may obtain and understand all the relevant information and decide *not* to follow medical advice or instructions. The nursing response to such patients will be discussed in more depth below, but could be briefly categorised into either a desire to understand the reasons behind the patient's decision, or a judgement that the patient is ill-informed or being 'difficult'.

Critical health literacy, as the name suggests, involves bringing advanced skills to the critical examination of health information, often in the context of changing or controlling the social determinants of health such as improved nutrition and exercise habits. A key part of critical health literacy is that it contributes to a community-based focus and has implications for the health of more than just the patient/person seeking the information. Other examples of critical health literacy include community advocacy for health promotion activities such as vaccinations and screening programmes, or protesting the placing of casinos or liquor outlets in disadvantaged communities.

There was considerable interest in health literacy following the publication of Nutbeam's expanded classification, resulting in further proposed definitions of health literacy across the range of health settings. These were analysed in a systematic review (Sørensen *et al.*, 2012) which identified the need to consider health care, disease prevention, and health promotion as separate strands of the existing conceptual dimensions of health literacy, and asserted that the key attributes for health literacy should be accessing, understanding, appraising and using information that relates to each of the three strands. While the recognition of differing health information needs and the inclusion of the social, emotional and cognitive aspects of health literacy is an improvement on early desires to develop a compliant patient, the flaw in these definitions was that the focus remained solely on the patient or person seeking improved health. This makes it very easy to blame the patient for not following instructions or changing their health behaviours, and doesn't take into account their political or cultural environment, the communication skill of health professionals, the usefulness of the resources that are available, or the rules, signage and culture of the health institutions they are involved with.

In the last four years critiques of health literacy have seen the more contextual inclusions of the patient's socio-cultural setting (Simpson *et al.*, 2015; Kidd *et al.*, 2014), the health professional's communication ability, the type of resources used and the environment and culture of the health organisation (Estacio *et al.*, 2013; Koh and Rudd, 2015; Brach *et al.*, 2012), and the policy environment that supports or constrains health literate service delivery (Rudd, 2015; Koh *et al.*, 2013). These latter aspects refer to *health literacy demands* (Estacio *et al.*, 2013) which are the knowledge, beliefs and behaviours the health professional, health organisation and health system expect of the patient and family in order for them to successfully engage with care. Health literacy demands can be extremely high, and range from finding and contacting the appropriate health service, communicating the need for an appointment and attending the right person, place and time, through to working with complex health jargon and activities such as self-managed medications or end of life care at home (Kidd *et al.*, 2014). Reviews of brochures and other written information, signage, and medical instructions almost always find that the health literacy demands for patients and families are high and could be reduced without losing the quality of information (Tong *et al.*, 2016; Tong *et al.*, 2014; Raynor *et al.*, 2007).

It seems that understanding health literacy from a nursing perspective is currently an almost incomprehensible process when you consider all the different viewpoints. A review of the paragraphs above reveals no less than 21 aspects to health literacy, and there is still more to consider. First, Koh and Rudd (2015) identify a 'paradox of health literacy', noting that people are 'awash in knowledge they may be unable to use' as a result of the sheer volume of often conflicting information that is sometimes too difficult for even health professionals to grasp. Next, in recent projects I identified that sometimes people understand the information very well, are able to access the relevant services, but do not want to because the services conflict with their cultural values (Kidd *et al.*, 2014; Kidd *et al.*, 2013). And finally, sometimes the systems and organisations that we work in create such significant barriers to understanding how they function that even the most health literate staff members can barely penetrate them, leaving the more vulnerable patient populations quite literally out in the cold.

To date the nursing perspective on health literacy is largely represented in the literature as being focused on functional health literacy, particularly adapting nursing communication styles to ensure that information is understood by patients (Sand-Jecklin *et al.*, 2010; Speros, 2011), yet it is clearly in the best interests of our patients and profession to become involved in exploring the full range of health literacies as a practice, education and research issue. However, it is not in anyone's best interest to jump into this very poorly defined and contestable area by announcing that nursing as a whole has an obligation to measure and address health literacy. Instead we should be carefully considering what health literacy on multiple different levels might look like in our practice areas, and what the consequences are for all stakeholders from its improvement.

The many concepts described so far have been drawn together in Table 8.1 by using questions to represent the key concerns that might be asked by a person or group who are engaged with accessing, understanding, appraising, choosing and using health information or care.

Reflect 8.1

- Pause for a moment and consider your own health care setting.
- Using Table 8.1 as a guide, write a list of health care demands your patients face, including what they must navigate in order to access, understand, and obtain the best care possible from you.

Health literacy for nurses: A double-edged sword?

Health literacy has not been universally embraced, with some authors arguing that it blurs the boundary between a person who knows enough to seek expert care and actually being the expert (Rubinelli *et al.*, 2009), and others noting that the

TABLE 8.1 Key health literacy questions

	Accessing	Understanding	Appraising	Choosing	Using
Individual and family	How do I find the service/information? Is it right for my needs?	What will it do for me? Do I know the people and resources involved?	Will it do what I want it to? Do I trust this provider and what they're offering?	Is this what I want? What other options do I have?	Do I have the physical, cultural, financial and emotional resources I need to be able to engage with this service?
Community	Is this service/information accessible for the whole community? Who does it privilege and who does it exclude? Have we been consulted during its development stages?	Does it meet our needs for healthy development? Are the resources adequate? Do we know the people and agendas in play?	How will it work with and for us? Are they willing to be flexible and responsive to our needs? Will it support our aspirations?	Will this service/information challenge or dismiss our cultural values? Is there a better option?	How do we adapt this service/information for the advantage of our community?
Health organisation including buildings, websites, portals, staff, and resources	Do we 'fit' with the needs and abilities of our target population? How will they find us? How and when will we engage with them?	Are we using the right language, images, people, and processes to meet the needs of this population? Are we communicating what we do, what we don't do, and who we work for?	Do we adapt our service at all levels to work more effectively? Do we respect the fundamental identity of the populations we serve?	Do we provide understandable and supported information and treatment options? Do we liaise effectively with other providers and use clear referral processes?	What systemic processes are in place to support individual, family and community uptake of this service or information? How do we build and support health literacy in all our employees?

persistent drive to make people self-manage their health is more consistent with a neoliberal risk-aversion approach than a patient-centred one (Morden *et al.*, 2012). This latter perspective is a challenge to grapple with, because although more engaged and informed decision-making by patients, families and communities is undoubtedly a positive goal, forcing people into independence as a way of rationing resources is not.

Nutbeam (2008) addresses this challenge when he characterises health literacy in two ways, as a risk factor and as an asset. Viewing health literacy as a risk factor is consistent with the way nursing has engaged with the topic so far. Patients with low health literacy are at risk of poorer health outcomes, so ongoing efforts to address health inequities and mitigate the effects of low health literacy on health outcomes tend to focus on measuring individual functional health literacy and managing the identified deficit. Taking care to ensure that patients and families understand their healthcare needs and how to follow treatment plans is clearly a good goal for nursing care that is likely to lead to improved patient engagement and positive clinical outcomes.

Health literacy as an asset, on the other hand, supports the development of control over one's health, including knowledge about health and illness, and empowering people to put that knowledge into action. This way of understanding health literacy has marked similarities to the field of health promotion and public health because it aims to improve 'personal, social and environmental' health determinants (Nutbeam, 2008), and has a broader aim of creating internal changes that drive health behaviour.

These characterisations offer two sides of a single coin; mitigating risk and improving health outcomes at the (metaphorical or literal) bedside, and building confidence and changing health behaviours at a community or population level. Both sides have benefits for patients, but equally they both present difficulties for nurses at a practical level. Nursing is not an autonomous profession, but an interdependent one. Nurses structure practice according to the needs and expectations of our patients, the other health professionals whose care intersects with our own, the health care system we work in, and the larger socio-cultural and political environment. We are guided and constrained by legislation, codes of ethics, and by written and unwritten codes of conduct. All of these factors will impact on our understanding of health literacy, and on our willingness and ability to fully develop health literacy in our patients.

Reflect 8.2

- In the three case studies below, consider the written and unwritten rules that are in play.
- What are the consequences for the other health professionals as well as the nurse and patient of increasing health literacy?
- What ethical principles are in play in these health literacy scenarios?
- What would you do?

Case study: Critical health literacy

Jo is a nurse in a primary health care practice in a suburb that has a high level of social and economic deprivation and a low level of health insurance. He is employed by the owners of the practice, a collaboration of general practitioners, to assess and treat minor injuries and to provide disease prevention and early intervention activities for their local community. Jo's employers receive incentive payments from the government based on how many activities such as vaccinations, cardiovascular and diabetes risk assessments, and well child checks are completed each month. The patients also pay individually at a slightly reduced rate for these consultations. While Jo acknowledges the value of proactive health interventions, he is concerned that the low income families in the community have to pay for these non-essential (but desirable) health care visits and believes that the practice and the community should be working together to minimise the costs while retaining the benefits of such care. Jo's employers say they cannot maintain their business without the consultation fees.

Case study: Interactive health literacy

Helen is a senior registered nurse in a psychiatric inpatient unit where the main patient population are experiencing symptoms of psychosis and are being legally compelled to stay in the ward and to accept treatment. The treatment of choice in Helen's unit is second generation antipsychotic medication, and a part of Helen's role is to administer the medication and monitor the effects and side effects. She is familiar with common side effects such as hyper-salivation, weight gain and constipation, but has only recently become aware of research that explores the potential life-limiting consequences of metabolic syndrome and prolonged QT interval associated with these medications (Raedler, 2010; De Hert et al., 2012; Morrison et al., 2015). Helen is a part of the treatment team that assesses people when they arrive in the unit, and knows that at that time they are generally highly distressed and thought disordered, and are generally not consulted about their treatment preferences. However, she believes that even in a crisis state they should be given information about their treatment and offered choices. She has so far held back from offering additional information about the side effects of second generation antipsychotics because she is worried about how her actions will be perceived by the rest of the multi-disciplinary treatment team.

Case study: Functional health literacy

Simon works the afternoon shift in a busy urban medical ward. He works closely with patients and families who are due to be discharged the following day to ensure that they clearly understand how to manage their medications when they get home. He creates information sheets tailored to each patient that simplifies their instructions to include the colour and shape of each tablet and a timeline showing when each tablet should be taken. He even includes tick boxes on the form so patients can note that they have taken each dose, which avoids the risk that they'll accidentally take a dose twice. Simon notices at times that patients don't fully understand their treatment, but explains that 'this one is for the waterworks, and this one keeps your heartbeat nice and strong'. Patients sometimes ask for more information, but Simon worries that if they have too much knowledge they will start deciding which meds to take and which to discontinue. He discourages the use of the Internet for his patients, warning them that none of the information online can be trusted.

Health literacy and the acceptance or rejection of care

An aspect of health literacy that has not yet been addressed in the literature is the lack of control health professionals have over the direction in which people's interactive and critical health literacy develops. There is an underpinning assumption in most calls for a health literate population that once people understand their health and illness they will agree that Western medicine has the answers, and that they will change their behaviour accordingly.

This raises some important questions about medical hegemony and its relationship with apparent 'low health literacy', particularly in relation to indigenous and other non-Western or non-medical belief systems. Examples of this include the uncomfortable joke in mental health nursing that 'lack of insight' in a patient's assessment really means that the person disagrees with their psychiatrist. At the time of writing there are tensions around people's interpretation of information about the fluoridation of public water supplies and about individual vaccination choices. Acupuncture, shamanism and herbal medicine specialists are viewed by some populations as being their practitioners of choice, and research with indigenous populations has clearly identified racism and cultural irrelevance as barriers to accessing many health services (Tang *et al.*, 2015; Dew *et al.*, 2015; Kidd *et al.*, 2014; Kidd *et al.*, 2013; Cram *et al.*, 2003). Thus the shortfalls of current Western ways of thinking about health and illness are already well established in the literature. The increasing availability of information about alternative approaches to health care, and the ability of health consumers to choose information that is consistent with their own spiritual and cultural belief systems makes it likely that such marginal views will also increase. Regardless of our own beliefs, nurses need to think about our responses to individuals and populations whose development of critical health literacy leads them to make decisions we may not be comfortable with. Simply abandoning people to live with their choices has historically been an option for some services, but this is an unacceptable response from the perspective of advancing holistic health strategies.

Reflect 8.3

- Does your health organisation systematically accommodate diverse belief systems?

- If so, how does it do this? If not, what changes would need to be implemented to improve responses to diversity at the organisational level?

The health literate nurse

Recognising that there are challenges to promoting and developing health literacy in patients, families and communities is an important step to its implementation. The paucity of nursing literature that engages in explorations beyond functional health literacy from a risk perspective is perhaps indicative of a lack of confidence, or even an act of resistance on the part of nursing researchers and authors. Perhaps many nurses are more comfortable aiming for simple understanding and compliance in our patients? Certainly the well documented concerns about increasing acuity, rapid bed turnover, and high patient loads (Hayward et al., 2016; Khademi et al., 2015; Alghamdi, 2016) would indicate that encouraging patients to question their care is an additional workload that nurses simply do not need or want. This is a perennial problem with a workforce that is struggling to meet the needs of their patients and employers, and is often in 'survival mode' as a result of burnout (Kidd and Finlayson, 2010). However, it also seems likely that low health literacy is contributing to the very factors that keep nurses so busy. Focusing on having compliant patients might be easier in the short term, but keeping people reliant on their expert nurses for health care effectively creates dependence in the long term. Shifting our health literacy focus towards interactive and critical health literacy should increase decision-making and independence in patients and families and ultimately create changes in how nurses work and who with, but making that change requires us to lift our heads from day to day activities and consider what changes we can make as individual clinicians, as a profession, and as a part of the health care system.

Reflect 8.4

- It's time to be brutally honest with yourself.
- Take some time to reflect (alone or with a trusted peer or clinical supervisor) on your beliefs about health literacy for your patients; do you withhold information from your patients?
- Why?
- How do you respond to patients who question your care?
- Are you confident about encouraging them to take control, or exasperated that they are taking up your valuable time?
- Do you consider them to be 'difficult patients'?
- Could you take a more health literate approach to your practice?

Getting practical, changing practice

Given the realities of resourcing and interdependent practice, there are still several actions nurses can take to improving both risk and asset focused health literacy (see additional resources at the end of this chapter).

- Understand your own health literacy, identify gaps and outdated knowledge, build your own confidence.
- Identify your own learning style, and build your knowledge about how other people learn so you can develop a 'tool kit' that you can use to help the full range of people to grow their health literacy.
- Understand the information resources (pamphlets, videos, websites, community organisations etc.) that are available, their strengths and weaknesses, and develop a range of processes that support you to pass this information on effectively to your patient population.
- Find out what the health literacy risks are for your patient population and explore strategies for mitigating these.
- Develop an understanding of what health literacy might look like as an asset for your patient population.
- Build your knowledge of the range of cultural values and beliefs in your patient population, and how health systems can adapt to work with those beliefs.
- Include health literacy in your nursing assessments, care plans, handovers, and referrals to support other nurses to take up this aspect of practice.
- Become a 'change champion' to support practice change for your colleagues and your organisation.

Summary

This chapter has focused on the evolving definitions of health literacy and how nurses can critically engage with the concept. Different perspectives relating to health literacy include functional, interactive and critical levels, and whether health literacy is viewed as a risk or an asset. Importantly, nursing's own responsibility as health providers also needs to be understood as a contributor to environmental health literacy, particularly because we can readily exert some influence on the level of health literacy demands on our patients, their families and communities.

Focusing on improving health literacy inevitably foreshadows significant changes in nursing practice. There is a point where high health literacy means that poorly thought out or inflexible nursing care, traditional Western health care mores, and 'business as usual' organisational approaches are rejected. Regardless of the motivation for change, whether it is to manage scarce resources or to genuinely create a healthier world population, nurses need to choose whether we will be fully engaged in how health literacy shapes our role or whether we will keep a narrow focus on achieving patient compliance. Our own approach to the 'flood of information' will shape our future. Is there a future for nurses where we are the supporters, navigators, facilitators, and sharers of information instead of expert instructors?

Additional resources

Find your learning style here: http://vark-learn.com/.
Information about organisational health literacy, including a questionnaire to test your organisation: www.cdc.gov/healthliteracy/planact/steps/index.html/.
A guide to assessing online health information: www.healthdirect.gov.au/health-information-online/.

References

Alexander, G. L., Madsen, R. W., Miller, E. & Wise, K. (2016) A national report of nursing home information technology adoption and quality measures. *Journal of Nursing Care Quality*, 31, 201–206.

Alghamdi, M. G. (2016) Nursing workload: A concept analysis. *Journal of Nursing Management*, 24, 449–57.

Batterham, R. W., Hawkins, M., Collins, P. A., Buchbinder, R. & Osborne, R. H. (2016) Health literacy: Applying current concepts to improve health services and reduce health inequalities. *Public Health*, 132, 3–12.

Brach, C., Keller, D., Hernandez, L. M., Baur, C., Parker, R., Dreyer, B., Schyve, P., Lemerise, A. J. & Schillinger, D. (2012) *Ten Attributes of Health Literate Health Care Organisations*. Washington DC: Institute of Medicine.

Cram, F., Smith, L. & Johnstone, W. (2003) Mapping the themes of Maori talk about health. *New Zealand Medical Journal*, 1170, 116.

De Hert, M., Detraux, J., Van Winkel, R., Yu, W. & Correll, C. U. (2012) Metabolic and cardiovascular adverse effects associated with antipsychotic drugs. *Nature Reviews. Endocrinology*, 8, 114–26.

Dew, K., Signal, L., Davies, C., Tavite, H., Hooper, C., Sarfati, D., Stairmand, J. & Cunningham, C. (2015) Dissonant roles: The experience of Māori in cancer care. *Social Science and Medicine*, 138, 144–51.

Dewalt, D. A., Berkman, N. D., Sheridan, S., Lohr, K. N. & Pignone, M. P. (2004) Literacy and health outcomes: A systematic review of the literature. *Journal of General Internal Medicine*, 19, 1228–39.

Estacio, E. V., Comings, J. & Rudd, R. E. (2013) Needed action in health literacy. *Journal of Health Psychology*, 18, 1004–1010.

Hayward, D., Bungay, V., Wolff, A. C. & Macdonald, V. (2016) A qualitative study of experienced nurses' voluntary turnover: Learning from their perspectives. *Journal of Clinical Nursing*, 25, 1336–45.

Huston, C. (2013) The impact of emerging technology on nursing care: Warp speed ahead. *Online Journal of Issues in Nursing*, 18, 1.

Johnson, A. (2014) Health literacy, does it make a difference? *Australian Journal of Advanced Nursing*, 31, 39–45 7p.

Khademi, M., Mohammadi, E. & Vanaki, Z. (2015) Resources-tasks imbalance: Experiences of nurses from factors influencing workload to increase. *Iranian Journal of Nursing and Midwifery Research*, 20, 476–83.

Kidd, J., Gibbons, V., Kara, E., Blundell, R. & Berryman, K. (2013) Oranga Tane Māori: A whānau ora journey of Māori men with chronic illness: a te korowai analysis. *AlterNative*, 9, 125–41.

Kidd, J., Reid, S., Collins, N., Gibbons, V., Blundell, R., Black, S. & Peni, T. (2014) *Kia mau te kahu whakamauru: Maori Health Literacy in Palliative Care*. Auckland: University of Auckland.

Kidd, J. D. & Finlayson, M. P. (2010) Mental illness in the nursing workplace: A collective autoethnography. *Contemp Nurse*, 36, 21–33.

Koh, H. K., Brach, C., Harris, L. M. & Parchman, M. L. (2013) A proposed 'health literate care model' would constitute a systems approach to improving patients' engagement in care. *Health Affairs*, 32, 357–67.

Koh, H. K. & Rudd, R. E. (2015) The arc of health literacy. *Journal of the American Medical Association*, 314, 1225–26.

Morden, A., Jinks, C. & Ong, B. N. (2012) Rethinking 'risk' and self-management for chronic illness. *Social Theory & Health*, 10, 78–99.

Morrison, P., Meehan, T. & Stomski, N. J. (2015) Living with antipsychotic medication side-effects: The experience of Australian mental health consumers. *International Journal of Mental Health Nursing*, n/a–n/a.

Nutbeam, D. (1998) Health promotion glossary. *Health Promotion International*, 13, 349–64.

Nutbeam, D. (2000) Health literacy as a public health goal: A challenge for contemporary health education and communication strategies into the twenty-first century. *Health Promotion International*, 15, 259–67.

Nutbeam, D. (2008) The evolving concept of health literacy. *Social Science and Medicine*, 67, 2072–2078.

Raedler, T. J. (2010) Cardiovascular aspects of antipsychotics. *Current Opinion in Psychiatry*, 23, 574–81.

Raynor, D. K., Blenkinsopp, A., Knapp, P., Grime, J., Nicolson, D. J., Pollock, K., Dorer, G., Gilbody, S., Dickinson, D., Maule, A. J. & Spoor, P. (2007) A systematic review of quantitative and qualitative research on the role and effectiveness of written information available to patients about individual medicines. *Health Technology Assessment*, 11, 1–160.

Rubinelli, S., Schulz, P. J. & Nakamoto, K. (2009) Health literacy beyond knowledge and behaviour: Letting the patient be a patient. *International Journal of Public Health*, 54, 307–11.

Rudd, R. E. (2015) The evolving concept of health literacy: New directions for health literacy studies. *Journal of Communication in Healthcare*, 8, 7–9.

Sand-Jecklin, K., Murray, B., Summers, B. & Watson, J. (2010) Educating nursing students about health literacy: From the classroom to the patient bedside. *OJIN: The Online Journal of Issues in Nursing*, 15. Available at www.nursingworld.org/MainMenuCategories/ANAMarketplace/ANAPeriodicals/OJIN/TableofContents/Vol152010/No3-Sept-2010/Articles-Previously-Topic/Educating-Nursing-Students-about-Health-Literacy.html/.

Simpson, M. L., Berryman, K., Oetzel, J., Iti, T. & Reddy, R. (2015) A cultural analysis of New Zealand palliative care brochures. *Health Promotion International*. doi: 10.1093/heapro/dav067.

Sørensen, K., Van Den Broucke, S., Fullam, J., Doyle, G., Pelikan, J., Slonska, Z. & Brand, H. (2012) Health literacy and public health: A systematic review and integration of definitions and models. *BioMed Central Public Health*, 12, 1–13.

Speros, C. I. (2011) Promoting health literacy: A nursing imperative. *Nurs Clin North Am*, 46, 321–33, vi–vii.

Tang, S. Y., Browne, A. J., Mussell, B., Smye, V. L. & Rodney, P. (2015) 'Underclassism' and access to healthcare in urban centres. *Sociology of Health and Illness*, 37, 698–714.

Tong, V., Raynor, D. K. & Aslani, P. (2014) Design and comprehensibility of over-the-counter product labels and leaflets: A narrative review. *International Journal of Clinical Pharmacy*, 36, 865–72.

Tong, V., Raynor, D. K., Blalock, S. J. & Aslani, P. (2016) Exploring consumer opinions on the presentation of side-effects information in Australian consumer medicine information leaflets. *Health Expectations*, 19, 543–56.

9

THE GLOBAL CONTEXT OF HEALTH CARE DELIVERY

Allison Squires

Why this chapter is important

While nurses are confident and well informed about their own safe practice, we are not always aware or understand how international institutions shape the context and care we deliver through their economic and social policies. This chapter provides an overview and beginning appreciation of the roles that international institutions and policies play in influencing our individual practice and the profession of nursing.

Chapter trigger question: Do global institutions, country contexts, and international development have a real influence on your everyday care delivery and the nursing profession?

Key words: Global institutions, international development, global health, health care systems, universal health coverage, Global Health Governance, WHO, World Bank.

Introduction

Nursing practice, research, and policy are all affected by where a nurse lives and works. When we consider nursing from a global perspective, we know there are many common threads in what we do. How we are able to do our jobs depends on the organisation for which we work, the place where we live, the health system design, whether or not the patients we care for have health insurance, the wealth of the country, and how a country's wealth is distributed to fund the health care system.

How does all of this translate into shaping the context of care? In truth, we know a lot but are still just beginning to understand the complexity of these relationships and how they translate into different care contexts. A 2016 study, for example, showed that a country's average education level of its population was strongly correlated with the nurse and midwifery-to-population ratio ($p=0.00$, $r=0.59$) (Squires, Uyei *et al.*, 2016). From a context perspective, that means if a country does not invest in education, they are less likely to have the number of nurses they need. The study further explored how context influences the number of nurses in a country to see if any of the factors predicted how many nurses there are in a country. Through an analysis that included education, political system, health system and economic data, the study's results also showed that contextual factors could explain as much as 62 per cent of the nurse and midwifery-to-population ratio. The take-home message from the study is that context matters when it comes to care delivery and it is quantifiable in its import.

What many nurses may not realise is how much influence international institutions have on the context of care. What is an international institution? An international institution is an organisation that was established to help regulate and monitor a specific issue that affects everyone across the world, including social and economic development. In the case of health, it is the World Health Organization (WHO). Other international institutions, however, also play a role in our ability to respond to the health issues our populations face in the context of where we work. Health care also needs to be financed and that money, in the case of low- and middle-income countries, comes in part from international development funds. These funds come from the World Bank, the International Monetary Fund, and some countries make direct grants to countries for health initiatives.

The purpose of this chapter is to familiarise nurses and their supporters with the most common international institutions that influence the global context of nursing care. We aim to offer a 'big picture' overview of a very complex topic. I hope as a reader you will come away with a basic understanding of how the key actors in Global Health Governance operate via their institutional arrangements and subsequently influence the contexts where we deliver nursing care.

Reflect 9.1

- Take a few minutes to recall any international organisations you know that influence global health care.
- Can you remember any recent news stories where one of those organisations was quoted?
- When you think about the term 'Global nursing' what words or images come into your mind?

Global institutions influencing nursing

International institutions play an important role in Global Health Governance (GHG). Their policies ultimately significantly affect what nurses are able to do for patients, both directly and indirectly. The institutions provide a basic international governance mechanism for addressing the world's health problems. Formally, this is known as Global Health Governance (GHG). GHG began to emerge in the early twenty-first century as a unifying theory, concept, and operation for how the world could manage the impact of globalisation on health (Fidler, 2007).

GHG helps ensure that policies and infrastructure are in place to prevent infectious diseases and other vector borne illnesses from spreading across borders in our increasingly globalised world (Ricci, 2009). GHG also ensures that there is a mechanism for countries to work together to address health problems that affect everyone, like non-communicable diseases and respond to epidemic crises. GHG will also play an increasing role in health systems strengthening as care delivery becomes increasingly standardised to a level that can ensure the public a minimum quality of care. This section will review four of the most influential international institutions that affect nurses and nursing and provide examples of how their role in GHG has affected nursing personnel or issues related to nursing in different regions of the world.

The International Council of Nurses (www.icn.ch)

A hallmark of a profession is a unifying body that creates a vehicle for political advocacy work and support for professionalisation issues as they arise (Abbott, 1991). The International Council of Nurses (ICN) is our international representative organisation that helps provide a voice for the world's 16 million nurses and the 130 national nursing associations. The ICN established the international definition of what is a nurse and what is nursing. Through that common definition, we have a way to describe ourselves to those who may not understand what nurses do.

The ICN's main role is to help establish policy about nursing practice and nursing workforce issues. They publish carefully considered and globally applicable position statements about nursing practice and the workforce. They also serve as a knowledge repository for policy analyses related to nursing. The organisation is the publisher of the well-respected *International Nursing Review* – which every country with a national nursing organisation receives for free – and the sponsor of one of the few international congresses for nurses that draws nurses from everywhere around the globe. The ICN provides us with a central place to network and connect with our nursing colleagues around the world to both celebrate our strengths and work together to find solutions to address our challenges as a profession and the health needs of our patients.

One limitation of the ICN is that it is not a wealthy organisation. Funds are dependent on member dues from national nursing associations and foundation grants. In many respects, this limits how much the ICN is able to do simply because they do not have the staff to broaden the scope of its work. Most resources are also prioritised for developing nursing in countries where it is moving from an occupation to a profession. More recently, however, the ICN has increased its engagement with international institutions through more policy collaborations and improved dissemination efforts around its resources.

The World Health Organization (www.who.int/en)

The WHO became an international institution specifically devoted to addressing global health issues shortly after World War II. Its predecessor, the Pan American Health Organisation (PAHO), had formed in the early 1900s as a way to combat vector borne illnesses in the Americas and throughout the Western hemisphere. PAHO's work proved effective in leading the way to addressing problems like malaria, improving vaccinations, and developing the health workforce in the region. Because of PAHO's early work, the WHO had a foundation from which to build its own work.

Today, the WHO has seven regions around the world and each regional office is assigned to address the regional health issues. The main role of the WHO is to help countries address their local health problems and to set the policy standards for the delivery of health care and how to treat and manage diseases (Ruger and Yach, 2009). The WHO is also expected to provide global leadership to organise international responses to epidemics, like Ebola or a very bad strain of influenza.

For nursing, the WHO has had a mixed history. Until 2010, there was an office dedicated to nursing and midwifery personnel alone and supporting their work. The efficacy of the office depended heavily on the quality of leadership within it. However, the WHO had to reorganise after the global economic crisis of 2009 and its funding was cut dramatically. Consequently, the nursing office was merged with a new Human Resources for Health division that has multiple nurses working on policy issues directly affecting our profession. Since the reorganisation, there has been more collaboration with nurses through the WHO collaborating centre networks. A WHO collaborating centre is a special designation assigned to a university or organisation that helps create the research and policy recommendations the WHO needs to be effective in its role. There are over 50 collaborating centres affiliated with nursing programmes around the world.

The World Bank (www.worldbank.org)

The role of the World Bank in health and health systems strengthening is multifaceted. The institution has a long history of investing in health services and health worker development as part of a global strategy to develop and sustain health care systems around the world. As an organisation, it commits more than a billion dollars a year to improve population health across the globe.

The World Bank was first started to help finance the reconstruction of Europe after World War II (Ruger, 2005). Throughout the rest of the twentieth century, the Bank provided the financing for countries to build hospitals, primary care clinics, and health professions education schools. All financing through the World Bank tends to occur through low or zero interest loans to countries that do not have the capital to invest in their health care infrastructure to meet the demand for care and services.

The twenty-first century World Bank's main priorities are to reduce poverty and promote shared prosperity – a way of saying they want to reduce inequalities. As we know, socioeconomic inequality contributes to health disparities and health disparities lead to higher health system costs (King *et al.*, 2012).

Many lessons have been learned through the World Bank's work with health systems. For example, in the early 1990s as the HIV/AIDS crisis began to reach epidemic proportions in sub-Saharan Africa, the World Bank and the International Monetary Fund forced countries to change how their health systems were financed (Squires *et al.*, 2013). These changes usually supported private sector health services development. What happened, however, was that the public sector (which delivered the majority of health care in low- and middle-income countries) could no longer deliver health care services. Many health workers also became infected with HIV and died from it. The scenario was the perfect storm of fewer resources and fewer personnel to meet population health needs. As the world observed the consequences of these policies, that is when the World Bank shifted its funding priorities toward improving population health, health systems, nutrition, and other social system strengthening investments (Ruger, 2005).

Today the institution sees nursing as a critical part of achieving universal health coverage (otherwise known as universal health insurance) in every country around the world. The main challenge they face with investing in nursing human resources development, however, is that there needs to be more evidence about nursing labour markets and targeted development needs in low- and middle-income countries since most of the research about nurses and the efficacy of our work comes from high-income countries (McPake *et al.*, 2015).

The International Labor Organization (ILO) (www.ilo.org/global/lang-en/index.htm)

The International Labour Organization (ILO) is an agency of the United Nations whose purpose is to bring governments, employers, and workers together so that everyone has a chance at decent work, equal human rights, and social justice. The ILO represents workers from all fields, all over the world. It is important to note that the ILO is not a labour union or syndicate. It is an international advocacy and policymaking organisation that believes safe working conditions are a key to peace and prosperity for all.

An important role that the ILO plays for nurses is monitoring international labour standards and the migration of people for work. Hundreds of studies from all over the world produced by nurses and their supporters form the research evidence that has established that nurses need supportive work environments with the right resources so they can provide patient care in a way that meets international standards. The research we have produced has helped the ILO work with the ICN to set minimum standards for safe working conditions for nurses.

In terms of international migration, the ILO plays an important role in monitoring international nurse migration. Nurses, especially those from low- or middle-income countries, are one of the health care workers most likely to migrate abroad for work with a primary goal of sending money, known as remittances, home to support their families (Squires and Amico, 2014). Many have written about the challenges internationally educated nurses face when they move abroad, and these include but are not limited to human trafficking, passport confiscation by employers, placement agencies with questionable business practices, practice differences that require substantial organisational investment in skilling up of workers, and all of the issues that come with culture shock when leaving home (Winkelmann-Gleed and Seeley, 2002; Schmid, 2004; Lee and Mills, 2005; Xu, 2007; Malvarez et al., 2008; Kingma, 2008; Reinhard et al., 2009; Kawi and Xu, 2009; Dywili et al., 2013; van den Broek and Groutsis, 2016; Pung and Goh, 2016; Squires, Ojemeni, et al., 2016). The ILO's role is to document these occurrences and raise an alarm when a problematic pattern seems to emerge. For example, when the international migration of health workers, including nurses, began to contribute to brain drain from low- and middle-income countries in a way that crippled health system operations, the ILO worked with the WHO, World Bank, ICN, and other international institutions to help create the Code for the Ethical International Recruitment of Health Workers. The WHO passed the Code in 2010 and it has helped mitigate some of the issues related to brain drain from low- and middle-income countries (Squires, Ojemeni et al., 2016).

The international institutions highlighted here are just a few of the many around the world that can and do affect nurses, their work, and patient outcomes. While we may not feel a direct impact from these institutions in our daily clinical practice with patients, their influence becomes clearer as we consider how globalisation has made us all more connected.

Reflect 9.2

- Are you able to recall any guidance or policy documents that you have used in your practice that were produced by either or both the ICN and WHO?
- By visiting the websites of the WHO and ICN are you able to find guidance on how the role of the nurse is defined by these organisations?

Economic development and nursing

The world spends US$6.5 trillion on health care every year (World Health Organization, 2016). Because of development differences, some countries will have more to spend than others. Some years there are crises, like Ebola or Zika, that force countries to shift their spending to fight an infectious disease. Health spending is a huge part of the global economy and since nurses are the single largest group of health workers in any country and the largest group of health workers on the globe, nurses make significant contributions to global health spending and their local economies.

With that much money spent on health in any given year, making sure those resources are used effectively and efficiently is an important role for international institutions. Many international institutions support nursing, health care, and improved population health through development investments. 'Development' or 'socioeconomic development' is a term familiar to many, but not always well understood. In nursing, researchers and policymakers are only just beginning to explore how development investments directly and indirectly impact nurses and their work.

It's important to note that the term 'developing country' is no longer an appropriate way to describe countries. In the past, data showed that 'developing' countries had similar characteristics but this is no longer the case (Khokhar and Serajuddin, 2015). Now there are two ways that policymakers think of development: economic as indicated by a country's income level and the Human Development Index managed by the United Nations. Why do we need to categorise countries in these ways? Through categorisation countries that want to invest in other countries can more easily figure out how to prioritise their investments and how the country's needs align with their own policy goals.

Let's define some key terms. All of these definitions relate to the 'country level' and draw from the World Bank's common definitions. Table 9.1 also provides descriptors of how economies are classified and their per capita (per person) income.

Investments: Money, people, or time directed toward improving a specific indicator or toward meeting a goal.
Development: The process by which a country prioritises social, economic, and political investments in its population as a way to improve the overall quality of life and well-being of anyone living in the country.
Economic Development: Investments made directly into growing or developing the economy of a country so that people can find paid employment and are able to purchase the things that are necessary for their daily lives.
Socioeconomic Development: Investments in sections of society with direct links to economic development. These include, but are not limited to, education, housing, and health. One of the main goals of socioeconomic development investments is to reduce extreme poverty.
Sustainable Development: Where investments are prioritised to effect lasting social and economic change in a country, thereby promoting economic stability and reducing inequality.

How do these concepts relate to nursing? Development investments are important for our profession just like they are important for health system and services development. For example, if a country does not have a national nursing

TABLE 9.1 Country income classifications

Income category	Gross national income per capita (in USD, 2015)
Low income	<$1,025.00
Low–middle income	$1,026.00–4,035.00
Upper–middle income	$4,036.00–12,475.00
High income	$12,476.00+

Source: https://datahelpdesk.worldbank.org/knowledgebase/
articles/906519-world-bank-country-and-lending-groups.

organisation, then development investments could help the nurses in that country form the organisation and help it operate. By having their own professional nursing organisation, nurses from that country then have a vehicle to have a voice in their own government and also contribute their perspectives to global health problems. Development investments can also help to create more nurses by helping to build new nursing schools, provide scholarships for nurses to become faculty to teach in those schools, provide scholarships for individuals to become nurses, and also create new career pathways that help keep people working in the profession but give them new opportunities for personal and professional growth.

But what about development investments that do not directly go to nursing, but may still benefit the profession? The interdisciplinary research literature suggests that there are a few key areas where development investments may benefit the nursing profession. A good example is women's development – and it's not just because most nurses globally are still women.

When countries have higher average education levels, they have more nurses (Squires, Uyei et al., 2016). So, investments in education for women and men have a greater chance of increasing the number of nurses in a country. Why? Logically, women need access to education to become a nurse. If a girl cannot go to primary or secondary school, she will not have the basic knowledge and skills needed to study nursing. Economic studies have confirmed this fact for many years (Owen and You, 2009; Self and Grabowski, 2009). At the same time, however, men also need to become more educated because when men are more educated, it is easier to overcome gender related cultural barriers toward women's education.

There are situations and times, however, when a country cannot invest in its own people because it simply does not have the resources to do so. This often happens because of internal conflicts, wars, terrorism, catastrophic climate events (e.g. tsunamis, hurricanes, typhoons and earthquakes) or other political changes. When countries do not have the resources to invest in their own development, this is where the international community steps in to help out through development aid. Development aid can be controversial but for nurses in most low- and middle-income countries it is critical for them to be able to do their work and help their patients achieve the best possible outcomes.

Let's take the example of a country that has just recovered from a war. Country A has just stabilised after a ten-year civil war and is now classified as a low income country. There are few health workers, just one hospital for a country the size of the United Kingdom, no medical schools, and two nursing schools. Primary care clinics are set up in temporary areas by international non-governmental organisations that specialise in operating in post-conflict states. There were no physical therapists, occupational therapists, or pharmacists before the war started, so the country did not even have that human resource to begin with. The country is lucky enough to have rich farmland so they can at least begin to recover their economy through agriculture and people will have some work.

Development aid will help the country to rebuild its health system infrastructure, educate more nurses and doctors, rebuild schools, and get the minimum necessary equipment and medicines to the population. It will be critical in the reconstruction phase of the country's history that people who can work are able to so that the economy can rebuild itself. As more people are able to work, they will generate more money for the local economy and eventually, the country will need less development aid. This process, however, can take decades. That's why development aid is given over long periods. Hopefully, the country is adopting a sustainable development approach toward its use of funds. Through sustainable development, there is a greater chance that the development investments will last for a long time.

Much like the section on international institutions, this one provides a very superficial overview of a complex topic. Nonetheless, economic development affects every nurse in every country. In order to understand how it affects nurses in your country, a basic familiarity with the terms and concepts is important. Said understanding can help make sense of what seems to be an increasingly complex world where globalisation affects everything around us, and especially our clinical practice and our patients.

An applied case example: Cholecystectomy

This chapter has focused on a lot of 'big picture' issues related to nursing. Through the following case example, we will try to show you how all these things relate to the 'real world' of clinical nursing practice. We will use the example of a cholecystectomy to show how everything ties together.

The gall bladder is located in the same location in 99.9 per cent of the population and makes for a good example to illustrate the impact of contextual factors on care delivery. When it needs to be removed, the cholecystectomy procedure will happen the same way in almost every location around the world. The nursing role in that procedure will also be fairly consistent across borders.

What may affect the patient's outcome from the procedure is the role of the context where the surgery occurred. The context of care consists of many levels: Organisational, geographic location within the country, and income status of the country (which affects health system financing and available resources).

From an organisational perspective, the type of hospital where the surgery took place may affect the outcome. Was it an urban or rural hospital? A teaching or non-teaching hospital? How many nurses were available to care for the patient before, during, and after surgery? Did the procedure occur laparoscopically or was it an open cholecystectomy? The latter is important because some countries cannot afford laparoscopic surgery equipment in all their facilities. Furthermore, when they get the equipment the surgeons, nurses, and any other member of the surgical team must be trained on how to use the equipment and sterilise it afterwards. Even though the evidence shows that patients recover more quickly from cholecystectomy with laparoscopic surgery and that it reduces costs, if there is no money to purchase and maintain equipment, then that changes the context of care and how nurses take care of patients receiving a cholecystectomy.

So why would the hospital not have money to purchase the laparoscopic surgery equipment? There are a number of reasons for that and all apply to both public and private hospitals. First, perhaps the hospital is in a rural location. The demand for laparoscopic surgery might be low, and therefore patients need to travel to another location (often hundreds of miles away) to receive the surgery. There might also not be a physician available at the site to conduct the surgery, nor an anaesthesiologist. We know that nurses are much more likely to work in rural areas than physicians (Anatole et al., 2012; Marsh et al., 2012; Stark et al., 1999; Chirwa et al., 2009; Yates et al., 2010; Hill et al., 2000; Gross et al., 2010), so the nurse's role is in getting the patient who needs a cholecystectomy referred to an appropriate location. Another reason why there might not be money for equipment is because the hospital cannot afford to hire staff to maintain the equipment nor can they contract with an outside company for that service.

Furthermore, even a hospital that can afford to get the equipment might not have patients who can afford to pay for the procedure. While the World Health Organization and World Bank are both pushing for universal health coverage (UHC) so patients will not have to worry about paying for significant portions of their health care costs, this has not happened yet in all countries. Many patients and their families still face considerable financial risks when trying to pay for medical care in many countries around the world. Ensuring that everyone has health insurance is a key strategy for improving population health, reducing financial risks for patients, and making sure that health systems have the resources they need to ensure that there is the right worker at the right place at the right time with the right resources to deliver care. And most of the time, that worker is a nurse.

Then there is the scenario of people migrating to other countries for health care. Sometimes this happens because they have migrated for work, because their country does not offer the procedure, or for medical tourism reasons. In the case of our cholecystectomy scenario, we may find an individual seeking care who has had their cholecystitis symptoms managed medically or through diet because it is the country's policy to try that first before going into surgery. If the patient doesn't have health insurance or if they have to wait a long time to get the surgery completed, they may opt to travel to another country for the surgery where the costs of the procedure are significantly lower than their home country. The latter is an example of medical tourism, a phenomenon driven by different health care contexts (Crisp and Chen, 2014; O'Brien and Gostin, 2011; Kanchanachitra *et al.*, 2011; Bhat, 2015).

For nurses caring for patients migrating to other countries for health services, this means they need to understand the cultures they come from and how to effectively work around a language barrier when present. The nurse has to be able to adapt to an increasing variety of patients and adapt practice to meet the care needs of the patient. For example, what if the nurse was completing discharge teaching with a patient post-cholecystectomy and did not adapt the dietary instructions to the patient's home country diet? The patient then becomes at higher risk for having post-operative complications or making lifestyle adjustments after surgery.

What the cholecystectomy example shows is how context can affect a single procedure and how nurses may need to adapt their practice due to different contextual factors. From the big picture perspective, we know that the contexts where care occurs and where patients seek treatment may be the result of the influence of international institutional policies. This was just one example. Consider how it all translates to hundreds and thousands of patients, procedures, nurses, and health systems around the world.

Summary

Nurses, their practice, and health systems do not operate in isolation in the twenty-first century. Globalisation means that we are all more connected than ever and there are many positives and negatives to that phenomenon. To focus on the positive, nurses are able to share more resources than ever before through international networks. Our practice differences are becoming less about knowledge differences and more about resource driven ones. More than any other profession, nursing is the most globally mobile of the health professions.

In summary, I hope this chapter has highlighted and helped you to explore the importance of thinking about nursing in a global context. There are many key actors who influence our practice and work lives through their policies. With a fundamental understanding of how these key actors shape what we do, we can start to become better advocates for ourselves and our patients. Through that, we will eventually achieve better health for all.

References

Abbott, A. (1991) The order of professionalisation: An empirical analysis. *Work and Occupations*, 18(4), pp. 355–384. Available at: http://wox.sagepub.com/content/18/4/355 (Accessed 25 September 2014).

Anatole, M. *et al.* (2012) Nurse mentorship to improve the quality of health care delivery in rural Rwanda. *Nursing Outlook*, 61(3), pp. 137–144. Available at: www.ncbi.nlm.nih.gov/pubmed/23164530 (Accessed 6 September 2013).

Bhat, T.P. (2015) International trade in health care services: Prospects and challenges for India. *India Quarterly: A Journal of International Affairs*, 71(3), pp. 239–254. Available at: http://iqq.sagepub.com/content/71/3/239.abstract?maxtoshow=&HITS=10&hits=11 0&RESULTFORMAT=1&andorexacttitle=and&andorexacttitleabs=and&fulltext=M exico&andorexactfulltext=and&searchid=1&FIRSTINDEX=0&sortspec=match&fdate =//&resourcetype=HWCIT (Accessed 18 August 2015).

van den Broek, D. & Groutsis, D. (2016) Global nursing and the lived experience of migration intermediaries. *Work, Employment & Society*, p. 950017016658437. Available at: http://wes.sagepub.com/cgi/doi/10.1177/0950017016658437 (Accessed 22 September 2016).

Chirwa, M.L. *et al.* (2009) HIV stigma and nurse job satisfaction in five African countries. *The Journal of the Association of Nurses in AIDS Care : JANAC*, 20(1), pp. 14–21. Available at: www.pubmedcentral.nih.gov/articlerender.fcgi?artid=2743864&tool=pmcentrez&r endertype=abstract (Accessed 3 April 2012).

Crisp, N. & Chen, L. (2014) Global supply of health professionals. *The New England Journal of Medicine*, 370(10), pp. 950–957. Available at: www.ncbi.nlm.nih.gov/pubmed/24597868 (Accessed 19 March 2014).

Dywili, S., Bonner, A. & O'Brien, L. (2013) Why do nurses migrate? – A review of recent literature. *Journal of Nursing Management*, 21(3), pp. 511–520. Available at: www.ncbi.nlm.nih.gov/pubmed/23409815 (Accessed 29 May 2014).

Fidler, D.P. (2007) Architecture amidst Anarchy: Global health's quest for governance. *Global Health Governance 2*, 1(1), pp. 1–17. Available at: http://ghgj.org/Fidler_Architecture.pdf (Accessed 4 October 2016).

Gross, J.M. *et al.* (2010) The impact of an emergency hiring plan on the shortage and distribution of nurses in Kenya: The importance of information systems. *Bulletin of the World Health Organization*, 88(11), pp. 824–830. Available at: www.pubmedcentral.nih.gov/articlerender.fcgi?artid=2971507&tool=pmcentrez&rendertype=abstract (Accessed 17 October 2013).

Hill, A.G. *et al.* (2000) Decline of mortality in children in rural Gambia: The influence of village-level primary health care. *Tropical Medicine & International Health : TM & IH*, 5(2), pp. 107–118. Available at: www.ncbi.nlm.nih.gov/pubmed/10747270.

Kanchanachitra, C. *et al.* (2011) Human resources for health in southeast Asia: Shortages, distributional challenges, and international trade in health services. *Lancet*, 377(9767), pp. 769–781. Available at: www.ncbi.nlm.nih.gov/pubmed/21269674 (Accessed 20 August 2014).

Kawi, J. & Xu, Y. (2009) Facilitators and barriers to adjustment of international nurses: An integrative review. *International Nursing Review*, 56(2), pp. 174–183. Available at: www.ncbi.nlm.nih.gov/pubmed/19646166.

Khokhar, T. & Serajuddin, U. (2015) Should we continue to use the term 'developing world'? | The Data Blog. *The Data Blog*. Available at: http://blogs.worldbank.org/opendata/should-we-continue-use-term-developing-world (Accessed 7 October 2016).

King, N.B., Harper, S. & Young, M.E. (2012) Who cares about health inequalities? Cross-country evidence from the World Health Survey. *Health Policy and Planning* (October 2012), pp. 558–571. Available at: www.ncbi.nlm.nih.gov/pubmed/23059735 (Accessed 12 August 2013).

Kingma, M. (2008) Nurse migration and the global health care economy. *Policy, Politics & Nursing Practice*, 9(4), pp. 328–333. Available at: www.ncbi.nlm.nih.gov/pubmed/19074203 (Accessed 8 June 2012).

Lee, R.J. & Mills, M.E.E. (2005) International nursing recruitment experience. *The Journal of Nursing Administration*, 35(11), pp. 478–481. Available at: www.ncbi.nlm.nih.gov/pubmed/16282824.

McPake, B. *et al.* (2015) *The Economics of Health Professions Education and Careers: Insights from a Literature Review.* Washington, DC: World Bank. Available at: https://openknowledge.worldbank.org/handle/10986/22576 (Accessed 21 September 2015).

Malvarez, S. *et al.* (2008) *Serie 55: Notas Preliminares Sobre Migración y Escasez de Enfermeras en América Latina.* Washington, DC: World Bank.

Marsh, L., Diers, D. & Jenkins, A. (2012) A modest proposal: Nurse practitioners to improve clinical quality and financial viability in critical access hospitals. *Policy, Politics & Nursing Practice*, 13(4), pp. 184–194. Available at: www.ncbi.nlm.nih.gov/pubmed/23528434 (Accessed 6 September 2013).

O'Brien, P. & Gostin, L.O. (2011) *Health Worker Shortages and Global Justice.* New York: Milbank Memorial Fund.

Owen, A.L. & You, R. (2009) Growth, attitudes towards women, and women's welfare. *Review of Development Economics*, 13(1), pp. 134–150. Available at: http://doi.wiley.com/10.1111/j.1467-9361.2008.00466.x (Accessed 8 June 2012).

Pung, L.-X. & Goh, Y.-S. (2016) Challenges faced by international nurses when migrating: An integrative literature review. *International Nursing Review*. Available at: http://doi.wiley.com/10.1111/inr.12306 (Accessed 8 September 2016).

Reinhard, B.S., Redfoot, D. & Cleary, B. (2009) Health and long-term care: Are immigrant workers indispensable? *The American Society on Aging*, 32(4), pp. 24–30.

Ricci, J. (2009) Global health governance and the state: Premature claims of a post-international framework. *Global Health Governance*, 3(1), pp. 1–18. Available at: http://ghgj.org/ricci3.1prematureclaims.htm (Accessed 4 October 2016).

Ruger, J.P. (2005) The changing role of the World Bank in global health. *American Journal of Public Health*, 95(1), pp. 60–70. Available at: www.ncbi.nlm.nih.gov/pubmed/15623860 (Accessed 6 October 2016).

Ruger, J.P. & Yach, D. (2009) The global role of the World Health Organisation. *Global Health Governance*, (Fall/Spring), pp. 1–11. Available at: www.ghgj.org.

Schmid, K. (2004) Strategies to manage migration of health professionals to protect national health systems will be successful only if all stake-holders are involved in the process. *Bulletin of the World Health Organization*, 82(8), pp. 621–622.

Self, S. and Grabowski, R. (2009) Gender development, institutions, and level of economic development. *Review of Development Economics*, 13(2), pp. 319–332.

Squires, A., Uyei, S.J., *et al.* (2016) Examining the influence of country-level and health system factors on nursing and physician personnel production. *Human Resources for Health*, 14(1), p. 48. Available at: http://human-resources-health.biomedcentral.com/articles/10.1186/s12960-016-0145-4 (Accessed 20 September 2016).

Squires, A. and Amico, A. (2014) An integrative review of the role of remittances in international nurse migration. *Nursing: Research and Reviews*, 5, p. 1. Available at: www.dovepress.com/an-integrative-review-of-the-role-of-remittances-in-international-nurs-peer-reviewed-article-NRR (Accessed 6 October 2016).

Squires, A., Ojemeni, M.T. and Jones, S. (2016) Exploring longitudinal shifts in international nurse migration to the United States between 2003 and 2013 through a random effects panel data analysis. *Human Resources for Health*, 14(S1), p. 21. Available at: http://human-resources-health.biomedcentral.com/articles/10.1186/s12960-016-0118-7 (Accessed 5 July 2016).

Stark, R., Nair, N.V. and Omi, S. (1999) Nurse practitioners in developing countries: Some ethical considerations. *Nurse Ethics*, 6(4), pp. 273–277.

Winkelmann-Gleed, A. and Seeley, J. (2002) Strangers in a British world? Integration of international nurses. *British Journal of Nursing*, 14(18), pp. 954–961. Available at: www.ncbi.nlm.nih.gov/pubmed/16237349.

World Health Organization (2016) WHO | Spending on health: A global overview. *WHO Fact Sheet #319*. Available at: www.who.int/mediacentre/factsheets/fs319/en/ (Accessed 7 October 2016).

Xu, Y. (2007) Strangers in strange lands: A metasynthesis of lived experiences of immigrant Asian nurses working in Western countries. *Advances in Nursing Sci*, 30(3), pp. 246–265.

Yates, V.M. *et al.* (2010) Management of snakebites by the staff of a rural clinic: The impact of providing free antivenom in a nurse-led clinic in Meserani, Tanzania. *Annals of Tropical Medicine and Parasitology*, 104(5), pp. 439–448. Available at: www.ncbi.nlm.nih.gov/pubmed/20819312 (Accessed 6 June 2012).

10

THE ECONOMIC CHALLENGE FOR HEALTHCARE SERVICES

Helen Myers and Di Twigg

Why this chapter is important

If nurses are to influence the policy debate in regard to healthcare reform, then all nurses must be able to articulate the evidence available to inform that debate. There is a clear relationship between nurse staffing (education, skill-mix and hours of care), the practice environment, and patient outcomes. There is also emerging evidence that improvements in nurse staffing can be cost-effective because of the associated reduction in adverse events and better discharge planning leading to shorter lengths of stay in hospital. This chapter will articulate this evidence and discuss the implications of this evidence and the challenges that lie ahead.

Chapter trigger question: Is it really possible to balance the scales between the need for major healthcare reform and quality patient care?

Key words: acute care, economic evaluation, patient outcomes, nurse staffing, nurse skill-mix, practice environment

Introduction

Modern healthcare is expensive. It is also highly complex and pluralistic, with multiple layers of healthcare workers, care settings, care delivery models, technologies, products and funding arrangements. Expectations amongst consumers and governments are high. The goal is for high quality care to be provided to all at an affordable price – the 'iron triangle' of cost, quality and access (Clarke, 2013). Yet there are often significant failings in achieving these goals. With the spiralling costs of healthcare, it is clear that health reform needs to take place to contain costs without adversely affecting quality or access but how best to do this is contested.

The impact on nurses from health reform agendas has been notable. Nurses are the largest hospital workforce, providing twenty-four-hour care, seven days a week. A critical role of the nurse in this setting is the continuous observation of patients resulting in the prompt detection of any deterioration in a patient's condition. This allows nurses to implement the necessary interventions to rescue the patient from harm. Nurses' ability to fulfil this critical role depends on personal characteristics such as their education and experience. It also depends on the ward structure such as the number of nurses on the ward, and the skill-mix of the nursing staff. Both of these staffing parameters have been shown to be associated with the quality of patient care. The practice environment in which nurses' work is also critical and a positive practice environment has been linked to better patient outcomes. However, staffing parameters and the practice environment are both threatened by health reform agendas.

Policy responses to economic and other pressures on the health system have focused on increasing reliance on unregulated nursing support roles and increasing productivity often coupled with embargoes on employing new staff and reductions in the use of agency staff. The evidence linking nurse staffing parameters to patient outcomes has had little policy impact. In addition, emerging research examining the economics of nurse staffing decisions suggests the benefit of improved staffing can be cost-effective; however, this evidence is often ignored.

This chapter will give an overview of some of the economic issues affecting healthcare systems to provide a broad picture of the context in which nursing care is delivered. It will also explore how health reforms have impacted on nursing and what this means for you as a nurse within the healthcare system. The focus of the chapter is predominantly on Western economies as there are specific considerations within developing countries that are beyond the scope of this chapter.

As you read this chapter there are some questions that you may like to consider:

- How can healthcare be delivered at an affordable price without sacrificing quality?
- How do we ensure that healthcare reforms are evidence based?
- How can nurses win the policy argument to ensure there are sufficient nurses of the right type to deliver quality patient care?
- Does the caring ethos of nursing suffer in the drive for cost efficiencies?

The political economy of healthcare

To understand the pressures on health systems it is important to have an understanding of some basic economic concepts. This chapter is not intended to give a full explanation of health economics, just a plain language summary of some of the important issues. For a full explanation of health economics, the reader is referred to Palmer and Ho (2008).

Economics is the study of the efficient allocation of scarce resources in order for people to meet their goals – or to put it another way, it is the study of who gets what (Maddison and Denniss, 2009). The discipline of economics contains many different viewpoints about the way in which efficient allocation can be achieved. Central to economic theory is the notion of opportunity cost. Opportunity cost reflects the fact that resources are scarce and therefore decisions have to be made about how to use them. Whenever you use a resource for one particular purpose, you lose the opportunity to use that resource for another purpose. For example, if you have five dollars and you use it to buy some chocolate, you give up the opportunity to buy fruit with that money. From an overall point of view decisions are said to be efficient if they make at least one person better off without making anyone else worse off. This is known as Pareto efficiency and is presented as a way to make social decisions about resource allocation that are value neutral. Some economists have argued that even if a decision would make some people worse off it would still be a desirable decision if the winners could compensate the losers (Palmer and Ho, 2008). However, in practice policy decisions around resource allocation generally produce winners and uncompensated losers.

In reality decisions about allocating scarce resources are not neutral but are based on values. The wider political context that shapes the economics of healthcare is referred to as the political economy of healthcare. It is described as 'political power (or control) over resource allocation' (Mooney, 2012, p. 15) emphasising the context dependent nature of economic decisions in healthcare. Decisions are shaped by the particular economic ideologies that underpin any analyses and the social and political milieu of the time. Take a different viewpoint and you will arrive at a different conclusion. This means that any economic viewpoint can be critiqued and challenged. It is therefore important to understand the dominant viewpoints that shape the current political economy of healthcare as these underpin healthcare reform strategies.

Neoliberalism

Neoliberalism, also known as economic rationalism or the new right, is the dominant economic viewpoint within Western democracies. It is based on ideas originally put forward by the Scottish economist Adam Smith in 1776 and revived in the 1980s, in which the 'free market' is seen as the best organising principle for the economy. Individuals are seen to act in their own best interests and this creates balance in the market through the mechanisms of competition and supply and demand. Government 'interference' in the free market is therefore seen as undesirable and inefficient (Maddison and Denniss, 2009; Steger and Roy, 2010). The result of this economic viewpoint is deregulation of the market, privatisation of public assets to 'remove inefficiencies', dismantling of trade unions to promote 'labour flexibility', tax cuts for high-income earners and businesses, reduction in public expenditure for social services such as health, welfare and education and the rise of individualism and individual responsibility. Neoliberal policies have led to substantial economic growth in some countries and for some corporations and some individuals. Critics of these policies point to the growing income inequalities between individuals which have become entrenched under neoliberal policies (Benatar, Gill and Bakker, 2011). Income inequality within countries has been shown to be a major source of health inequality (see Wilkinson and Pickett, 2010 for a full discussion of the health effects of income inequality). Neoliberal policies within healthcare manifest in many ways such as the privatisation of health assets including hospitals, the view that health is a commodity rather than a social good, and the transforming of government health providers into commissioning groups.

Globalisation

Globalisation is the application of neoliberal policies in the international arena to allow the free circulation of capital, goods, services and labour across the world. It includes the introduction of free trade agreements with the removal of restrictions and tariffs and the removal of barriers to investment to allow capital accumulation at a global level. It has resulted in the creation of global agencies such as the World Bank, World Trade Organization and the International Monetary Fund to facilitate the conditions required for a world market. Critics of these agencies claim they have promoted the interests of capital and transnational corporations at the expense of the public, social and environment interests of nation states (Stiglitz, 2002; Teeple, 2000). Globalisation impacts on health in a number of ways. For example, it affects the affordability of medicines for developing countries through the protection of patents by trade agreements. It also creates the conditions that allow high levels of migration of health professionals across the globe, particularly from poorer to richer countries which adversely affects the health of developing nations. Additionally, increased movement of people across the world changes the epidemiology of disease transmission. Globalisation also contributes to environmental degradation, particularly in developing countries, which impacts on health outcomes (Palmer and Ho, 2008).

New public management

New public management (NPM) also grew out of neoliberal policies and resulted in a shift in what is required of public service managers. Rather than focusing on service and the public good, managers are now primarily expected to focus on business efficiencies in the *management* of public services. New public management ushered in a world of performance-based management, risk management strategies, strategic plans, cost–benefit analyses, outcomes monitoring, benchmarking, accreditation and efficiency drives (Newman and Lawler, 2009; Steger and Roy, 2010). In healthcare it has resulted in a change of focus for managers from someone who safeguarded patients by acting as advocates and maintaining professional standards to someone who is concerned with efficiencies, targets and budgets (Newman and Lawler, 2009). Patients are now consumers or clients rather than patients, and managers are entrepreneurs rather than health professionals. This can create tensions for nurse managers as they try to balance the competing demands of professional values and responsibilities with the values and focus favoured by NPM (Aiken, 2002).

Reflect 11.1

- As a nurse, your working environment is structured and shaped by the influence of neoliberal policies.
- Try to identify some of the ways this view manifests in the organisation of your working environment and your working conditions.
- Discuss your thoughts on neoliberal policies with a colleague to identify if you have similar or differing views.

What do we spend on healthcare?

In addition to understanding the political economy of healthcare it is also useful to have an overview of the level of spending on healthcare at a country level to help you understand why there is so much pressure on governments and health administrators to reduce healthcare spending. Resources are scarce and spending on health reflects value judgements about the importance of health to individuals within society relative to the importance placed on other public goods such as education, infrastructure and welfare. There are always trade-offs, both within healthcare and between public services, as it is not possible to fund every social good within existing budgets. Even in economies with large proportions of healthcare provided outside the government purse, inequalities within healthcare provision are still evident.

Healthcare spending has been slowly rising in many countries and unless cost containment measures are implemented the level of growth will become unsustainable. Figure 10.1 illustrates this trend for six Organisation for Economic Co-operation and Development (OECD) countries. This upward trend is noticeable in the majority of other OECD countries as well. Although the global economic crisis slowed the growth in healthcare spending to approximately 1 per cent in 2013 compared to 3.8 per cent per annum between 2000 and 2009, predictions are that overall spending will continue to rise slowly in subsequent years (OECD, 2015a).

Gross domestic product (GDP) is used as an indicator of the health of a country's economy. Within the OECD datasets GDP is defined as 'final consumption plus gross capital formation plus net exports. Final consumption of households includes goods and services used by households or the community to satisfy their individual needs. It includes final consumption expenditure of households, general government and non-profit institutions serving households' (OECD, 2015a, p. 166). The proportion of GDP spent on health indicates the 'relative importance of health expenditure in the national economy' (Palmer and Ho, 2008, p. 76). Figure 10.2

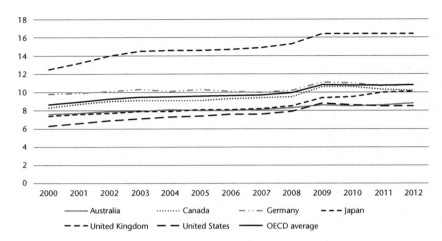

FIGURE 10.1 Growth in healthcare spending (as a percentage of GDP) of selected OECD countries

Data source: https://stats.oecd.org/ - Health expenditure and financing dataset.

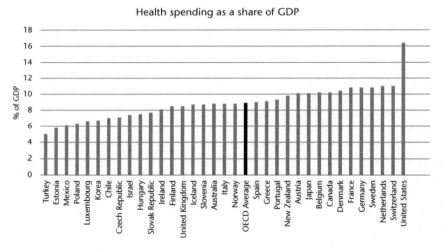

FIGURE 10.2 Proportion of GDP spent on health in 2012 for OECD countries

Data source: https://stats.oecd.org/ - Health expenditure and financing dataset.

shows the proportion of GDP spent by OECD countries on health. These figures include both public and private expenditure. The country with the largest proportion of health spending as a share of GDP is the United States (US) at 16.4 per cent, nearly twice the OECD average of 8.9 per cent.

Another useful statistic is health expenditure per capita, which shows the total public and private expenditures on health as a ratio of total population. To enable comparisons across countries the amounts are converted to US dollars (as the common currency) and adjusted to reflect the purchasing power of different currencies using economy–wide (GDP) purchasing power parities (PPPs). Statistics for 2012 for OECD countries are shown in Figure 10.3. The US spends more than any other country, $8454 per capita, and more than twice as much per person as the OECD average of $3389. Turkey and Mexico spend the least amount per person.

Impact of health spending on life expectancy

You would expect that countries that spend more on health would produce better health outcomes for the population. In general, this is the trend. When you compare life expectancy and healthcare spending as either a proportion of GDP (Figure 10.4) or health spending per capita (Figure 10.5) you see an increase in life expectancy in countries that spend more on health. The US is again an outlier. It spends more on health than any other country and yet this does not translate into a proportional increase in life expectancy. This gives some indication that you can implement efficiencies in the system without affecting health outcomes.

Reflect 11.2

- How much do you consider the cost of care when you are delivering care?
- Do you think there is a mismatch between professional values and the need to implement efficiencies in the health system?

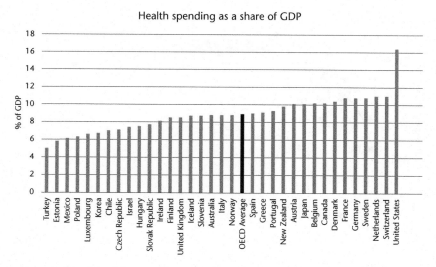

FIGURE 10.3 Total health expenditure per capita expressed in US$ adjusted for PPP (2012 figures)

Data source: https://stats.oecd.org/ – Health expenditure and financing dataset.

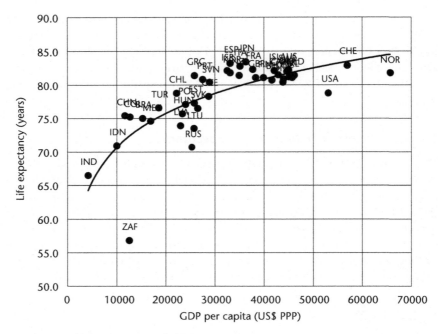

FIGURE 10.4 Life expectancy and GDP per capita

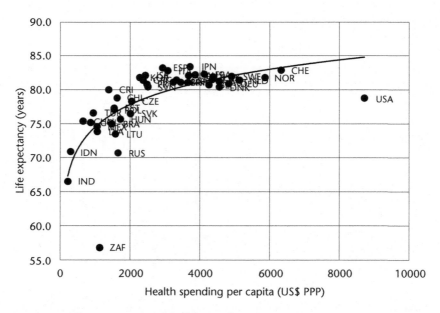

FIGURE 10.5 Life expectancy and health spending per capita

Source: OECD Health Statistics 2015, http://dx.doi.org/10.1787/health-data-en/.

- Read the article by Thompson, Cook and Duschinsky (2014) about nurses' experiences of funding arrangements in nursing homes. Can you relate to the nurses' experiences?
- Should nurses be concerned about the cost of care or should their primary focus be on the provision of quality care? Discuss your views with a colleague.

Economic challenges for the healthcare system

There are many challenges for the healthcare system which impact on both the availability of funding for healthcare, as well as on the cost of providing healthcare. Some of the major challenges include the global economic crisis, the ageing population, the rise of chronic diseases, the ageing healthcare workforce, and healthcare workforce shortages. These challenges are outlined in the following section.

Global economic crisis

The global economic crisis, or global recession, originated in the collapse of the sub-prime mortgage market in the US, and led to the collapse of financial institutions and subsequent bailouts by governments. The crisis initially affected the US and Europe with many countries remaining largely unaffected. However, there has been a flow-on effect to other countries due to globalisation and the interdependency of markets (Nanto, 2009). The economic crisis has had a number of effects including a reduction in credit availability, business contraction, reduction in the value of stocks and currencies, rising unemployment rates, reduced government revenues and the implementation of austerity measures such as reductions in government spending and higher taxes (Nanto, 2009). These effects have not occurred uniformly across countries, with some countries experiencing more difficult times than others (Phillips, 2012).

The global economic crisis affects health systems because governments tend to spend less on health services during times of recession. This may be experienced at the local level as the withdrawal of funding for some services such as community programmes, job redundancies or freezes on filling job vacancies, and amalgamation of departments or services. Recessions increase unemployment and so health professionals, including nurses, are less likely to leave their jobs because their alternative options are limited (Buchan, O'May and Dussault, 2013).

Ageing population

One of the biggest challenges for the healthcare system is the ageing population and the associated increase in healthcare costs for people as they age. Populations are growing in overall size in addition to changing their composition. The world population in 2015 was 7.3 billion, up 1 billion from 2003, and is projected to increase by another billion by 2030 (United Nations, 2015). Life expectancy has also increased across the world, and the population over 60 is the fastest-growing portion of the population. Globally 12 per cent of the population is over 60 and this is predicted to rise at a rate of 3.26 per cent per annum, doubling by 2050. The number of people over 80 years is expected to triple by 2050 (United Nations, 2015). The changing age composition of the population is best illustrated by population pyramids which show the increase in the proportion of older people over time. If you would like to see the population pyramids for your country or explore this further go to the United Nations website (http://esa.un.org/unpd/wpp/Graphs/DemographicProfiles/).

As an example, select the population pyramids for the years 1950, 2015 and projected for 2050 which clearly show the ageing of the population for countries such as Japan, the UK and Australia.

As the population ages there is a rise in healthcare costs primarily due to a rise in care needs. As people live longer with a greater number of healthcare problems their need for health services increases.

Rise of chronic diseases

Chronic, non-communicable diseases now account for the majority of the burden of disease across the world. Chronic diseases cover a range of conditions, but typically they are conditions that cannot be cured but instead need to be managed over a long period of time. Many people have multiple chronic conditions as they tend to stem from the common risk factors of unhealthy eating, excess alcohol, physical inactivity and smoking. The World Health Organization (WHO) (2014) reported that four chronic conditions, namely cardiovascular diseases, cancer, chronic respiratory diseases and diabetes accounted for 82 per cent of chronic disease deaths. These diseases have a significant impact on the demand for healthcare services and healthcare costs as people live with increasing levels of disability from their chronic conditions.

Ageing workforce

In line with the ageing of the population, the workforce is also ageing. This is evident within the nursing workforce where the average age of nurses has been increasing, as well as the proportion of nurses who are over 45. This means that workplaces will have to adapt as older workers may experience a higher level of disability such as back injuries which require more workplace support.

Additionally, older workers are more likely to work part-time and require more flexible working conditions. As these nurses retire it will mean costs for employers to recruit new nurses. An illustration of these changing demographics is given in Figures 10.6 and 10.7 which are based on Australian data and show the change in the average age of nurses between 1995 and 2012 as well as the proportions of nurses in each age category over the same time period. The average age of Australian nurses has continued to rise from 39.3 years in 1995 to 44.6 years in

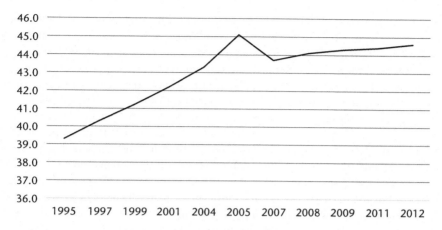

FIGURE 10.6 Average age of Australian nurses 1995–2012

Data source: Australian Institute of Health and Welfare (AIHW)
http://aihw.gov.au/workforce-data/.

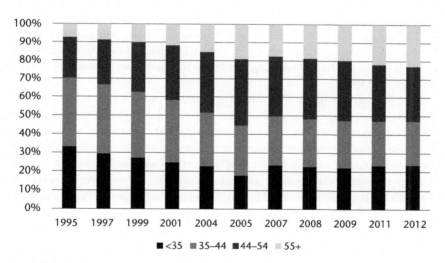

FIGURE 10.7 Proportion of Australian nurses in age groups 1995–2012

Data source: AIHW http://aihw.gov.au/workforce-data/.

2012 although the change between 2007 and 2012 has been minimal. The proportion of nurses who were 45 or over has increased from 30 per cent in 1995 to around 53 per cent in 2012.

Workforce shortages

Health workforce shortages for medicine, nursing and other health professionals have been widely predicted in many countries. This has implications for the healthcare system as workforce shortages impact on the quality of care that can be delivered which will increase healthcare costs. What does it mean to say that there is a nursing shortage? Buchan (2006) argues that the 'nursing shortage' is not easy to define as it may mean different things in different countries at different times. There is wide variability in the supply of nurses between countries. Figure 10.8 shows the number of nurses per 1,000 population in OECD countries. Numbers range from 1.8 nurses per 1,000 population in Turkey to 17.4 nurses per 1,000 population in Switzerland with the OECD average being 9.1 nurses per 1,000 population. However, these figures in themselves do not indicate which countries have a nursing shortage and which don't. For example, Australia, which has 11.5 nurses per 1,000 population, above the OECD average, generally regards itself as having a nursing shortage. Workforce shortages are generally defined by workforce modelling procedures which attempt to identify the supply and demand issues affecting a particular country and then projecting these into the future.

In general, nursing shortages exist when there is a gap between the supply of nurses and the demand for nurses although as Buchan (2006) points out supply may be more to do with a shortage of nurses who are willing to work under the current conditions rather than an actual lack of qualified nurses. Additionally, shortages at the bedside may not be reflective of overall nurse availability, but may be as a result of policy decisions by health services to restrict the number of nurses employed or to fail to supply the type of working conditions that nurses are attracted by (Buchan and Aiken, 2008).

Many countries have predicted nursing shortages into the future. However, the situation is not static as the system responds to predicted shortages by increasing enrolments in nurse education courses, making efforts to increase nurse retention by changing the practice environment or offering incentives to nurses to return to the workforce. The nursing labour supply is cyclical and also responds to broader changes in wage levels, general economic conditions, unemployment levels and the working conditions provided by employers making future workforce numbers

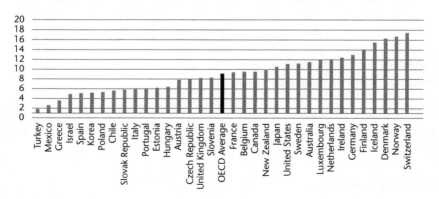

FIGURE 10.8 Nurses per 1,000 population in 2012 or closest year in OECD countries

Data source: OECD Health Statistics 2015 Frequently Requested Data.

hard to predict. For example, in the early 2000s the US was predicting a severe nursing shortage into the future. However, conditions have changed and the US is now predicting a surplus of both registered nurses (RN) (340,000 FTE excess) and licensed practical nurses (LPN) (59,900) into 2025 (US Department of Health and Human Services, 2014).

Healthcare reform

The current political economy of healthcare combined with the economic challenges facing the healthcare system have produced an era of almost continual healthcare reform. Healthcare reform, also known as redesign or restructuring, is a process of changing elements of the health system in order to obtain efficiencies, without compromising access or quality. This may include changes in healthcare delivery, funding, education or coverage. To survive, nurses need to be flexible and proactive in ensuring that they understand any proposed changes and are able to identify the impact on nurses and the quality of patient care. Nurses also need to be able to identify how their ways of working need to change and be able to adapt to these changes. A good example of a proactive response to healthcare reform is the American Academy of Nursing Edge Runner programme which you can explore on their website (www.aannet.org/edgerunners).

Reflect 11.3

• Consider the 'iron triangle' of healthcare reform in Figure 10.9.

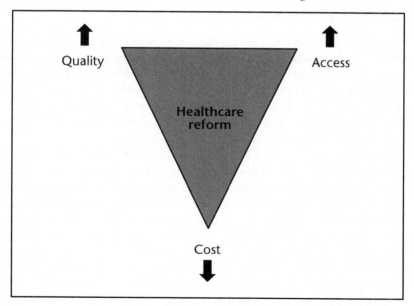

FIGURE 10.9 The iron triangle of healthcare reform

- If the aim of healthcare reform is to decrease costs whilst maintaining or improving quality and access, how can this be done?
- Think of an example from your own life where you have to make this kind of decision. For example, when you go shopping how do you make decisions about what to buy and where to buy it from?
- How would your shopping patterns change if you lived in a city or a country area? Try to see the trade-offs that are made.
- What happens if you add limited time into the mix?

Health workforce reform

Healthcare reform measures often centre on the healthcare workforce, particularly nurses as they are the most expensive item of any health system (Addicott et al., 2015; Behner et al., 1990; Dubois et al., 2006; Needleman et al., 2006; Twigg and Duffield, 2009). Nurses outnumber doctors, the second-largest health professional group, at a rate of three to one in Australia – 214,321 nurses compared to 73,980 doctors (Health Workforce Australia, 2013): four to one in the United States – 3,528,000 nurses compared to 806,000 doctors (Deloitte Centre for Health Solutions, 2012): and three to one in the United Kingdom – 347,944 nurses compared to 110,957 doctors (Health and Social Care Information Centre, 2013). Workforce reform usually involves decreasing the number of staff working, changing the skill-mix of staff through staff substitution or changing how care is delivered, for example, moving more care into the community.

Impact of reducing the number of nurses

One area of health workforce reform that has received a lot of attention in the literature is the relationship between nurse–patient ratios and patient and nurse outcomes. Reducing the overall numbers of nurses working in hospitals has been one cost-cutting measure that has been frequently used by health services. However, research indicates that reducing nurse staffing numbers has a detrimental effect on patient outcomes and may in fact end up costing more due to an increase in adverse events and the associated costs of these (Twigg et al., 2015).

Landmark studies by Needleman et al. (2001, 2002) and Aiken et al. (2001, 2002) have paved the way for a landslide of studies into the relationship between nurse staffing levels and patient and nurse outcomes across many countries and settings. The main patient outcomes that have been studied are mortality, central nervous system complications, deep vein thrombosis, pressure ulcers, upper gastrointestinal bleeding, hospital-acquired pneumonia, hospital-acquired sepsis, shock/cardiac arrest, urinary tract infection, failure to rescue, metabolic derangement, pulmonary failure, wound infections, medication errors, falls, care not done, patient and nurse perception of the quality of care and length of stay. The main nurse variables that have been studied are job satisfaction, burnout, turnover, intention to leave, satisfaction with the practice environment, and exposure to violence.

There have been a number of systematic reviews of the literature on nurse staffing and patient outcomes. Of particular note is a systematic review and meta-analysis conducted by Kane *et al.* (2007). They reviewed 28 studies published between 1990 and 2006 and found that increased RN staffing was associated with lower hospital-related mortality in intensive care, surgical and medical patients, lower hospital-acquired pneumonia, unplanned extubation, respiratory failure and cardiac arrest in ICUs and a lower risk of failure to rescue in surgical patients. They also found a significant reduction in length of stay for surgical patients and those in ICUs when RN staffing was increased.

In 2013 Brennan *et al.* published a systematic review of reviews of nurse staffing and patient outcomes and identified eight systematic reviews and 21 literature reviews around the topic highlighting how far the science has progressed. The authors reported that there was evidence of an association between nurse staffing and some patient outcomes indicating an overall trend towards improved outcomes when staffing levels were improved. However, they also identified that review authors reported inconsistencies in the results of the primary studies leading to an inability to clearly define optimum staffing levels. This is why there are currently no evidence based staffing guidelines that recommend specific nurse to patient ratios as studies do not provide a consistent picture that can be used to determine a specific ratio.

Despite these numerous studies and reviews healthcare managers and policy-makers do not readily accept the conclusions or recommendations of these studies which usually include increasing staffing levels and improving the nursing skill-mix. This highlights the limitations of studies that are based on associations which cannot attribute causality. More longitudinal studies which more precisely measure the nurse and patient variables are needed to drive an evidence based practice change and to influence policy-makers and managers.

Impact of changing the skill-mix

Another way to reduce the cost of the healthcare workforce is to change the skill-mix of staff. This generally means substituting one type or level of staff for another. Within the nursing workforce this occurs in three main ways.

The first is enabling nurses to practice at an advanced level, often taking on some responsibilities traditionally seen as part of the medical role.

The second is to substitute assistants in nursing for registered nursing staff to perform 'basic care duties' that don't require the level of skill that registered staff can offer.

The third is to change the balance of the nursing staff when there is more than one level of nurse. For example, Australia and the US both have more than one level of licensed or registered nurse. Skill-mix can be changed by having fewer registered nurses and more second-tier nurses such as enrolled nurses or licensed practical nurses. Changing the skill-mix has been found to adversely impact patient outcomes, with studies showing that a poorer skill-mix is associated with increased adverse outcomes for patients (Blegen *et al.*, 1998; Needleman *et al.*, 2002; Roche *et al.*, 2012; Sovie and Jawad, 2001; Thungjaroenkul *et al.*, 2007; Tourangeau *et al.*, 2002; Twigg *et al.*, 2011).

Advanced nursing roles

Nurses working in extended nursing roles are generally termed advanced practice nurses although the actual titles may vary across settings (Duffield *et al.*, 2009). Advanced practice roles lend themselves to research studies as it is relatively easy to randomly assign patients to receive care by advanced practice nurses. A recent systematic review of nurse practitioners and clinical nurse specialists identified 43 randomised controlled trials evaluating the cost-effectiveness of these roles (Donald *et al.* 2014). Results from studies of advanced nursing roles report favourable results with advanced practice nurses delivering cost-effective quality care (Newhouse, 2011).

Assistants in nursing

Unregulated nursing support roles are ubiquitous in the healthcare system. These health workers may be known as assistants in nursing, nursing aides, healthcare assistants, certified nursing assistant, unlicensed assistive personnel, healthcare support worker, and nursing auxiliaries. Their use has increased in recent times as they are seen as a cheaper option than licensed or registered nurses, who can deliver basic nursing care not requiring the skills of highly trained nurses. Nurses are not necessarily happy with this move which is often seen as underpinning an agenda to reverse nurses' professionalisation drive (Aiken, Clarke and Sloane, 2000). A high percentage of unskilled workers have been linked to numerous negative patient outcomes (Griffiths *et al.*, 2016; Kane *et al.*, 2007; Needleman *et al.*, 2011; Roche *et al.*, 2012; Spilsbury and Meyer, 2005).

Reflect 11.4

- Read chapter 23 in Volume 3 of the Francis (2013) report into the Mid Staffordshire NHS Foundation Trust which focuses on nursing.
- Consider what went wrong. Do you agree that it was a lack of compassion that led to the adverse outcomes for patients or was it to do with the structure of the environment such as low staffing numbers and poor skill-mix that created these issues?
- Read Paley (2014) and Traynor's (2014) critiques of the Francis recommendations.
- What would you do if you were in an environment with low staffing numbers, depleted skill-mix and a practice environment that wasn't very positive?
- How do you think you would behave?
- How would you go about changing this?

Impact of changing how care is delivered

Care is increasingly moving into the community and out of institutions as this is seen as both a cheaper and more preferable way of delivering care. This change is also driven by the increasing health literacy of the population, changes in consumer expectations and changes in technology which make community care more attractive and attainable. For example, there has been an increase in technologies which allow people to be in control of their care at home. Health workers need to be able to work in multidisciplinary teams and provide integrated care across traditional care sector boundaries. This will change the way in which nurses work. It also changes the demand for nurses, for example, a recent report suggests that practice nurses or community matrons could undertake aspects of care traditionally provided by GPs to deliver more cost-effective care (Ewbank, Hitchcock and Sasse, 2016).

Are nurses a cost or a saving?

To achieve healthcare reform that includes the employment of appropriate levels of nursing staff, along with the right skill-mix, evidence on the cost-effectiveness of nurse staffing strategies is needed. This is a two-step process. First you need to provide evidence that increasing the number of nursing staff or improving the skill-mix by increasing the proportion of registered nurses decreases adverse patient outcomes and/or reduces patients' length of stay. The second step is to show that the cost of employing more nurses is less than the costs incurred from the increased adverse patient outcomes or longer lengths of stay that would have occurred if you hadn't improved the staffing levels/skill-mix. If you can show both a benefit, in terms of improved patient outcomes, and a cost saving, then increasing nurse staffing levels can be said to be a cost-effective intervention.

In the last ten years there have been seven literature reviews that have assessed the evidence on economic evaluations of nurse staffing and/or nurse skill-mix. The first was in 2004 and the latest was in 2015. A list of the reviews and the number of articles they assessed is given in Table 10.1.

TABLE 10.1 Literature reviews of economic evaluations of nurse staffing

	Years covered	Number of economic articles reviewed
Lang et al. (2004)	1980–2003	9
Spetz (2005)	No dates given	5
Thungjaroenkul et al. (2007)	1990–2006	17
Unruh (2008)	1980–2006	12
Goryakin et al. (2011)	1989–2009	17
Shekelle (2013)	2009–2012	4
Twigg et al. (2015)	No date limits	9

Although many individual studies included in the reviews found that improving nurse staffing or nurse skill-mix was a cost-effective intervention for improving patient outcomes, all of these reviews concluded that it was not possible to assess overall whether or not adding additional nurses or changing the skill-mix was a cost-effective intervention for improving patient outcomes. The main reason for this was that the underlying evidence studies, that is, the studies that assessed whether or not increasing the level of nurse staffing or improving the skill-mix reduced adverse patient outcomes or decreased patient length of stay, were not of sufficient quality to be able to state conclusively that improving nurse staffing had a beneficial effect on patient outcomes. They specifically identified the lack of intervention studies in this area as being a major barrier to allowing the cost-effectiveness of nurse staffing to be assessed. Other issues identified were the lack of standardised methods used in the studies which meant that different studies were difficult to compare as they measured different things. They also identified the mixed study results in that some studies reported nurses saved money, while others found that they cost money, making it difficult to draw any conclusions about the overall cost-effectiveness of nurse staffing initiatives.

If nurses are to win the argument for improving staffing levels, then one area that requires attention is improving the quality of the evidence. Better-quality evidence may help to reduce the variation in results, particularly if studies are conducted using a set of standardised guidelines. Additionally, more evidence is needed. There are a large number of studies that have assessed the impact of nurse staffing levels and skill-mix on patient outcomes. There are relatively few studies that have investigated the cost-effectiveness of nurse staffing changes.

The overall conclusion that can be drawn from these reviews is that nurse staffing levels and nursing skill-mix are important variables for improving the quality of patient care; however, this improvement comes at a cost. This means that it is up to society to determine whether or not they are willing to pay for this. From a hospital perspective it may be that improving nurse staffing is not cost-effective but from a societal perspective it is. It is also important to consider the effect on nurses from poor staffing levels and to include the cost of nurse turnover in economic studies. Additionally, the perception of poor-quality care being delivered by too few stressed nurses is an intangible cost that is often only counted when there are significant failures in care such as occurred in the Mid Staffordshire NHS Foundation Trust.

Summary

Nurses are aware of and know that these bigger economic issues impact on daily nursing practice. Your ability to practise nursing is enabled or constrained by the resources you have available. Perhaps the hospital or community service you work for decides to put a freeze on filling staff vacancies and you find yourself looking after more patients each shift because there are not enough nurses available. Or maybe your hospital implements nursing assistants and you find yourself working for the first time with another group and you have to develop new ways of delivering care. Or perhaps your hospital has a funding cut and some advanced nursing roles are no longer funded. All healthcare reforms will impact on your ability as a nurse to give quality patient care but not necessarily in a negative way. The important point is to pay attention to the reform going on around you and try to understand the impact it will have on you and the people you care for. If you think that something will have an adverse impact on patients, you need to be able to produce evidence for this and also be able to present this to policy-makers and healthcare managers.

Healthcare reforms are inevitable. Nurses can influence the debate over which reforms will be implemented by becoming aware of the 'big picture' issues that drive changes in the healthcare system, by researching and defining the nursing contribution to quality patient care, and by articulating credible policy options to governments and administrators. Nurses can also become proactive by collectively asking the question – how can we maintain good patient outcomes and reduce the cost of nursing services? By seeking answers to this question nurses can become innovators in healthcare reform rather than passive observers of continual change implemented by others.

References

Addicott, R, Maguire, D, Honeyman, M & Jabbal, J (2015) *Workforce Planning in the NHS.* London: The Kings Fund.

Aiken, LH (2002) Superior outcomes for magnet hospitals: the evidence base. In *Magnet Hospitals Revisited: Attraction and Retention of Professional Nurses,* ed. ML McClure & AS Hinshaw. Washington, DC: American Nurse Publishing, pp. 61–79.

Aiken, LH, Clarke, SP & Sloane DM (2000) Hospital restructuring: does it adversely affect care and outcomes. *Journal of Nursing Administration,* vol. 30, pp. 457–465.

Aiken, LH, Clarke, SP, Sloane, DM, Sochalski, JA, Busse, R, Clarke, H, Giovannetti, P, Hunt, J, Rafferty, AM & Shamian, J (2001) Nurses' reports on hospital care in five countries. *Health Affairs,* vol. 20, pp. 43–53.

Aiken, LH, Clarke, SP, Sloane, DM, Sochalski, JA & Silber, JH (2002) Hospital nurse staffing and patient mortality, nurse burnout and job dissatisfaction. *Journal of the American Medical Association,* vol. 288, pp. 1987–1993.

Behner, KG, Fogg, LF, Fournier, LC, Frankenbach, JT & Robertson, SB (1990) Nursing resource management: analysing the relationship between costs and quality in staffing decisions. *Health Care Management Review,* vol. 15, pp. 63–71.

Benatar, SR, Gill, S & Bakker, I (2011) Global health and the global economic crisis. *American Journal of Public Health,* vol. 101, no. 4, pp. 646–653.

Blegen, MA, Goode, CJ & Reed, L (1998) Nurse staffing and patient outcomes. *Nursing Research,* vol. 47, no. 1, pp. 43–50.

Brennan, CW, Daly, BJ & Jones, KR (2013) State of the science: the relationship between nurse staffing and patient outcomes. *Western Journal of Nursing Research,* vol. 35, pp. 760–794.

Buchan, J (2006) Evidence of nursing shortages or a shortage of evidence? *Journal of Advanced Nursing,* vol. 56, no. 5, pp. 457–458.

Buchan, J & Aiken, L (2008) Solving nursing shortages: a common priority. *Journal of Clinical Nursing*, vol. 17, no. 24, pp. 3262–3268.

Buchan, J, O'May, F & Dussault, G (2013) Nursing workforce policy and the economic crisis: a global overview. *Journal of Nursing Scholarship*, vol. 45, no. 3, pp. 298–307.

Clarke, SP (2013) Healthcare reform in 2013: enduring and universal challenges. *Nursing Management*, vol. 44, no. 3, pp. 45–47.

Deloitte Centre for Health Solutions (2012) *Issues Brief: The New Health Care Workforce: Looking around the Corner to Future Talent Management.* Washington, DC: Deloitte.

Donald, F, Kilpatrick, K, Reid, K, Carter, N, Martin-Misener, R, Bryant-Lukosius, D, Harbman, P, Kaasalainen, S, Marshall, DA, Charbonneau-Smith, R, Donald, EE, Lloyd, M, Wickson-Griffiths, A, Yost, J, Baxter, P, Sangster-Gormley, E, Hubley, P, Laflamme, C, Campbell-Yeo, M, Price, S, Boyko, J & DiCenso, A (2014) A systematic review of the cost-effectiveness of nurse practitioners and clinical nurse specialists: what is the quality of the evidence? *Nursing Research and Practice.* doi: 10.1155/2014/896587/.

Dubois, C, McKee, M & Rechel, B (2006) Critical challenges facing the health care workforce in Europe. In *The Healthcare Workforce in Europe: Learning from Experience*, ed. B Rechel, C Dubois & M McKee. Trowbridge: European Observatory on Health Systems and Policies, pp. 1–18.

Duffield, C, Gardner, G, Chang, AM & Catling-Paull, C (2009) Advanced nursing practice: a global perspective. *Collegian*, vol. 16, pp. 55–62.

Ewbank, L, Hitchcock, A & Sasse, T (2016) *Who Cares? The Future of General Practice.* London: Reform Research Trust.

Francis, R (2013) *Report of the Mid Staffordshire NHS Foundation Trust Public Inquiry*, Volume 3: *Present and Future, Annexes.* London: The Stationery Office.

Goryakin, Y, Griffiths, P & Maben, J (2011) Economic evaluation of nurse staffing and nurse substitution in health care: a scoping review. *International Journal of Nursing Studies*, vol. 48, pp. 501–512.

Griffiths, P, Ball, J, Murrells, T, Jones, S & Rafferty, A (2016) Registered nurse, healthcare support worker, medical staffing levels and mortality in English hospital trusts: a cross-sectional study. *BMJ Open*, vol. 6, pp. 1–7.

Health and Social Care Information Centre (2013) *NHS Workforce Statistics, September 2013: Provisional Statistics.* Leeds: Health and Social Care Information Centre.

Health Workforce Australia (2013) *Australia's Health Workforce Series: Health Workforce by Numbers.* Adelaide: Health Workforce Australia.

Kane, RL, Shamliyan, TA, Mueller, C, Duval, S & Wilt, TJ (2007) The association of registered nurse staffing levels and patient outcomes. *Medical Care*, vol. 45, pp. 1195–1203.

Lang, TA, Hodge, M, Olson, V, Romano, PS & Kravitz, R (2004) Nurse-patient ratios: a systematic review on the effects of nurse staffing on patient, nurse employee, and hospital outcomes. *Journal of Nursing Administration*, vol. 34, pp. 326–337.

Maddison, S and Denniss, R (2009) *An Introduction to Australian Public Policy: Theory and Practice.* Port Melbourne: Cambridge University Press.

Mooney, G (2012) *Health of Nations: Toward a New Political Economy.* London: Zed Books.

Nanto, DK (2009) *The Global Financial Crisis: Analysis and Policy Implications.* Washington, DC: Congressional Research Service.

Needleman, J, Buerhaus, P, Mattke, S, Stewart, M & Zelevinsky, K (2001) *Nurse Staffing and Patient Outcomes in Hospitals: Final Report for Health Resources Services Administration.* Boston, MA: Harvard School of Public Health.

Needleman, J, Buerhaus, P, Mattke, S, Stewart, M & Zelevinsky, K (2002) Nurse staffing levels and the quality of care in hospitals. *New England Journal of Medicine*, vol. 346, pp. 1715–1722.

Needleman, J, Buerhaus, PI, Stewart, M, Zelevinsky, K & Mattke, S (2006) Nurse staffing in hospitals: is there a business case for quality? *Health Affairs*, vol. 25, pp. 204–211.

Needleman, J, Buerhaus, P, Pankratz, VS, Leibson, CL, Stevens, SR, & Harris, M (2011) Nurse staffing and inpatient hospital mortality. *New England Journal of Medicine*, vol. 364, no. 11, pp. 1037–1045.

Newhouse, RP, Stanik-Hutt, J, White, KM, Johantgen, M, Bass, EB, Zangaro, G, Wilson, RF, Fountain, L, Stwinwachs, DM, Heindel, L & Weiner, JP (2011) Advanced practice nurse outcomes 1990–2008: a systematic review. *Nursing Economics*, vol. 29, no. 5, pp. 230–250.

Newman, S & Lawler, J (2009) Managing health care under new public management: a Sisyphean challenge for nursing. *Journal of Sociology*, vol. 45, no. 4, pp. 419–432.

OECD (2015a) *Focus on Health Spending: OECD Health Statistics 2015*. Paris: OECD Publishing.

OECD (2015b) *Health at a Glance 2015: OECD Indicators*. Paris: OECD Publishing.

Paley, J (2014) Cognition and the compassion deficit: the social psychology of helping behaviour in nursing. *Nursing Philosophy*, vol. 15, pp. 274–287.

Palmer, GR & Ho, MT (2008) *Health Economics: A Critical and Global Analysis*. Basingstoke: Palgrave Macmillan.

Phillips, N (2012) A 'global' economic crisis?' *Political Insight*, vol. 3, no. 3, pp. 24–27.

Roche, M, Duffield, C, Aisbett, C, Diers, D & Stasa, H (2012) Nursing work directions in Australia: Does evidence drive the policy? *Collegian*, vol. 19, no. 4, pp. 231–238.

Shekelle, PG (2013) Nurse-patient ratios as a patient safety strategy: a systematic review. *Annals of Internal Medicine*, vol. 158, pp. 404–410.

Sovie, MD & Jawad, AF (2001) Hospital restructuring and its impact on outcomes. *Journal of Nursing Administration*, vol. 31, no. 12, pp. 588–600.

Spetz, J (2005) The cost and cost-effectiveness of nursing services in health care. *Nursing Outlook*, vol. 53, pp. 305–309.

Spilsbury, K & Meyer, J (2005) Making claims on nursing work: Exploring the work of healthcare assistants and the implications for registered nurses' roles. *Journal of Research in Nursing*, vol. 10, no.1, pp. 65–83.

Steger, MB & Roy, RK (2010) *Neoliberalism*. Oxford: Oxford University Press.

Stiglitz, JE (2002) *Globalisation and its Discontents*. London: Penguin.

Teeple, G (2000) What is globalisation? In *Globalisation and its Discontents*, ed. S MacBride & J Wiseman. Basingstoke: Palgrave MacMillan, pp. 9–23.

Thompson, J, Cook, G & Duschinsky, R (2014) 'I feel like a salesperson': the effect of multiple-source care funding on the experiences and views of nursing home nurses in England. *Nursing Inquiry*, vol. 22, no. 2, pp. 168–177.

Thungjaroenkul, P, Cummings, GG & Embleton, A (2007) The impact of nurse staffing on hospital costs and patient length of stay: a systematic review. *Nursing Economics*, vol. 25, pp. 255–265.

Tourangeau, AE, Giovanetti, P, Tu, JV & Wood, M (2002) Nursing-related determinants of 30-Day mortality for hospitalized patients. *Canadian Journal of Nursing Research*, vol. 33, no. 4, pp. 71–88

Traynor, M (2014) Caring after Francis: moral failure in nursing reconsidered. *Journal of Research in Nursing*, vol. 19, no. 7–8, pp. 546–556.

Twigg, D and Duffield, C (2009) A review of workload measures: a context for a new staffing methodology in Western Australia. *International Journal of Nursing Studies*, vol. 46, pp. 131–139.

Twigg, D, Duffield, C, Bremner, A, Rapley, P & Finn, J (2011) The impact of the nursing hours per patient day (NHPPD) staffing method on patient outcomes: A retrospective analysis of patient and staffing data. *International Journal of Nursing Studies*, vol. 48, pp. 540–548.

Twigg, DE, Myers, H, Duffield, C, Giles, M & Evans, G (2015) Is there an economic case for investing in nursing care: what does the literature tell us? *Journal of Advanced Nursing*, vol. 71, no. 5, pp. 975–990.

United Nations (2015) *World Population Prospects: Key Findings and Advance Tables*. New York: United Nations.

Unruh, L (2008) Nurse staffing and patient, nurse, and financial outcomes. *American Journal of Nursing*, vol. 108, pp. 62–71.

US Department of Health and Human Services, Health Resources and Services Administration, National Center for Health Workforce Analysis (2014) *The Future of the Nursing Workforce: National- and State-Level Projections, 2012–2025*. Rockville, MD: US Department of Health and Human Services.

Wilkinson, R and Pickett, K (2010) *The Spirit Level: Why Equality is Better for Everyone*. London: Penguin.

World Health Organization (2014) *Global Status Report on Non-Communicable Diseases 2014*. Geneva: World Health Organization.

11

POLITICAL AND POLICY INFLUENCES ON HEALTH CARE

Are nurses political and do they need to be?

John S.G. Wells and Jennifer Cunningham

Why this chapter is important

Nurses have a tendency to be 'apolitical' in terms of engagement with politics and policy as they get focused on the day-to-day challenges of practice. However, nurses' work in terms of what they do and how they do it is largely framed and shaped by political decisions and contexts (Goodman, 2016). This chapter considers why nurses should be involved in politics and describes and discusses the forces that constrain and shape the political responses of nurses and the nursing profession to politics and change in order to encourage the nurse to reflect on the political process and the degree to which they are currently, and should be in the future, politically engaged with current and future issues that will shape their practice.

Chapter trigger question: How does the nursing profession engage with politics and to what degree does it have the capacity to do so?

Key words: political action, capacity and training to be political, constraints, current and future issues for the nursing profession

---

Introduction

In 1985 a UK nurse and journalist, Jane Salvage, wrote an influential book entitled *The Politics of Nursing* (1985). In it she bemoaned a political passivity which she perceived within the British nursing profession and called upon it to 'wake up and get out from under'. Her call was subsequently taken up by many writers on nursing to promote a greater political engagement by the profession (Goodman, 2016; Twibell *et al.*, 2012; Austin *et al.*, 2007).

The degree to which this call to political action has been successful forms the subject of this chapter, which examines the question 'are nurses political and do they need to be?' At first sight the question may seem naïve for of course nurses, as citizens, are political beings with a self-interest as to how society is organised and as such they often, as individuals, take part in the political process. In this regard they act politically on an individual basis. However, nurses as part of the profession of *nursing* do not in most countries have a reputation for being significantly politically active. This is despite the fact that throughout its modern history nursing has been affected by politics in terms of how the profession is maintained and structured as part of the wider political discussion on how society should organise its health care, particularly as this relates to resourcing (Wells and White, 2014). In addition, nurses in their everyday practice are often in the frontline as both witnesses and managers of the consequences of a range of social and political injustices (Stuckler and Basu, 2013). In this context, the very concept of nursing has been called into question within the political arena on foot of a series of scandals in a number of countries involving an apparent loss of compassion for patients within the profession in nurses' day-to-day practice (Francis, 2013; Health Information and Quality Authority, 2013).

The second part of the question, 'should nurses be political?' in the light of what we have said in relation to the first, would appear easy to answer – yes. However, as we shall discover, this is not a question so much of *should* but rather of *capacity* to act politically and the *nature* of that political action. This chapter explores these issues through a consideration of some of the historical legacies of the nursing profession and how they empower and constrain both nurses and the wider profession to act politically. It then goes on to explore the nature of policy and how this can impact on nursing at an individual level and at an organisational level through an exploration of some of the recent and current challenges facing the profession in many countries.

Political and policy influences in nursing

Nurses in nearly all countries comprise by far the biggest professional group within health services, often accounting for half of the total workforce and work most closely with patients on a day-to-day basis of all compared to all other health professions (Kunaviktikul, 2014). As an occupational group their sheer size and the nature of their relationship to patients means that they are often the most affected professional group in relation to political and policy developments in health care. It is therefore important that they both understand and engage with the political structures and processes in their respective countries. Furthermore, as Michael Lipsky (1980) on Street Level bureaucracy indicates, nurses, because of their pivotal one-to-one relationship with patients, often occupy a powerful agency position in determining whether government health policies are successful at the 'felt' end of the patient experience and can influence patients' views on the politics of health care (Wells, 2004).

There are three political agencies at national level that directly influence nursing in Western democratic societies. These are the executive or government (including the civil service); the legislature, consisting of representatives drawn largely from party political groups and directly elected by a citizen electorate; and the judiciary, which interprets and pronounces on the law as it is applied to health care and nursing practice. At local level, there is usually some form of local executive and assembly supported by a local group of administrators often responsible for running social care related services that interface with health care and nurses.

At the next level of political and policy influence are trades unions – not only those that represent nurses but also those that represent groups alongside whom nurses work. In addition to these labour representative organisations, there are lobby and advocacy groups (these groups are either associated with particular causes or clinical conditions that are associated with the health care industry in the broadest sense). Finally, there is the media (principally TV and newspapers but increasingly social media).

These agencies all influence the day-to-day practice of nurses with the national political agencies defining nurses' working conditions, pay and what they are allowed to do in practice. However, perhaps the most powerful in terms of influence is the media, for often poor practice in nursing has come to light not because nurses have reported it but because the media has exposed it (Wells and White, 2014). As such the media plays a significant part in shaping the public and political perceptions of nurses and the nursing profession and it is these perceptions that often lead the executive and legislature to act in relation to health and nursing care.

Despite the clear importance of these political agencies in shaping both the context of practice and the direct experience and rewards available for nursing work, nurses and nursing appears resistant to taking on an overt lead in health care politics (Oestberg, 2013) despite calls by major international health care agencies to do so (WHO, 2002). So we need to explore what lies at the heart of this resistance. Most recently, the UK All Party Parliamentary Group on Global Health (2016) stated the following:

> There is an urgent need globally to raise the profile of nursing and enable nurses to work to their full potential if countries are to achieve universal health coverage. Nursing can and must take the lead on these issues but cannot achieve them without the support of politicians, policy makers and non-nursing health leaders.
>
> (All Party Parliamentary Group on Global Health, 2016, p. 7).

However, despite this 'editorialising call to arms' on the part of nurses to become more 'political', the report illustrates in both its editorial and in its recommendations a common unsaid precept – a lack of confidence in nursing being able to take the lead without the underpinning support of others – something which is articulated, for example, in relation to the political power of the medical profession. Thus the

All Party Parliamentary Group on Global Health (2016, p. 7) goes on to call for convening of,

> a high level global summit on nursing aimed at political and health leaders outside nursing, to raise awareness of the opportunities and potential of nursing, create political commitment, and establish a process for supporting development.

Thus, based on this statement, nursing should be more politically active, but within limits imposed by other political actors.

Reflect 12.1

- Would you describe yourself as politically aware?
- Think about the last time you were interested in a political debate or discussion; what was it about the issue that raised your interest?
- Are there any issues in your current working environment that you would describe as having a 'political' dimension?
- How empowered do you feel to effect change in your current working environment?
- Who has the most power to effect change and why?

The legacy of nursing's origins and how they serve to constrain a 'political challenging' nursing

Clarke (1999) points to a tendency amongst nurses not to reference their day-to-day work to political and/or social systems. In this sense it may be argued that there is an innate social conservatism within nursing which militates against the profession challenging the construction of society, even when that construction demonstrably impacts on the health of the people for whom nurses care (Mossé *et al.*, 2011). This characteristic of the nursing profession as a whole has its roots in its early history, first in terms of the control exercised over nursing by the religious orders, for example in Germany and Ireland (Wells and Bergin, 2016; Foth *et al.*, 2014) and, in particular, in the work at St Thomas' Hospital in London and the international dominance of Florence Nightingale and her system of nursing with its emphasis on a nursing professionalism characterised as a vocational calling differentiated from other forms of work through an ethos of self-sacrifice and acceptance of hierarchy and authority (Godden, 2005). As such, a profession which emphasises a deference to authority does, by its nature, place a great emphasis on system stability (for without such how can hierarchical based authority operate effectively?) and thereby dislikes system challenge and change.

This, of course, is deeply ironic when one considers that Nightingale in her early days at Scutari Hospital during the Crimean War challenged the traditional order of military care and on her subsequent return to the UK, was politically highly active in establishing a better service of military medical care, promoted public health improvements for the poor and fought to establish a professional training for nurses (McDonald, 2006). However, she always, at the end of the day, emphasised her own authority of nurses when she was faced with challenge to her own system, even in the Crimea (Wells and Bergin, 2016), which became the abiding feature of her successor in their approach to nursing leadership and therefore subsequently ensured that nursing would not attempt to change society but rather reflect that which was socially and politically acceptable.

This tradition of social and political conservatism is further reinforced through the organisation of entry to and regulation of the profession through state licensure to practise. The first such licence registration system was introduced in 1891 in Cape Colony, South Africa; this was followed in 1901 by New Zealand regulating those who could be nurses with the introduction of a national licensure system through registration. A national registration system was introduced in the UK in 1919. National licensing empowers the state not only to decide who is suitable to enter the profession of nursing but also to control the curriculum and thereby ensure that nurse education is broadly reflective of the prevailing political ethos. The most overt example of this perhaps was the nursing curriculum established in Nazi Germany in 1938 with its emphasis on racial values as the most significant element in informing nursing practice (Foth *et al.*, 2014).

It is notable that within the context of what is and what is not approved of in terms of inclusion in nursing curriculum, as set by state licensing bodies, skills training in relation to policy and political engagement is not featured as a significant component of education. And yet many research studies have highlighted that nurses' lack of political engagement, as nurses themselves report, derives from feeling unprepared by their training to engage (Taft, 2008; Arabi *et al.*, 2014).

Nursing as part of the establishment

The term 'the establishment' denotes the interface of official centres of power within society with the matrix of political and social relations through which power is defined and exercised; usually to maintain and defend an established status quo of social relations and practices. Nursing as a profession (as opposed to individual nurses) tends to conform to the prevailing views of 'the establishment', which sets the parameters in which the profession is allowed to engage and act politically (as the recent All Party Parliamentary Group on Global Health report [2016] illustrates). Indeed, as its history shows, the profession of nursing is in effect a part of 'the establishment'.

The manifestations of being part of the 'establishment' with regards to centres of power and social relations includes the fact that in most jurisdictions in the Western world there is a senior civil servant position reserved for a nurse in health ministries, for example the Chief Nurse for England in the United Kingdom and the Chief Nurse in Ireland – both ministerial advisers in their respective Departments of Health. In addition to this high level political representation, nurses' trades unions tend to adopt the characteristics and attitudes of professional associations, for example the Royal College of Nursing in the UK, where the approach to industrial relations engagement with both government and health services' management tends to look for consensus, with the threat of strike action very rarely invoked and not vigorously pursued. And finally, with nurse education now largely established within a university setting, nurses are enabled to build social relations with other social and political elites as they rise through the education process, thereby ensuring that they take on the values of those elites as promoted through a university education.

As a result of being embedded with 'the establishment' the nursing profession often tends to either support or adjust to the prevailing political constructs and usually refrains from vigorously and proactively promoting an alternative perspective even when prevailing political constructs directly impact (sometimes negatively) on the position of the profession as a whole. In his seminal work *One-Dimensional Man*, published in 1964, Herbert Marcuse referred to the flattening of discourse, imagination, culture and politics into the perspective of the dominant order, where there is a loss of a gap between two dimensions – if you like, the critique – between what is and the alternatives. Some examples from very recent history will illustrate this proposition.

Reforming nurse management and care as a political project – the case of the United Kingdom

During the 1980s and 1990s the United Kingdom saw a series of profound changes in the organisation of health care and, most profoundly for the nursing profession. The significant restructuring of the managerial role of nurses within the hospital sector diminished the nursing 'voice' to an advisory one in determining clinical priorities and how they should be addressed within services (Wells, 1999). In effect nursing management was removed from the executive position it had traditionally occupied (Keen and Malby, 1992). This was a result of the confluence of two reports on the National Health Service (NHS) in the mid-1980s – the Griffiths Report (1983) and a report on reorganising the NHS by an American economist, Alain Enthoven (1985), for the Nuffield Trust, which heralded the introduction of the hospital Trust movement and the establishment of market forces within health care in the UK.

There was professional opposition to these changes within the NHS. What is notable, however, was that this was led by the British Medical Association, on behalf of doctors, rather than the RCN, who voiced their concerns but did not engage in outright opposition to the downgrading of the nursing voice in management. The result was that medicine secured a much stronger voice within the proposed management structures of the new Trust hospitals through the establishment of the post of 'Clinical Director' at an Executive Board level, with defined powers, compared to nursing.

Ireland

The second example relates to Ireland and the changes that were initiated within the Irish health care system as a result of the 2008 economic crisis. Between 2009 and 2013 the Irish government introduced severe cuts to the health service budget which resulted in a draconian impact on nurses (as the biggest staff cost in the health service) and the nursing profession. These cuts included an employment moratorium relating to the replacement of vacancies (resulting in a fall of nurses employed in the health service of over 5,000 between 2009 and 2013; that is a reduction of 13 per cent in the nursing workforce); an immediate cut to the number of training places available for undergraduate nursing; accumulated salary cuts amounting to pay being 25 per cent less than commensurate salary grades of other health professionals; increased working hours from 37 to 39 per week and an annual leave reduction of two days and incentivised early retirement schemes resulting in the loss of experience and expertise to the profession (Wells and White, 2014).

Yet despite the severity of the impact on nursing and whilst the nursing trades unions (the Irish Nurses and Midwives Organisation and the Psychiatric Nurses Association) protested against this impact, they took no industrial action and eventually accepted the reductions. It should be noted, however, that medicine fought a much stronger fight which resulted in fewer salary cuts to medical pay (particularly at the higher end) compared to nurses and over the same period of 2009 to 2013 actually saw a rise in the number of junior medical posts within the health service (ibid.).

Reflect 12.2

- How do you define a nurse as being 'professional' in terms of their demeanour and practice?
- Think about the programme content and clinical experiences during your training and the values both promoted. Do you feel it equipped you to understand how politics (both national and local) affects you as a nurse and nursing care?
- Do you feel your education programme equipped you with political skills and to be engaged with politics and policy development in nursing and health care?
- For the purposes of receiving a licence to practise is there a declaration you or your training establishment have to make to the licensing board? What values does this declaration emphasise?
- How do you feel about voting for and taking industrial action as a nurse? What issues, if any, would lead you to withdraw your labour?

Contemporary political issues that will shape the future of nursing

As indicated earlier, nurses are the largest professional group employed in health services and therefore have received particular attention from politicians and governments in relation to pay, workforce planning and reconfiguration of services and indeed, of the profession itself (Wells and White, 2014). Such reconfigurations are aimed at delivering what is termed cost-effective approaches to care. Such approaches have tended to focus on doing more clinical activity over a shorter period of time with fewer staff (Scott *et al.*, 2013). However, this approach, which has dominated health care discourse and action since the 1990s and, in particular, since the economic collapse of 2008, has now become highly politicised as this relates to patient experience of care and the stress it places on nurses and other health care professionals (Wells, 2011). We will now look at these issues and consider their political nature and therefore why nurses and the profession of nursing need to take a leading political role in terms of determining their outcome.

Quality of care, patient outcomes and compassion in nursing as a political issue

International research and public inquiries on health services demonstrate that there is a relationship between nurse staffing levels, patients' experiences and safe clinical outcomes (Ball and Catton, 2011; Keogh, 2013; Cavendish, 2013; Berwick, 2013). Most significantly the European Union-funded RN4CAST (Aiken *et al.*, 2014) indicates that nurse staffing levels have a significant impact on patient outcomes as this relates to nurse–patient ratios, patient acuity and the level of training nurses have. The RN4CAST study (Aiken *et al.*, 2014) found that nurses are among the largest components of hospital operating expenses and are therefore a 'soft target' because savings can be made quickly by reducing their numbers. However, the cost of meeting financial targets through such nursing reductions is that there is a significant threat to patient safety and clinical outcomes as these relate to morbidity and mortality (Aiken *et al.*, 2014).

Whilst this research in and of itself made some telling points, what politicised it was the fact that it was published shortly after the release of the Francis Report on the lack of nursing care and compassion at the Mid Staffordshire Hospitals NHS Trust (2013) and the Keogh Report (2013) on the quality of care in 13 NHS hospitals and patient mortality. The Francis Report in particular touched a nerve with the public, not only in the UK, but in many other jurisdictions, such as Ireland, in which there is a growing public perception that nursing has become too technocratic, uncaring and disconnected from the patient experience – what has been popularly termed 'too posh to wash' (Wells and Norman, 2009).

The ironic feature of the Francis Report in this regard was that the critique of care largely, though not exclusively, focused on an over-reliance on relatively poorly skilled health care assistants delivering direct patient care and a lack of supervision of their activities by qualified nursing staff. The public, however, has not made this differentiation (and neither may it be said has the discourse in much of the commentary within the nursing profession itself). As far as the public are concerned nursing is less compassionate than it used to be. For example, Wells and White (2014) have pointed to a survey of public attitudes to nursing conducted by the Nursing and Midwifery Board of Ireland which, though overall, still indicated high public confidence in nurses, however a third of all those surveyed said that they felt the health care system was not producing nurses with the right skills. This is a warning that the public are more likely than they used to be to be critical of nurses and the nursing profession.

The recognition of a public crisis in confidence in nursing as a political problem may be seen in the release of policy guidelines by the Chief Nursing Officer for England entitled 'Compassion in Practice' (Department of Health [DoH], 2012), supported another document called 'Values Based Recruitment' (VBR) (Health Education England [HEE], 2014). 'Compassion in Practice' in particular illustrates the current political agenda to re-establish public confidence in a particular type of nursing vision. Thus the policy document emphasises that nurses should demonstrate *care, compassion, competence, communication, courage* and *commitment* which places an emphasis on the individual and their failings as opposed to the failings of the system in which they have to operate (Goodman, 2015).

Reflect 12.3

- What would you consider are the local drivers for setting nurse staffing levels in relation to patient care?
- How aware are you of public attitudes to nurses and what do you think these attitudes are?
- What aspects of the care that you deliver do you think might have a political dimension and why?
- Can you think of any examples in your organisation where issues of care became either a local or national subject of political debate? How were these issues resolved?
- Are you aware of policy guidance relating to compassionate care and how were you made aware of this? How do you feel nurses can improve public confidence in relation to compassion and care?

The issue of unregulated health care workers and changes to skill-mix

As indicated in the above section, workforce planning and particularly skill-mix is now a significant element in the reconfiguration of nursing (Department of Health, 2016). Skill-mix has been described as the mix of posts, grades or occupations in an organisation. It may also refer to the combination of activities or skills needed for each job within the organisation (Buchan, 2002). According to the RCN

(2015), since 2010 in the UK there has been a 33 per cent increase in the health care assistant workforce in the NHS, a rise from 42,122 to 56,215. This has significant implications for registered nursing staff as health care assistants require supervision and this should be taken into account when looking at staffing levels and setting the appropriate skill-mix to deliver safe and quality care (RCN, 2015).

Appropriate skill-mix and care is one of the biggest staffing challenges in health care today (WHO, 2011). The Willis Commission on Nursing (2012) reported that skill-mixes in the United Kingdom were being diluted by the expanded, uncontrolled use of non-registered and often untrained staff to carry out tasks that were previously the remit of registered nurses. To a degree, the findings of the Francis Report (2013) validated these conclusions. However, this does not mean that non-registered staff should not be used to deliver care. Rather, it poses the question what type of care and who supervises these practitioners. Fundamentally, these are questions of policy and politics for they will only be resolved through ministerial and political decisions as they relate to the resourcing of nursing care.

The Royal College of Nursing (RCN) staffing guidance in the UK suggests that the split should never be more than 65 per cent qualified nurses to 35 per cent non-qualified nursing staff in acute, medical and surgical wards (Royal College of Nursing, 2012). However, because of the cost of nursing, the temptation to breach these guidelines when resources are constrained is considerable. Furthermore, as there are shortages of nurses (WHO, 2016) within specific sectors of health care – for example, mental health (Gilburt, 2015) – managers may have no choice but to replace nurses with less-qualified staff in order to deliver a service.

In 2008 in Ireland, a review of the Health Care Assistant (HCA) role took place (HSE, 2008). Since the publication of this report the Irish Nurses and Midwives Organisation (INMO) highlighted a lack of consistency in the number of HCAs employed in health services across the country. In terms of safe staffing levels the INMO has taken a more conservative view of the skill-mix numbers compared to the RCN, recommending a mix of 80 per cent registered nurses and 20 per cent HCAs.

The fact that there is this variation of views in terms of appropriate balance between qualified nurses and unqualified staff delivering nursing care suggests that this issue is as much being driven by local conditions and professional role protection as it is by rational calculations. The political difficulty nursing has in this scenario is twofold. First, how does it engage on this issue of replacement without projecting an image that it is seeking professional exceptionalism and protectionism in relation to maintaining its exclusive control of domains of care? This is particularly difficult when the nurse's role is expanding into areas that were the traditional preserve of medicine and which medicine itself argues against (Iglehart, 2013). The second difficulty relates to the fundamental question of availability as this relates to numbers of qualified nurses (Commission of the European Communities, 2008). If the nursing numbers are not there, is the profession's position that the service cannot be provided? The controversy that such positions might engender in the political arena would be considerable.

An ageing workforce and recruitment issues

It is well documented that there are insufficient numbers of younger people entering the nursing profession to replace those who are leaving due to retirement or 'burnout' resulting from demanding work conditions in many European countries (WHO, 2016; RCN, 2015; Commission of the European Communities, 2008; OECD, 2008; Wiskow, 2006).

Across Europe, most health services are facing a demographic time bomb as the nursing workforce becomes a predominantly 'grey' one (Wells and Norman, 2009; Buchan et al., 2015). Recently, the RCN reported that in the NHS in the UK, around 45 per cent of the nursing workforce is aged over 45 (RCN, 2015) in a system where the retirement age, depending in which clinical service one is working, can be either 55 or 65 years. Thus increasing numbers of nurses will be due to retire over the next decade with insufficient entry into the profession to replace them. An international comparison of policies regarding the nurse workforce in the UK, Australia, US and Portugal indicates that an ageing workforce is likely to drive projected shortages and highlights the vulnerability of the future supply of nurses (Buchan et al., 2015).

A complicating factor in this regard relates to nursing faculty, which like their clinical colleagues, is an ageing one. The result is that even if recruitment were to improve, there will be insufficient numbers of educators to train student nurses (Nardi and Gyurko, 2013).

Such demographic shifts are particularly worrying at a time when European health services are underpinned by economic and political uncertainty, compounded other significant demographic challenges such as the recent refugee crisis and the rise of right-wing politics (Commission of the European Communities, 2008; Baeten, 2013; European Commission, 2013).

The recent UK decision to leave the European Union, popularly referred to as Brexit, has meant that issues of recruitment to nursing in the UK, as this relates to foreign nurses, has become a significant political issue in the context of these demographic issues. The issue of who can and cannot be a nurse and stay in the UK, therefore, is now on the cusp of not only being a significant domestic political issue, but one which may well poison international relations between the United Kingdom and other European nations (McKenna, 2016). Therefore, politics and nurses in these circumstances are now likely to have international and ethnic dimensions which previously did not exist. Thus nurses need to become far more aware not only of the domestic political scene but also the international because of the impact this will have on the future make-up of the profession.

Improving the image of nursing

As indicated earlier, fewer young people are entering the workforce, as they have a greater range of professional opportunities, particularly women. This is combined with the increasingly low social value placed on nursing as a career and the negative perceptions of working conditions for nurses (Simoens *et al.*, 2010). Wells and Norman (2009) highlight the need for nursing to be made a more attractive career choice if it's going to compete successfully with other career opportunities.

Government initiatives such as 'return to practice' campaigns are advocated by the European Commission in order to attract those who have left the nursing profession (Commission of the European Communities, 2008). Recently there has been increased emphasis on campaigns to attract people into nursing in countries such as Ireland, for example. The Irish Health Service Executive (HSE) initiatives to recruit former nurses back to nursing have failed. The failure of such recruitment initiatives highlight the damage that has occurred to the perception and image of nurses and nursing in recent years and, more particularly, the political failure of nursing representation at a political and social level to counter the overall decline in the image of the profession.

Reflect 12.4

- What are your attitudes to health care assistants?
- Are health care assistants a threat to your professional status or a vital group of people in the delivery of good health care?
- Should the nursing profession resist their employment in clinical settings?
- Do you work alongside foreign nurses and do you see this as becoming an issue in terms of local and national politics?
- What do you think will be the implications of an ageing workforce in health care in terms of the image of nursing amongst the general public?
- Are you aware of any recruitment or retention strategies targeted at the nursing profession? Have these strategies been successful or unsuccessful?
- Do you think nursing is an attractive career choice?
- How have political decisions affected the image of nurses and consideration of nursing as a career choice?
- What factors do you think would contribute to increasing the attractiveness of nursing as a career choice?

Summary

This chapter has highlighted the need for nurses and the profession to adopt a more proactive stance in relation to political action, particularly in the light of issues such as skill-mix and increasing protectionism in relation to the composition of the health care workforce in the light of such developments as Brexit. However, to do this nursing must overcome its innate tendency, as a result of the profession's history to be conservative and conformist when confronted with change. Training nurses to be more politically active needs to become part of their education if the nursing voice is to play a significant role in decision making as this relates to the future of the profession.

References

Aiken, L.H., Sloane, D.M., Bruyneel, L., Van den Heede, K., Griffiths, P., Busse, R., Diomidous, M., Kinnunen, J., Kózka, M., Lesaffre, E., McHugh, M.D., Moreno-Casbas, M.T., Rafferty, A.M., Schwendimann, R., Scott, A., Tishelman, C., van Achterberg, T. & Sermeus, W. (2014) Nurse staffing and education and hospital mortality in nine European countries: a retrospective observational study. *The Lancet*, 383:9931: 1824–1830.

All Party Parliamentary Group on Global Health (2016) *Triple Impact: How Developing Nursing Will Improve Health, Promote Gender Equality and Support Economic Growth*. London: APPG.

Arabi, A., Rafii, F., Cheraghi, M.A. & Ghiyasvandian, S. (2014) Nurses' policy influence: a concept analysis. *Iranian Journal of Nursing and Midwifery Research*, 19:3: 315–322.

Austin, W., Burcher, B., Carlin, K., Chavez, F., Leadbeater, S., Oberle, K. & Storch, J.L. (2007) Call to action to advance the human right to health care, economic justice and mitigation of climate change. *Canadian Nurse*, 103:1: 5–5.

Baeten, R. (2013) Evolutions récentes dans l'UE ayant un impact sur les systèmes nationaux de soins de sante. Paper Series. Briefing Paper 9. Brussels: OSE.

Ball, J. & Catton, H. (2011) Planning nurse staffing: are we willing and able? *Journal of Research in Nursing*, 16:6: 551–558.

Berwick, D.M. (2013) *A Promise to Learn – A Commitment to Act: Improving the Safety of Patients in England*. London: Department of Health.

Buchan, J., Twigg, D., Dussault, G., Duffield., C. & Stone, P.W. (2015) Policies to sustain the nursing workforce: an international comparison. *International Nursing Review*, 62: 162–170.

Cavendish, C. (2013) *The Cavendish Review: An Independent Review into Healthcare Assistants and Support Workers in the NHS and Social Settings*. London: Department of Health.

Clarke, L. (1999) *Challenging Ideas in Psychiatric Nursing*. London: Routledge.

Commission of the European Communities (2008) *Green Paper on the European Workforce for Health*. Brussels COM(2008), 725, final.

Department of Health (DoH) (2012) *Compassion in Practice: Nursing, Midwifery and Care Staff: Our Vision and Strategy*. London: The Stationery Office.

Department of Health (2015) *Draft Interim Report and Recommendations by the Taskforce and Skill Mix for Nursing on a Framework for Safe Staffing and Mix in General and Specialist Medical and Surgical Care Settings in Adult Hospitals in Ireland*. Department of Health.

Department of Health (2016) *Interim Report and Recommendations by the Taskforce on Staffing and Skill Mix for Nursing on a Framework for Safe Nurse Staffing and Skill Mix in General and Specialist Medical and Surgical Care Settings in Adult Hospitals in Ireland*. Dublin. The Stationery Office.

Enthoven, A. (1985) *Reflections on the Management of the National Health Service: An American Looks at Incentives to Efficiency in Health Services Management in the UK*. London: Nuffield Provincial Hospitals Trust.

European Commission (2013) *Social Policy Reforms for Growth and Cohesion: Review of Recent Structural Reforms 2013*. Report of the Social Protection Committee. Luxembourg: Publications Office of the European Union.

Foth, T., Kuhla, J. & Benedict, S. (2014) Nursing during Nazi Germany. In Benedict, S. & Shields, L. (eds), *Nurses and Midwives in Nazi Germany: The Euthanasia Programmes*. London. Routledge, pp. 27–47.

Francis, R. (2013) *Report of the Mid Staffordshire NHS Foundation Trust Public Inquiry*. London: The Stationery Office.

Gilburt, H. (2015) *Mental Health under Pressure. A Briefing.* London. King's Fund.

Godden, J. (2005) Nightingale's legacy and hours of work. In Rafferty, A.M., Robinson, J. & Elkan, R. (eds), *Nursing History and the Politics of Welfare.* London: Routledge, pp. 177–190.

Goodman, B. (2016) The missing two Cs – commodity and critique: Obscuring the political economy of the 'gift' of nursing. *Journal of Research in Nursing.* doi: 10.1177/1744987116630023/.

Griffiths, R. (1983) *NHS Management Inquiry.* London: Department of Health and Social Security.

Health Education England (HEE) (2014) *Values Based Framework.* Available at: http://hee. nhs.uk/wp-content/blogs.dir/321/files/2014/10/VBR-Framework.pdf (accessed 2 November 2016).

Health Information and Quality Authority (HIQA) (2013) *Investigation into the Safety, Quality and Standards of Services Provided to Patients, including Pregnant Women, at Risk of Clinical Deterioration including those Provided by University Hospital Galway and as Reflected in the Care and Treatment Provided to Savita Halappanavar.* Dublin: Health Information and Quality Authority.

HSE (2008) *National Review of the Role of the Healthcare Assistant in Ireland.* Dublin: Health Service Executive.

Iglehart, J.K. (2013) Expanding the role of advanced nurse practitioners: risks and rewards. *New England Journal Medicine,* 368: 1935–1941.

Keen, J. & Malby, R. (1992) Nursing power and practice in the United Kingdom National Health Service. *Journal of Advanced Nursing,* 17: 863–870.

Keogh, B. (2013) *Review into the Quality of Care and Treatment Provided by 14 Hospital Trusts in England: Overview Report.* London: NHS.

Kunaviktikul, W. (2014) Nursing and health policy perspectives. *International Nursing Review,* 61: 1.

Lipsky, M. (1980) *Street Level Bureaucracy.* New York: Plenum Press.

Marcuse, H. (1964) *One Dimensional Man: Studies in the Ideology of Advanced Industrial Society.* Boston, MA: Beacon Press.

McDonald, L. (2006) Florence Nightingale as a social reformer. *History Today,* 56:1: 9.

McKenna, H. (2016) *Five Big Issues for Health and Social Care after the Brexit Vote.* Available at www.kingsfund.org.uk/publications/articles/brexit-and-nhs (accessed 9 July 2016).

Mossé, P., Harayama, T., Boulongne-Garcin, M., Ibe, T., Oku, H. & Rogers, V. (2011) *Hospitals and the Nursing Profession: Lessons from Franco-Japanese Comparisons Paths to Modernisation.* Montrouge: John Libbey Eurotext.

Nardi, D. & Gyurko, C. (2013) The global nursing shortage: status and solutions for change. *Journal of Nursing Scholarship,* 45:3: 317–326.

Oestberg, F. (2013) Getting involved in policy and politics. *Nursing Critical Care,* 8:3: 48.

Organisation for Economic Co-operation and Development (OECD) (2008) *The Looming Crisis in the Health Workforce: How Can OECD Countries Respond?* Paris: Organisation for Economic Co-operation and Development.

Royal College of Nursing (2012) *Mandatory Nurse Staffing Levels.* London: RCN.

Royal College of Nursing (RCN) (2015) *Frontline First: The Fragile Frontline.* London: RCN.

Salvage, J. (1985) *The Politics of Nursing.* London: Heinemann Nursing.

Scott, A., Kirwan, M., Matthews, A., Lehwaldt, D., Morris, R. & Staines, A. (2013) *Report of the Irish RN4CAST Study 2009–2011: A Nursing Workforce under Strain.* Dublin: Dublin City University.

Simoens, S., Villeneuve, M. & Hurst, K. (2010) *Tackling Nurse Shortages in OECD Countries.* Paris: OECD Publishing.

Stuckler, D. & Basu, S. (2013) *The Body Economic. Why Austerity Kills.* London: Allen Lane.

Taft, S.H. (2008) What are the sources of health policy that influence nursing practice? *Policy, Politics and Nursing Practice,* 9:4: 274–287.

Twibell, R., St Pierre, J., Johnson, D., Barton, D., Davis, C., Kidd, M. & Rook, G. (2012) Tripping over the welcome mat: why new nurses don't stay and what the evidence says we can do about it. *American Nurse Today,* 2016: 7.

Wells, J.S.G. (2011) Guest editorial: The impact of stress amongst health professionals. *Journal of Mental Health,* 20:22:111–114.

Wells, J.S.G. (2004) Community mental health policy in the 1990s: A case study in corporate and 'street level' implementation. PhD Thesis, King's College, University of London.

Wells, J.S.G. (1999) The growth of managerialism and its impact on nursing and the NHS. In Cowley, S. & Norman, I.J. (eds), *The Changing Nature of Nursing in a Managerial Age.* Edinburgh: Blackwell Science, pp. 57–81.

Wells, J.S.G. & Bergin, M. (2016) British icons and Catholic perfidy: Anglo-Saxon historiography and the battle for Crimean War nursing. *Nursing Inquiry,* 23:1: 42–51.

Wells, J.S.G. & White, M. (2014) The impact of the economic crisis and austerity on the nursing and midwifery professions in the Republic of Ireland: 'boom', 'bust' and retrenchment. *Journal of Research in Nursing,* 19:7–8: 562–577.

Wells, J.S.G. & Norman, I.J. (2009) Guest editorial: The 'greying' of Europe: reflections on the state of nursing and nurse education in Europe. *Nurse Education Today,* 29:8: 811–815.

Willis Commission on Nursing Education (2012) *Quality with Compassion: The Future of Nursing Education. Report of the Willis Commission on Nursing Education.* London: Published by the Royal College of Nursing on behalf of the independent Willis Commission.

Wiskow, C. (ed) (2006) *Health Worker Migration Flows in Europe: Overview and Case Studies in Selected SEE Countries – Romania, Czech Republic, Serbia and Croatia.* Geneva: International Labour Office.

World Health Organization (2002) *Conceptual Framework for Management of Nursing and Midwifery Workforce.* New Dehli: Regional Office for South East Asia, World Health Organization.

World Health Organization (2016) *Global Strategy on Human Resources for Health: Workforce 2030 Draft for the World Health Assembly.* Geneva: WHO.

INDEX

Page numbers in *italics* denote figures, those in **bold** denote tables.